The Institute for Therapeutic Learning

◆

Finding True Magic

◆

Sourcebook for
Transpersonal Hypnotherapy/NLP
Certification Training Program

Jack Elias, Director and Instructor

published by Five Wisdoms Publications

1999

Five Wisdoms Publications
P.O. Box 17229
Seattle, WA 98107

Finding True Magic

ISBN: 0-9655210-0-1

First printing 1996
Second Printing 1999

Printed in the United States of America

◆◆◆

Preface

<u>Finding True Magic</u> is used as a training manual for a Transpersonal Hypnotherapy/NLP Certification Program at the Institute for Therapeutic Learning. As the subtitle indicates, this book and the Hypnotherapy training are appropriate for lay people to foster personal growth as well as for therapists and healers intent on developing therapeutic skills. In fact, about 50% of the student body who take the training do so strictly for personal development and healing.

This book explores the possibilities of recognizing and freeing ourselves from a destructive process of perceiving, thinking, and acting that can be viewed as a worldwide epidemic infection that is pernicious because, unlike other diseases which we strive to isolate and cure, inherent to this infection, this fever, is the characteristic that it causes us to identify with it as our very own true self.

We speak of it lovingly as our ego, our sense of limited separate selfhood. I prefer to call it 'egoic-minding', because it is a process, not a thing. It is a fragmented, biased way of perceiving and thinking that can be viewed as a destructive hypnotic trance that causes us to experience each other as strangers, as different, as threats. The delirium of this feverish trance causes us to do violence to each other and to our world, never recognizing "it," egoic thought processes, as the true enemy.

I believe this 'egoic-minding' process to be the one source of all disease and strife on earth - the Great Killer and Destroyer next to which such subordinates as AIDS, cancer , and heart disease pale. Indeed, they would not exist except for having been birthed by the egoic process.

Through a synthesis of Eastern and Western philosophical and psychological insights and techniques, **<u>Finding True Magic</u>** explores understandings and processes that disperse this feverish trance, heal the trauma it causes, and wake us up to the Sacred Magic of our True Selves.

It is time that we recognize that essential insights and dynamics of healing communication need to be directly available and understood by all, without necessarily the need for a long term and expensive professional intermediary. The model of that professional relationship is starting to change because of the financial burdens it places on our medical system. But finances aside, it should change simply because there is a better way to approach healing. It relies on the Inherent Goodness of our Shared Being which can be accessed surprisingly easily in the space between egoic thoughts. Most of us don't experience that space in the normal course of thinking. Most of us may be surprised to be told such a thing, given our experience of the seemingly impenetrable stream of thoughts. But this space is the very Space of Silence, the Silence of God, that we all may have experienced on occasion through prayer or in a tender moment of love or awe. We generally haven't been taught, and haven't known that this Silent Presence is always so close and available. The new emerging Mind/Body therapeutic techniques, such as presented here, derive transformative power when they help us to tap into this Willing Presence of Grace.

It has been my experience from teaching the **Finding True Magic training** since 1988, that such concepts and approaches are virtually unheard of, or understood only in a very limited way, amongst a majority of therapists and lay people alike. In my opinion, this is not because the ideas are so esoteric, but because our basic educational system and societal support systems have become so degraded. For example, at the heart of healing work, as presented here, is a simple process of self-inquiry. We seem to have lost a sense of how important self inquiry, contemplation, is. Thus, it's not surprising that we have forgotten how to do self-inquiry effectively, and comprehensively, and, therefore, we don't teach it to our children.

This can be the case for highly educated therapists, as well. As a result, in the Institute's trainings, this general lack of familiarity with self-inquiry and the accessability of Silence "levels the playing field" between lay people and professionals. Ph.D. and MA. trained therapists are challenged in the same way lay people are challenged. They don't have an edge, in spite of their training.

Quite frankly, in the beginning, I feared the presence of highly educated professionals in my classes. My fantasy was that they would be bored and critical of short-comings in the material. Over the years their response has totally contradicted my fearful fantasies. They have consistently claimed that the material presented in **Finding True Magic,** and the training course and tapes, has opened their eyes and revolutionized their therapy work.

It is also not uncommon for "lay people" to more easily comprehend the material than a professional, because they are not burdened with prejudicial preconceptions about models and processes of healing. Everyone becomes truly equal - just folks - in the challenge of learning these approaches to healing communication.

If you find the ideas here intriguing and want to explore them further, there are several options open to you. At the back of this book is an order form explaining how to receive a free brochure about attending a live training, and about how to order tapes for independent study.

Master Table of Contents

Phase I

Phase II

Phase III

Phase IV

Phase V

Phase VI

◆ ◆ ◆

Table of Contents
Phase I

1. Introduction

This course is designed with several objectives in mind:

1) To provide a comprehensive package of specific tools and guidelines to enable students to achieve a level of understanding and skill as hypnotherapists that will make it possible for them to confidently begin a counseling career.

2) To make clear to students how to incorporate these skills and understandings for their own benefit.

3) To contextualize these skills in an awareness of the underlying principles governing egoic mental functions as elucidated in various psychological/religious traditions throughout the ages.

The objective of this approach is to awaken in students **a living, moment by moment <u>heartfelt</u> sensitivity** to the limitations of the thinking mind as supporter and director of our lives. Developing this sensitivity softens the mind:

- When the mind is softened, concepts and preconceived ideas about who we are and what is going on become transparent.

- When our ideas become transparent, the light of the ever present brilliance of our life force can literally be seen as well as **felt in our bodies.** (This course is based on the presumption of inherent, basic purity and goodness of our life force, and its basic identity with Source, God - or whatever term one may choose to point at the ineffable.)

- When our ideas become transparent, we are not limited by habitual patterns of behavior which are maintained by opaque, i.e., **fixed, solid ideas** about who we are and what is going on, moment by moment, in our lives. We will learn that such fixed ideas are hypnotic trance states, most commonly experienced as **<u>ordinary waking consciousness</u>.**

- When we are not so limited, the resulting softness of mind constantly provides the opportunity for spontaneity to arise, and *spontaneity is the highest expression of freedom and appropriateness, **moment by moment, in <u>any</u> situation, including the so-called therapeutic situation.***

One quality that arises with a continuous experience of spontaneity is a playfulness when relating with ideas, a recognition of ideas as models -- descriptive approximations of experience, but not the truth of experience. This diffuses melodramatic seriousness, and pride. We begin to understand that experience itself is not the arbiter of truth, in the sense of defining who we are and what is possible. *But you will find prevalent in clients the attitude that they are defined, i.e. fixed, by past experience. They believe their right and power to choose are somehow irrevocably limited by their past experience. This is a pop-psychological cultural trance state. To what degree do you believe it about yourself?*

There is no experience without ideas. The ideas that define experience, when they short circuit the spontaneous play of our energies, become restricting "truths" (trance truths) for us and about us. They are no longer models over which we have power as creators, but they have power over us as our "definers."

This is what I view as hypnosis -- the *fundamental* underlying hypnosis that is the nature of the thinking mind in its relationship to the inherent spontaneity and purity of our being:

> *The fixating thinking mind is the **Great Hypnotizer** of us all!*

Without an awareness of this fundamental hypnosis, one might only play the game of self improvement. One would be doing hypnosis, therapy, or whatever, within the realm of the goals defined by fixating thinking mind. One would be *improving the self one thinks one is*, attempting to secure peace and happiness without ever noticing that living in the worlds of the fixating thinking mind (or living in the world as defined by the fixating thinking mind, on a **moment by moment** basis) is *always* a trap, an illusion, however beautiful.

In the person acting as therapist, this comes across as a certain mechanicalness and formality in relating to the client, the skills, and the techniques of therapy. There is a lack of heart, a lack of a warm living quality to what is being communicated. *One focus in this course is to dissolve the dominance of the fixating thinking mind in the therapist -- to free her from this kind of limiting trance state.*

Clients generally come to therapists to modify their experience more pleasantly. Therapists who believe in the mind, who are hypnotized by the mind, will agree with this idea/model of experience that such modifications are the goal. As graduates of this course, I hope you will understand that the happiness sought lies beyond the mind, beyond any *idea of self* getting happier. Hopefully you will learn to recognize THAT as apparent FACT not merely as idea.

It is my contention that those who believe in the mind and apparently have achieved a great deal of happiness *seemingly* by following the dictates of the mind, still are experiencing the happiness beyond the mind *as it is identified by and usurped by the mind as its own accomplishment*. This tendency, like taking credit for a sunny day, does make it hard to identify happiness, and the source of happiness, for what it is.

We do not create happiness through modifications of our lives. Our being is inherently happy, and, through our attempts at self improvement, we may create gaps in our mind-trance through which we experience the happiness of our innate purity. As long as we identify these experiences as the product of the mind, the product and creation of our efforts, we will miss the fullest appreciation of ourselves and our lives.

The conviction that this already happy state exists within us in its fullness and shines through our trances, rather than being produced by the modification of our trances, is the view that is central to the orientation of this course.

The ITL Approach to Hypnotherapy

My approach is to hypnotherapy is transpersonal in the sense that I think the client's goal, whether she realizes it or not "consciously," is to be whole and at peace with herself, moment by moment, in any and all situations, and, that regardless of the "presenting problem," the "cure" will ultimately only be satisfying if it is rooted in, and merely an expression of, this wholeness and peacefulness.

- *Exploring attaining this wholeness and peace is what this course is about.*
- *What constitutes this wholeness and peacefulness? Where is it?*
- *How do we create it or find it?*
- *Do we create it or find it?*
- *Did (does) it create us; does it find us?*

In my view, these questions need to be contemplated by prospective hypnotherapists with passion, curiosity, and perseverance, and their success with clients will be directly proportionate to how deeply they cultivate this contemplation and make it relevant to their own secret and shadowy inner life.

Contemplation of this sort, in order to be passionate and curious, has to be free of any standard of success regarding the contemplation. You have to be free of fear or hope that you will or will not be successful. You have to be doing it for the sake of learning...learning for its own sake...discovering that even so-called success or failure are merely labels for certain kinds of learning whose fundamental value lies beyond these conditioned judgments. Learning is not something you do with your head; it is a whole body/being process.

To be fully engaged in the process of learning is to be fully alive moment by moment. To understand that is to experience it -- *to experience being fully alive is the ultimate goal of this course.* To experience it is to be awake from all forms of hypnosis.

Hypnotic processes are redundant. It is important to recognize that almost any therapeutic process partakes of redundancy. Learning how to appreciate and work within this atmosphere of redundancy is one of the most important principles of this course. You do not have to put people in trance -- they already are in trance. Their problems are the fruit born of their trances. You can use standard hypnotic processes, which you will learn in this course, in the same way that poisons are used in proper fashions to make medicines. But I want you to do that alchemy with the greater viewpoint of recognizing that the goal is not to become established in comfortable trances, but to be free of trances - which is to be present, at ease, and free of fear - whole and peaceful.

This course will blend the nuts and bolts of learning hypnotic processes for therapeutic and clinical uses with a dance of metaphors and perspectives and challenges to wake you up from your own limiting trances. Learning how to awaken from your own trances is the best way to learn how to help your clients awaken from theirs, and it generates an essential compassion for yourself and your client.

Humility will also arise from genuine wakefulness - humility in renewed appreciation of the sacredness and mystery of life, *your life*, and, regarding your work as therapists, humility in honoring your clients' efforts to rediscover that same sacredness in their lives.

If you can contact, cultivate, and maintain an active sense of compassion and humility, moment by moment, situation by situation, these qualities will be your protectors and guides -- magical spiritual powers worthy of attainment.

This course is my attempt to make the above statements understandable in a way that is useful and transformative-not merely intellectual.

2. What is Hypnosis?

Hypnosis has many definitions and many books have been written debating whether it even exists. To my mind, these debates and the variety of definitions are themselves within the realm of what I consider to be the most basic and profound definition of hypnosis. This definition takes the perspective that the discursive thinking mind, what most of us identify with as our ordinary sense of self, is an on-going hypnotic process. This perspective recognizes that ordinary conscious mind contains all the process-elements of what more traditionally are called trance phenomena or characteristics and, though conscious mind approximates reality and makes it seem workable, it is never accurately in touch with reality. More and more people in this quantum age are beginning to subscribe to such notions. In fact, this approach to hypnotherapy could be called quantum hypnotherapy as well as transpersonal hypnotherapy.

This implies:

1) *You are not who you "think" you are. Who you think you are is your deepest trance state. (Actually a "bundle" of trance states.)*

2) *To the degree that your awareness is absorbed in and identified with your thoughts, you are in a hypnotic state-a <u>defined</u> state rather than a spontaneous "real" state, an "awake" state.*

3) *All communication, both intrapersonal and interpersonal, to the degree that it is a sharing of thoughts "about" reality rather than a direct experience of reality, is a sharing of hypnotic states, dream states, even deluded states.*

The Hypnotic Trance of Self

Not being who we "think" we are is the root of our dilemmas. (Or, more accurately, believing we are who we think we are, and not noticing that we are not, is the root.) We are *selectively attending** to our ideas about ourselves in order *to make choices** which define and determine our lives. If the root idea of who we are is a mistake, our whole process of strategizing about our lives is a **"mishap"** with varying degrees of painful and pleasurable consequences.

The most profound aspects of the hypnotic trance of self, or, more accurately, the bundle of trances of self, are established in our childhood prior to the time of the organic development of a discriminating perspective. As children, we had to accept the overwhelming *vividness and prestige,* good and/or bad, of the stimulus and messages impacting on us as "truth." Learning to identify our sensory functions and our bodily delineation could happen quite naturally, but the healthy extension of that process of mind/body coordination in interpersonal relationships is very rare. The degree to which those relationships were unhealthy, i.e. shaming, confusing, or threatening, determined how profoundly we developed the trance of false, hypnotic self - the fixed idea of a defined self, rather than the *felt sense of well-being* of an on-going self that doesn't need to keep track of itself with ideas. *When you're fully involved in being who you are, you don't waste time keeping track of who you are; it isn't necessary if there is no shame or threat to ward off.*

The hypnotic self is a powerful set of trance phenomena. Growing up is to be in the cultural and familial hypnotist's arena 24 hours a day! And everyone is hypnotizing you -- telling you what everything means; telling you what you are, and what your actions *mean* regarding your worthiness to be **with repetition and emotional force.**[*]

Children learn by modeling; they are master pantomimes. Thus begins the process of self hypnosis (self talk in adult terms). Have you ever had the opportunity to eavesdrop on a young child playing with their toys as they repeat the judgments of others about themselves in an innocent sing song voice? We all began to master these hypnosis skills very early.

We develop the veils of perception - we no longer see a tree, or hear a bird, or taste a hamburger, or experience ourselves simply and directly without a running commentary going on inside. The stimulus of a tree, or a bird, or a hamburger, or the spontaneous movement of our organic being, triggers what seems to be an on-going, instantaneous, uninterrupted barrage of associations, judgments, and memories, filling our mind with sights, sounds, and sensations referenced to the past and projected into the future with such force and speed that, not only do we not notice we haven't really seen the tree, but we don't notice that we've been distracted from seeing the tree and anesthetized to the pain of having our relationship to the tree cut off. How many of us are so habitually numbed to the pain of being cut off in relationship to our world that the notion that *"to not really see a tree, is painful,"* seems a strange idea?

Distraction by association, forgetfulness, spontaneous anesthesia, positive hallucination (seeing something that isn't there), negative hallucination (not seeing something that is there), time distortion and time displacement, spontaneous regression - these are all qualities listed as indicating hypnosis of significant depth in the traditional notions of hypnosis, and yet in these examples, they have transpired *in ordinary waking consciousness.*

Let's examine the signs and qualities of hypnotic depth from the traditional stand point, and then explore how they blend into what is traditionally considered the non-hypnotic or "conscious" state.

Therapeutic Hypnosis Defined

Conscious, subconscious, unconscious - these concepts are very pervasive in our culture, and people freely use them in talking about themselves. To the degree that we do this without having contemplated the meaning of these terms in the context of various kinds of personal experience, or, to the degree that we haven't determined the usefulness of labeling various kinds of experience with these terms, we really don't know what we are talking about. We are merely engaged in hypnotizing ourselves by the very familiar process of sloganeering.

A political slogan - "America! Home of the free!" which has no agreed upon specific meaning, but it is capable of triggering strong emotional response of varying kinds depending on the audience. Likewise, a phrase such as, "I know this problem is in my subconscious but I can't get at it," gives a person a false sense of knowledge which is really a confusion state (i.e. hypnotic state) that contributes to the dilemma expressed of not being able to "get at it."

---

[*] *Essential ingredients recognised by all hypnotists as being essential to the development of trance.*

Here's one we all can identify with: "I know that intellectually, but I can't stop...". The phrase, "I know intellectually," is one of the most common supports of on-going trance. Its most important characteristic is that it short circuits the possibility of accessing or maintaining an awake learning mode, while affording a bit of comfort in seemingly knowing something. What it usually means is, not that we know something - knowing meaning that it is alive and active as a resource within us capable of causing change - but that we can mimic the words, saying them over and over in our head like a lullaby, *and with the same effect on our awareness.*

I point this out because I want you to be alert to the tendency, **especially as a student,** to settle for this kind of "learning." It is what most of us have been conditioned (hypnotized) to do. With that in mind, here are a couple of attempts at defining hypnosis by very successful and recognized hypnotists.

"Hypnosis is the use of suggestion, whether direct or indirect, to induce a heightened state of suggestibility in which there is bypass of the critical faculty of the mind, and selective attention to suggestions given." --Dave Elman

"Hypnosis is a state of awareness dominated by the subconscious mind." -- Michael Preston, M.D.

"Hypnosis is a 'shrinking of the focus of attention.'" -- Milton Erickson

What sense can be made out of these statements that is useful? "...the use of suggestion...to heighten suggestion..."?"...the bypass of the critical faculty..."? "selective attention to suggestions given." Or, "...a state of awareness dominated by the..." (what?)"...subconscious mind." ?

What are they trying to describe? Can you relate the terms used to personal experience? First, recognize that labeling, like trying to create a nice neat box (this is what we all have been trained [hypnotized] to do, not just clients) *dissociates* you from the experience you are labeling and creates subtle and not so subtle limitations.

It is important to keep in mind the difference between *labeling,* which diminishes a level of interest and awareness in on-going phenomena, and *descriptive activity*, which keeps you engaged with the phenomena. When descriptive interest changes into labeling, something alive and vital is lost. But the capability to label is, nevertheless, a valuable one when used appropriately. One place it is not appropriate is in the learning process where it satisfies the urge to reach the goal of *being able to say* "I know that intellectually," because as soon as we can say that, we are going into the trance, *living in the box of our words.*

We all do this - in fact, it is at the root of all our worldly difficulties, personal and political, social and cultural. For once we have a box *to hold on to*, we grasp on to it and defend it, usually in the face of irrefutable evidence to the contrary. You can recognize this everyday in the prejudice and politics of our times, but have you ever thought about some of your problems from this point of view? See yourself in the grip of some limitation - where you act and feel like a helpless two year old - in spite of the irrefutable presence of your *six-foot-two-hundred-pound-body-having-taken-care-of-yourself-daily-for-years* experience. ***That's hypnosis!***

The phenomena these men are trying to describe as hypnosis are marked by the same qualities that pervade our conscious functioning. There is no clear distinction. **Even the critical faculty is a trance state.** From this perspective, it's not so important to make a neat definition that clearly defines the labels applied to the phenomena, because that so easily leads to a lazy false sense of knowledge. It is more a challenge to develop and access more resourceful trance states that expand the client's awareness of choice and power to benefit to the point where they ultimately awaken to an awareness beyond trance states altogether.

Buddhism calls this the state of No-Mind. Trance states are all states where the thinking mind is dictating what reality is vs. the No-Mind state which allows the perception of reality directly with no *conceptual mediation* (that's a euphemism for distortion and interference). **It is a state where the heart/mind and head/mind functions are joined releasing one's true clear intelligence. The mark of this union is reliance on the spontaneous guidance of intuition - direct perception and recognition of identity between subject and object. This intuition of identity engenders spaciousness, luminosity, and love. It manifests as the revival of the capacity to be moved by the beauty of a flower, to see the focus, love, and attention of the whole universe in the movement of a fly's wings, and to care for one's life and the life of all beings.**

I prefer to define therapeutic hypnosis as the use of the very same mental functions we are using continuously to *contract* our focus and numb our sense of being, or to maintain the status quo of an already acceptable contracted state, to *expand* our awareness of being organically alive. Therapeutic hypnosis alters these functions to *release the contraction* - the nature of which is fear, into an *expansiveness* - the nature of which is love. As with natural medicine, **we distill the very poison in such a way that we produce an antidote.**

In this definition, there is no conscious or unconscious boundary solidified; no borderline beyond which certain mental processes cannot go without destroying the hypnotic state. If one understands this definition, not as a label, but because they can actually see it being displayed by the mind, it becomes very delightful to do hypnotherapy. We don't have to be concerned about who can be hypnotized and who can't be. We simply need to develop the sensory acuity to notice **how each person does it to themselves, how we do it to ourselves,** and then make the adjustments this course intends to teach.

To do this kind of work, the emphasis has to be on the therapist's daily personal practice to cultivate the awareness of their own habitual states, of when they are triggered and what triggers them, within a growing capacity for spacious kind-hearted acceptance of their presence. This is the antidote to what is called trance-ferance (sic) and counter trance-ferance (sic) in traditional therapy. This daily practice should include some form of body-mind co-ordination through physical activity, and some form of meditation/contemplation practice to develop the capacity to dissociate from the hypnotic force of the turmoil of subconscious thoughts and feelings - the constant "subconscious gossip" that we all generally accept as a given in life and therefore rarely challenge.

◆ ◆ ◆

3. How to Induce and Facilitate Trance

This section includes some practical preliminary requirements for establishing a hypnotic state in a traditional sense and rules for the formulation of effective suggestions. These are followed by some tips on how to do a hypnotic session, including environmental considerations, aesthetic considerations, and basic information that should be discussed with a client prior to induction to insure, as far as possible, that they feel safe, secure, and free of disruptive preconceptions about the experience of being hypnotized. Hopes and expectations, as well as fears, can limit the spontaneous appearance of the most unbiased, truthful and needed information and resources. Therefore, it is necessary to cultivate a relaxed, alert, yet passive aspect of awareness in the client that will allow them to experience and report on content of experience without suppressing, altering, or doubting the content.

Establishing Hypnotic Trance

1) Eye fatigue and eye closure

While not necessary for the poison, eye closure is very conducive to the antidote. By the simply reducing visual stimulus, it robs the mind of fuel for unnecessary distraction, and allows you to further distract the client from their habitual thought pathways.

2) Relaxation- physical and mental

Generally, it is best to relax progressively from the head down to the fingertips. This relaxes about 80% of so-called conscious functioning -- what I would call a reduction in *speed and claustrophobia* of mental functions rather than a reduction of the *type* of function (as in **conscious vs. subconscious.**)

3) Trust or rapport

This is actually primary. Without the trust of your client, your suggestions and instructions won't be followed. In order to gain their trust, you must be able to establish rapport, and maintain it. As the motto of a Colorado real estate company, Moore & Co., says, *"People don't care how much you know, until they know how much you care."* As we will discuss later, rapport is a function of communication (of caring), over 90% of which is non-verbal and, therefore, "unconscious."

4) Well-formed suggestions, both linguistically and ecologically

A suggestion is well formed linguistically when it meets the following criteria:

a) They must be stated in the **present tense**. Once a level of relaxation is reached mentally, a characteristic of mind that is recognized as "subconscious" must be appreciated - it lives in the NOW. The mind that can cause change lives in the now and changes things in the now. Everything is happening, and you DO things, you don't "try" to do things. For example:

"The sound of my voice causes you to relax more and more," **NOT**, *"The sound of my voice will cause you to relax."* Or, *"You are losing weight quickly and easily, moment by moment, day by day..."* **NOT** *"You will lose weight easily..."* (Note: you can use "will," "shall," etc. if you designate a specific point in time for completion, as in: *"You will release this tension at the count of three...")*

b) Goals must be stated as a **present fact or presently engaged process (process language is almost always better than fixed language)** rather than as a possible or potential goal. Not *"I can be assertive when it is necessary"* but *"I am assertive when it is necessary."* If the factual structure leads to a problem of believability, which is another of the necessary criteria (below), switch to present process, *"I am becoming more assertive moment by moment, day by day, when it is necessary."*

c) **Suggestions must be believable,** which is more a function of the *phrasing of the goal* rather than the goal itself, as shown above. Generally, be sensitive to phrasing goals as **currently developing process** rather than a finished achievement that might be rejected.

d) **It is important to be positive** or to <u>finish</u> your suggestion in the positive, since **the last suggestion given has the power of change.** Also, appreciate that negative statements can only be understood by accessing the meaning of what is being negated. In order to understand, "Don't fall!" you have to access falling internally, which could induce you to fall! (This, in fact,

through intonation, can be utilized for indirect suggestion which we'll cover later.) It can be important to state negatives to gain rapport and establish believability, which is fine as long as you figure out a way to end in the positive. "you can't lose weight.. until you do." (Again, intonation here, could change the message, though negative in form, to positive by emphasis- "you can't...LOSE Weight..." the pause, though brief, plus the emphasis has the effect of making it two separate phrases.)

e) Generally, **suggestions are better if they are dramatic or have a "hook" of some kind.** Commercials rely heavily on this: *"gotta have it,"* *"Where's the beef?"* *"the real thing."*

f) **Positive emotion/negative emotion - strong and appropriate.** Strong emotion impresses the mind, causing it to give power to the thoughts to which it is linked. Generate positive emotion to move towards what is desirable, and negative emotion to move away from what is undesirable. e.g., *"the wonderful feelings of lightness and freedom that come with a healthy body; the acrid disgusting smell of poisonous cigarette smoke."*

g) **Suggestions must be personal**- you can't give suggestions to change anything else or anyone else but the client. Not *"your husband is nice to you now,"* but *"you are making the changes you can make to have the most positive relationship possible..."*

h) **Accurately represent what you really want.** Your unconscious mind is connected to your true heart desires and needs. But it can also be given directives to violate or override those needs. When it does so, inner conflict and pain result. Yes, that model looked good at 98 lbs. and in a size 2 dress, and you'd like to look like that, but is really the proper weight for your optimum health? Target what is truly beneficial!

i) A suggestion will be ***well-formed ecologically*** when it is congruent with the whole set of agendas present in the client - taking into account all issues of *secondary gain.* For example, a typical one is when someone stops smoking and then gains weight. **The negative effects of problems are always fused with genuine needs.** If you don't give the client effective ways of meeting the needs, they will find another ineffective way of attempting to meet the need. Another example common with women is putting weight back on because they have no other skills to deal with the stress of new found attractiveness.

5) *Repetition and emotional impact*

These are the two qualities of experience which determine how powerfully a given experience will cause change in a person's perception, belief structure, and behavior. It is important to appreciate both, and to develop the skill to generate both. *Develop the skill to be repetitive with presence and focus so that each repetition is the first time you have ever said it.*

Emotional impact, mentioned in (f) above is generated by the vividness of your imagery, your tone and your presentation. It has long been recognized that *the so-called subconscious mind determines reality by the strength and vividness of the stimulus encountered.* NLP (Neuro-Linguistic Programming), which we will cover more later, has coined the term "4-tuple" to designate what is required to achieve such vividness. A 4-tuple is a created internal experience that has at least four primary elements of sensory channel information: sight, sound, taste, touch, and smell. *If you include elements to stimulate four of these in your imagery, there is a much greater likelihood that the mind will accept the images as real experience.*

6) *Bring heart to the suggestion*

Don't be satisfied with superficial suggestions. Contemplate what is being asked for at a deeper level and address that issue. We'll work with this in Phase III in a more complex and comprehensive way. Examine any proposed suggestion to find if it has life to it, some heart. If not, go deeper. e.g., *"I'll keep my desk organized."* So what?

Conditions for Hypnosis - Summary

1) Eye fatigue & eye closure
2) Relaxation
3) Trust or Rapport
4) Well-formed Suggestions- both linguistically and ecologically
  a) Present tense
  b) Goals as present fact or present process
  c) Be believable
  d) Be positive, or finish in the positive
  e) Be dramatic, create a hook
  f) Use strong positive/negative emotion appropriately
  g) Keep it personal: change yourself & notice how the world changes as a consequence
  h) Accurately represent what you want
  i) Well-formed ecologically - congruent with all secondary issues
5) Repetition and Emotional impact
6) Bring Heart to the Suggestion

Exercise: *Creating Hypnotic SuggestionsCompose three well-formed suggestions that you actually would like to have presented to you in trance.*

Atmosphere and Setting

Hypnotherapy is theater; *hypnotherapy is play* (play is inherently creative); hypnotherapy is ritual; **hypnotherapy is the appreciative use of pretense,** hence it offers tremendous opportunity to explore - space, time, language, choice, perception, thinking, sensing, relating, actions, cause and effect, feelings, memory,...human-beings-in-process, in general -- a Vast Freedom of play, exploration, and learning.

People's problems and limitations (as well as their resources and skills) are theatrical; they are inherently play (although all the playfulness has more or less been frozen...that, in itself, is a playful act, however); they are ritual, however inelegant and painful, that gives meaning and structure to the vast unpredictable nature of the open space of reality.

Atmosphere and setting are elements of the hypnotic stage that you must consider as you begin any session. As you prepare for a client, ask yourself: What are you going to do in the session and how are you going to play with the space? That vast unpredictable open space includes your office and you. Most of us are so habituated to the process of filling up the space - moment by moment, that we have lost all recognition <u>that</u> we do this, and all recognition of the <u>significance</u> of doing it, and of <u>how</u> we do it and the <u>significance</u> of how we do it. In other words *we have forgotten that we are playing...*<u>with our minds</u> -- **it's all we really have to play with.** So how are you going to facilitate the playfulness...in a way that helps people remember they are playing and to take back the power over the control panel of play? In other words, to come out of trance, and regain the power to use trance states...our toys... for our benefit and enjoyment.

> *"Brahma's creative activity is not undertaken by way of any need on his part, but simply by way of sport, <u>in the common sense of the word</u>."* (Brahma Sutras, *bold and underline, mine.*)

In my opinion our goal should be to become so playful that we can make use of anything any time. But, since we are just starting out, let's take an orderly somewhat formal approach -- it would be a great accomplishment to make formal approaches always playful and creative as well!

1. Subdue and utilize the senses

Since you're beginning with a formal approach in practice, *while maintaining a playful view*, you want to foster the inclination to relax. You want to provide stimulus that subdues the senses:

- <u>Visually</u> - Use pleasant subdued colors and lighting; eliminate any glare or harshness from windows or lighting. Blues and greens are most soothing; reds are generally too irritating. These considerations include your attire. I'll always remember the delightful effect of one therapist's office. From where I sat, wherever I looked, there was some item of beauty or magic, from flower arrangements, to vases, hummingbirds hung from the ceiling, a wonderful ink brush painting, beautiful blankets... I just sat there and took it all in...these displays communicated a caring for the environment, for the activity of living, and it made me feel very happy inside. For those of more esoteric bent, visual shapes and mandalas can be used as inductive and meditative devices.

- **Physically** - Maintain a comfortable room temperature to invite physical relaxation. Have blankets and pillows available to accommodate any possible requests. For example, if people are lying down, have pillows available not only for their heads, but for under the knees, if necessary.

- **Smells** - The sense of smell is the only sense that goes directly to the brain without critical filtering, and therefore is a powerful force in the creation of trance. Flowers or incense can foster an altered state and be established as an *anchor* between a person's state and being in your office. Some familiarity with aromatherapy would generate useful ideas. If you are so inclined, aromatherapy can be incorporated as a healing modality in your work.

- **Sound** - The power of music and sound to enhance the capacity, speed, and depth of communication with the unconscious are becoming appreciated more and more in this field. It can be well worth it to investigate many forms of music from classic to New Age to find pieces that foster as well as induce trance states. Of course, avoid any music with lyrics, since the client needs to listen to you. Monotonous sounds can also be helpful- the constant ticking of a clock, the whir of a fan, etc.

- **Touch** - You generally won't engage in a lot of touching- especially initially. But you should be sensitive to the fact that communication is always going on, and that physical contact is a very powerful statement. Be sensitive to the information carried even in an initial handshake. Unless you are licensed to do massage, you can't do moving touch, but an appropriate light touch to the forehead or arm or hand can induce a desired suggestive effect.

2. Physical considerations

Generally you need to check in with the client to find out if they have anything bothering them: are they over-tired, ill, taking medication, and, rarely, are they intoxicated in anyway. The prevailing notion in the latter case is that it inhibits hypnosis. I know of some therapists who make it clear to clients that they will not work with them unless they are sober. I know other therapists who claim that when they hypnotize a drunk client, they are sober when in trance. You have to find your own way, and decide what your boundaries are going to be.

3. Emotional considerations

You need to become very sensitive to clients' emotional states. Over time and with experience, you will learn how close to expressing powerful emotions an otherwise "together" acting client can be. This capacity to recognize a client's true state is a tremendous tool in establishing rapport, and in initiating trance, since *releasing the flow of an emotional state is an immediate shift into relating to trance states that need attention.* For example, having a client "get into" a feeling and instructing them to follow it to its source can be a complete regressive hypnotic process. Freeing frozen emotional energies bound up in **chronically regressed trance states of identity,** is the primary skill we will be working to develop throughout this course. It is important to cultivate the remembrance, moment by moment, that you are rarely relating to a "whole" person, or as a "whole" person. We know this very well - this is why it takes time to get to know someone. But it serves to remember this fact from this perspective in therapy where you will be relating to **chronically regressed trance states of identity** most of the time - working to release them.

4. Cheerfulness and humor

Skillful use of humor and a sense of lightness can very powerfully diffuse the seriousness and affect of long-standing negative trance states and even obviate the need to delve into them. In other words, your humor gives the client: 1)the awareness of a *healthy dissociative position* they **can and may** give themselves permission to take regarding the problem, and 2) your humorous and cheerful behaviors *model* for them <u>how</u> they can take such attitudes for themselves, and that these attitudes are acceptable, valid alternative interpretations of their experience.

5. Total modeling considerations

We are in total communication, consciously and unconsciously all the time. Therefore, what you are communicating in therapy is your total self, whether you realize it or not, in spite of what your agendas might be. This doesn't mean you should *try* to be better or more than you think you are. Quite the contrary - nothing is hidden, and *part of the magic is in acceptance; the other part is in genuine effort to open and grow in alignment with the Truth of your being,* as much as possible resisting the egoic tendencies to *"cocoon"* or *"plateau"* in a perceived safe haven of trance identity: *"I've got it made now."*

<u>The magic of acceptance is that being willing to let something be itself without hope of **ever** changing it, paradoxically releases the resources that allow it to change in the quickest and most appropriate way.</u>

Thus, if you truly can embody and model acceptance and spaciousness, and cheerfulness, that in itself, as it is picked up and "learned " unconsciously by your client, will effect the greatest changes. Developing this capacity is one of the primary aspects of **genuine self-inquiry** and *self*-acceptance.

Beware of the therapist's trap of being accepting of your client's stuff, while still being hard on yourself for your own stuff. Beware of using your work with others as an avoidance for working on yourself. This is a particular danger with smart people who can master techniques to use on others, all the while maintaining distance from their own insecurities. Being smart doesn't necessarily diminish the fearful resistance to working on one's nightmarish illusions about ourselves. Intelligence can become the slave of the fearful master of denial, building the hardest shell there is to crack: pride of knowledge. The hypocrisy of this is communicated, even if the conscious mind is fooled.

In my opinion, you have to be alive in your own efforts of self-alignment, on a moment by moment, day by day basis, to do therapy work with integrity.

Pre-Induction Talk

Now that the client is comfortably in your office - what are you going to say about hypnosis?

Typically, clients come with many unusual preconceptions about hypnosis. It is very common that they imagine hypnosis to be a sleep state devoid of awareness.

1) **Therefore, never use the word "sleep" unless you make it very clear that you are referring only to relaxation of bodily functions, not to awareness.**

   Another common misconception is that you can make them "cluck like a chicken" against their will. This is not possible (see guideline #5 below).

2) **It is important that you address all the concerns that could inhibit the therapeutic process.** From the expanded viewpoint of understanding the on-going pervasive nature of hypnosis, it follows that it is very important to explain that **the fact that they can think, hear, and feel able to "take control," is <u>not</u> an indication that hypnosis is not occurring.** It also happens to be a very powerful suggestion that aids the hypnotic process-*" whatever you experience makes you relax pleasantly into a beneficial hypnotic state where you can easily follow my suggestions and accomplish your goals."*

3) Since hypnosis is all pervasive in the nature of mental functions, it follows to make clear to clients that **it is a natural state of mind.** It is actually happening all the time, but there are two times when everyone can identify it: that momentary, dreamlike state when just falling asleep, and just when waking up. *"These hypnotic procedures merely serve to establish you in that state for a constant period of time in order to do therapeutic work."*

4) **It feels good!** *"You have this opportunity to relax, both physically and mentally, and, at the same time, to experience a capacity to learn and to change in beneficial ways you might not have realized were available to you. The more you relax, the better you feel. (And the better you feel the more you relax.)"*

5) **You can not be made to do anything against your moral and ethical codes-** make this clear in pre-induction, and even build it into your preliminary suggestions so it will serve to safeguard and relax them.

6) **Affirm that they are in control** by telling them they can count themselves out at any time simply by counting up from 1 to 5, (or 1 to 3, whatever), Again, build this into preliminary suggestions (i.e. the official preliminary suggestions) to add to the sense of safety. The implication of this information needs to be made explicit:

7) **All hypnosis is self-hypnosis, and the therapist is guiding and assisting rather than controlling.** Make it possible for them understand that they are responsible for developing this capacity, with your help, but it is their skill of inner communication that is being enhanced. <u>Make this attractively compelling.</u>

   In the scripts which follow, you'll find language to this effect where you impress upon them that the suggestions you give them are theirs to accomplish. *"Make this happen...you have to do it...I can't do it for you."*

It serves to repeat and elaborate here that, in order to have this information accepted by the client:

8) You have to establish rapport, not only with the client, but with the material. You have to be able to present it in such a way that they sense that you believe it--that you are **congruent in your conviction about it**. You need to convey a sense of **sincerity, calmness, poise and confidence**. If it happens that you find they have an expectation of the hypnotists "steady gaze," you may have to develop one.

Common Sense - Hypnosis Do's and Don'ts

A couple of years ago a man who had completed some hypnosis training somewhere physically endangered a hypnotic subject by hypnotizing him in a hot tub, after he had been drinking. The person almost drowned, and the hypnotist lost his license.

The golden rule will always be your best guideline:

> ***DO UNTO OTHERS AS YOU WOULD HAVE THEM DO UNTO YOU,***

and conversely:

> ***DON'T DO ANYTHING TO ANYONE UNDER HYPNOSIS YOU WOULDN'T WANT DONE TO YOU.***

Because of what you may have seen stage hypnotists do, you might be curious about trying some things like:

1) testing the strength of a person beyond their normal capacity - **DON'T.**

2) putting them through emotional extremes, e.g. from happy to sad quickly and back again - **DON'T.**

3) exposing them to physical harm when they are anesthetized - e.g., putting pins in the arm --**DON'T.**

4) **Don't** subject them to sudden shocks when they are so open and receptive -- e.g. don't announce the death of a loved one.

5) **Don't** humiliate them; don't attempt to violate their moral or religious standards.

6) Be sure to remove all suggestions of hallucination or rigidity so that there is **no inappropriate carry over** once they have left your office. For example, don't leave in place a suggestion that could put them in trance in an inappropriate situation upon the perception of a trigger stimulus. *"When you hear the word "dog," you will go deeply into trance."*

7) **Don't** abruptly awaken them in response to a strong emotional abreaction on their part: 1) let it run its course and bring them out gently, or 2) help them rise above the experience by counting them up out of the experience, e.g., *"On the count of three, rising higher and higher to a safe place...one...two...three...".*

8) **Don't** leave a client alone without proper notice and suggestions of reassurance. If you should have to leave for some reason prior to awakening them, make sure they are comfortable and let them know that they can come out when they are ready. It's a complete myth that someone could go so deep that they would not come back.

9) Regarding therapy models and strategies: **Don't** reinforce internal splits, fragmentation, or the autonomous existence of parts. Our goal is to integrate these energies into the experience of wholeness - to break down the trance experience of their fixated "thingness" and antagonistic separateness, and sense of needing to struggle to survive. (More on this later in the course.)

◆ ◆ ◆

4. Levels of Trance

Until Walter Sichort discovered deeper levels of hypnosis in the 1960's, there were thought to be only three: light, medium, and somnambulistic. The transition from "awake" to light, called *hypnoidal,* is characterized by fluttering of the eyelids, swallowing, changes in breathing patterns, general signs of relaxation, and closing of the eyes.

1) Light state

The **light state** allows for the suggestions of eye, limb, or body catalepsy (although, in practice, I have not seen body catalepsy in a light state). *Catalepsy* generally means immobility, and insensitivity with rigidity, but here rigidity is not implied. An initial sense of light anesthesia can also be induced at this stage.

2) Medium state

The **medium state** can include bodily sensations of metabolic change, personality changes such as talking in a child's voice because of regression, deluded forms of thought, partial amnesia, and suggested post-hypnotic anesthesia.

3) Somnambulistic state

The **somnambulistic state,** formerly considered the deepest, allows for many interesting psycho-physical phenomena including: spontaneous amnesia (instantaneously forgetting as with a vivid dream that disappears/not remembering the hypnotic session), positive and negative visual and/or auditory hallucinations, time distortion and time displacement, eyes open while in deep hypnosis, the ability to perform post-hypnotic suggestions for amnesia or almost anything else without conscious participation. This is familiar to most as weird hypnotic suggestions given to people by stage hypnotists, but it can be put to beneficial use. The senses are also generally heightened at this depth level.

4) Coma

Coma - the first state below somnambulism. The body, being very deeply relaxed and flaccid, will not respond to *physical suggestion* but the mind can be very alert to its surroundings and can respond to suggestion internally, just not physically.

5) Catatonia

Catatonia - It's really arbitrary to call it a state, given that it cannot be verbally suggested - you go to coma and see if you've got it - mainly by being able to induce, with physical signals, a state of rigidity in the limbs or body which is not dependent on the muscles, and can be maintained without fatigue. Hence the name - catatonia. I think it could be considered a capacity which can be activated in the coma state rather than a separate state, if its only mark is this ability to create physical rigidity.

6) Ultra depth

Ultra Depth is the deepest state. Again. it can't be suggested. but a person can "slide" into it. It is a wonderful state of being, characterized by complete relaxation, euphoria, complete anesthesia, a great awareness of surroundings that could be called psychic. It releases the capacity for miraculously fast healing of injury or surgery, and generally includes amnesia.

Signs and feelings while hypnotized are so numerous and varied, it is always useful, and even important, to impress on a client that *whatever they feel is fine*, and will just help them relax more and lets them know that they are easily going into a beneficial state. And if properly delivered, with rapport etc., they will !

Truly almost anything goes, from laughter to tears, from itching and scratching to sighing, twitching, yawning, and tingling. Changes in body temperature often occur, sensation of body weight from lighter to heavier, to floating and sinking. Of course, there is relaxation, both mental and physical, but there could also be tension *(which might not necessarily be created so much as brought into awareness)*. The most important thing is that whatever it is, *it's good!*..."*and makes it easier for you to go into trance.*" Even fear or anger can arise - it's O.K. You will be learning the communication skills needed to work with these phenomena to make them resources for and enhancements to the therapeutic process.

After a session, you can notice the eyes- they will generally be somewhat red. Rapid eye movement is not an indication of any particular depth of trance. It is, however, an indication that visualizing is taking place.

Having a client open and close their eyes while in trance, accompanied by appropriate suggestions, is a way to deepen trance. A demonstration of this is incorporated into scripts you will be practicing.

◆ ◆ ◆

5. Elements of Hypnotic Communication
Theatrical Devices for the Mind

Remember, **hypnosis** is theater; **problems** are theatrical; they are all pretense, albeit very serious and powerful. That's the point of good theater: to make us forget it is pretense, to absorb us completely within the scope of its laws and boundaries. The author is the God of the theater, determining universal laws, defining boundaries, choosing events and outcomes, and providing all the props and dialogue. The client and the therapist are entering into a collaborative endeavor as co-authors of new scenarios, and hopefully and more significantly, entirely new perspectives on the creative process itself. In my opinion, these new perspectives should embody living/learning skills that foster and expand the enrichment and freedom of the learning process forever, as opposed to learning some new technique and solidifying it into a new limitation.

Following are some important tools, approaches, and mental functions you need to recognize and master to enhance your role as co-creator.

1. *The personal law of cause and effect*

There is a "real" law of cause and effect, of course, but, relative to therapy and regaining sanity, it is the client's personal laws of cause and effect that you need to comprehend. Their assumptions about cause and effect govern their thinking and perceptual processes and action in the world. They underlie the structure and maintenance of their problems, their resources, and their very identity. Once formulated, generally at a very young and 'magical' age, they operate primarily unconsciously, unexamined, and unchallenged.

You need to recognize that you have the freedom to create your own laws as needed to enhance therapeutic communication. You are generating assumptions about causal relationships all the time, <u>just like your clients</u>. The point of your training is to learn to do it with great competency in achieving beneficial outcomes. It is one of your greatest tools. You get to define the linkages between anything that "is," and anything you need "to be:"

> *"Hearing the sound of my voice <u>causes</u> your eyelids to grow heavy..."*

> *"Each breath you take <u>causes</u> you to go deeper into trance..."*

> *"These noises used to distract you, now they <u>cause</u> you to relax easily and delightfully..."*

2) *Pacing and leading*

Pacing and leading is similar to the law of causation explained above. The law of causation relies on the phenomena of pacing and leading in that the indisputable, verifiable existence of the sensory information mentioned - the *"sound of my voice,"* *"each breath,"* *"these noises,"* fosters the inclination to agree with what follows -

relaxing, going into trance, etc. It differs in that it is more subtle - you don't mention the causality. Stating the causality, any statement by nature, leaves an opening for refutation. Pacing and leading is more subtle. You simply mention verifiable sensory phenomena (*and, if they are on the periphery of the client's awareness, their impact is greater*) - two or three in a row, watching for agreement **(pacing),** then shift to an observation of what you want to create **(leading).**

> *"You see me sitting before you, you feel the weight of your head on the pillow, your eyes are blinking... (all pacing statements)...as you shift into a more relaxed state." (leading)*

> *"You hear my voice...you have a sense of holding your balance in the chair...as you notice your right knee <u>on the edge of your visual field</u>* (peripheral) (pacing)...*your eyelids become heavy and close* (leading) (and to combine with causality) ...*<u>causing you to easily glide into a relaxing trance that feels good...</u>"* (Do you see the causality here - defining how it's going to feel?)

3) Make it pleasant

As demonstrated above, once you have created a condition, suggest that it is good, that it is getting better, that it is making everything happen effortlessly. This is a specific causal link you want to impress on the client - that what you are doing feels good and benefits him/her. This is why they want to allow or make it happen. A simple formulation for effectiveness would be: 1) Do (the task), 2) How to do (the task), and 3) It feels good (to do the task).

4) Confusional techniques

A favorite form of confusional technique is the use of counting numbers or reciting letters. In order to occupy the client's so-called conscious attention, you have them count backwards from 1000 by 3's, or backwards from 100 by 1's making the numbers disappear, for example, while you continue to give them suggestions. You will know it's effective when they lose track, or stop counting, falling into trance. With "tough" cases, you can ask them to recite the alphabet backwards or to spell words backwards, while visualizing them forwards, all the while giving them trance inducing suggestions.

You can create confusional overload by packing a story full of confusing directions where the words have double or ambiguous meanings: "

> *"He said to turn right, I think that's right, or was it left? What am I left with if left isn't right, I began to feel it is right to be left with nothing to do but go right into trance and relax..."*

Or by building quotes within quotes to generate ambiguity:

> *"That reminds me of the time Bill saw Bob running from the house and <u>he</u> (which he?) said...*

The underlying principle here is that little blips of uncertainty have the effect of undermining a person's on-going sense of orientation and groundedness. Stopping, or opening, or "gapping" the mind with such confusion is very threatening to most peoples' sense of stability and safety within their own experience of themselves and, when that happens, most peoples' minds are very pliable, very suggestible, very willing, *even compelled to grasp on to the first bit of solid ground offered to them, even if it is a new structure of orientation and experience: "drop into trance..."*

This effect can be powerfully utilized through double induction - two people giving suggestions at the same time, one in each ear.

Milton Erickson was a pioneer and master of these sorts of techniques. You are encouraged to study his work and to take from it whatever works for you. Experiment! (His work is an excellent resource with which to structure on-going mentorship and tutorials through the Institute for continuing education credits.)

5) Requirements for creating suggested conditions

When attempting to create a suggested condition (or psycho-physical state, attitude or behavior), **suggestions have to be <u>actively rejected</u> or they are accepted. The deeper someone is in trance, the less time they have to actively reject (exercise critical faculty) a suggestion.** Also, when giving several suggestions in a row, **it is the last suggestion that has the power.** This dynamic allows you to pace so-called resistance. You can fearlessly suggest the maintenance of their limitation, ending with a way out:

> *"You don't want to feel that, and you don't have to feel that, you can block that feeling as long as you want to...until <u>you are ready to feel it</u>..."*

6) Testing a suggested condition

When attempting to create a condition, **don't assume you have it unless you have created it with proper suggestions. <u>Then test</u>.** And if a test response is not what you are expecting, generally do a different test, otherwise you will be reinforcing a notion that it's not working. However, since you have such total freedom in this process, even a so-called "failure" can easily be turned to your advantage:

> *"Your arm is so relaxed now...it just won't move...try to move your arm...[it moves]...good...you've just demonstrated you have the control to move your arm...<u>now demonstrate that you have the control to relax that arm so completely, it just won't move...even if you try</u>...*

Arm moves:

"Good...now you are going to notice the feeling in you left foot...and as you are noticing the feeling in your left foot that causes your right arm to become lighter and lighter..."

7) Be flexible

A) Remember the freedom you have to create what you need (cause and effect); and B) remember the implied <u>validity and prestige</u> of pretense - especially when a subject is unconscious of the fact that the assumption is arbitrary, i.e., pretense - no exercise of critical faculty. Utilize pretense - DreamPower!:

"You know how outlandish things can happen in a dream?...and yet they look and feel so real?...just relax now and imagine you're in that kind of dream realm where you can safely imagine any outlandish thing you like and make it look and feel really real...a place where you can eeeasily dream yourself doing 'X' fully and completely and vividly...that's right...or dream yourself as you are after having succeeded at doing 'X' and look back and see how you did it..."

Hypnotic communication is a conversation, a **non-judgmental** conversation, which means you are free to *release all notions of failure.* Any response you get is information, data. If it is contrary to what you hoped for or expected, it is **not** a failure - it is valuable information about the process of communication you are engaged in. Stay loose, **learn from it,** find a way to apply it. Don't let it throw you into a self-conscious trance.

8) Act on inspiration and intuition

Learn to be more aware of your own inspirations and to act on them, even if they aren't in a script. Develop an appreciation for the notion of being in total communication already, "consciously and unconsciously," *even before you develop the awareness of it.* Learn to trust your inner promptings in relationship to your clients. Over time you may notice you have random thoughts about them prior to or after they leave...*that turn out to be very relevant.* Learn to let your inner mind think about your clients, and learn to accept its messages. You can tell which thoughts to honor and which to suspect by noticing the degree of *self-conscious involvement* that is present in the experience of the thoughts:

One day I was driving to see a client who never went very deep into trance. As I drove along, I suddenly knew just what to say to him to get him in a deep trance. I went in and described to him a long involved imagery of him taking a wonderful Jacuzzi [completely ad lib]. He went sooo deep, and, at the end of the session, he said, somewhat mystified, *"I didn't know you could go so deep and still be conscious."*

9) Use metaphors, stories, indirect suggestions

As the above example illustrates, creative indirect suggestion can be more powerful than direct with some people. I never told him to relax or that anything was causing relaxation. I just had him imagine this wonderful situation, and he went there. These techniques are powerful ways of demonstrating to a person in a non-threatening way, without expectation, that other perspectives and choices exist beside those they have *fixated on.* If you can help someone change the way they think about a problem (or themselves), they have changed the problem (or themselves).

(*Metaphor:* a figure of speech by which something is spoken of as being something else: He's a lion. *Simile:* a figure of speech relating, likening, one thing to another using 'like' or 'as': He's like a lion. She's hungry as a bear.)

10) Attention and modeling

Cultivate whole body/mind attention and modeling, and nonverbal pacing and leading. As you become more confident of your ability to communicate, and develop an appreciation for the nuances of communication, your capacity to be relaxed, present, and focused with your whole being on your client will increase. And, naturally, out of that will flow the ability to intentionally or effortlessly pace and lead and maintain a strong sense of rapport. The key is letting go of your own contractions and relaxing into the space of shared inherent goodness that is *always* available to you and to your client to contact.

Words communicate only about 8% of the message. The other 90+% is communicated through tonality (~40%) and physiology (body language, ~50%). If you can recall noticing people conversing who obviously liked each other, check your memory to see if the reason you could tell they **liked** each other wasn't in large part determined because they acted **like** each other:

a) From a gross level of dressing alike or in complimentary fashion,

b) To the subtle level of moment by moment mirroring and matching of body expression [posture, facials - including eyes and blinks}, gestures, and unconsciously, even of breathing!].

c) Didn't they "sing" together in their discussion, mixing and matching tempo, tone, timbre, and volume to create a symphony of warmth?

d) On an even more subtle level, you can bet they "talked the same language" in respect to perspective, the size of information bytes they presented for assimilation, and unconsciously matching internal accessing predicates.(More of this in Phase II -- NLP)

Come to think of it, the recognition of **acting alike and its by-product of affection** is probably what gave rise to the use of the term "like" to denote affection.

11) *Ask leading questions that presume the outcome you want*

For example:

> *"Can you imagine what it might be like to go into trance?" "Can you remember your deepest trance?"*

In other words , ask questions that require the client to do what you want them to do, in order to answer your question. Note: these understandings are widespread in the field of sales. So, if you hadn't noticed, <u>until now</u>, that you have been thinking that this is different from sales communication (or different from any kind of communication) - notice it, and think about art, literature, and situations other than the therapist's office that can provide you with an opportunity to gather information about the nature of communication and TO LEARN! Hypnotherapy really is a set of generalized communication skills -- don't put it in a box of "therapy." You could gain a wealth of insights and story-telling information, if you appreciate the opportunities that present themselves in all kinds of situations. *Reality is always expressing itself, always exposing itself, always trying to get us to notice.*

Remember, telling stories about what others can do, and about how others think, is a wonderful indirect way of suggesting that they can do and think in those ways, too.

12) *Don't necessarily point out things about a client that they are unaware of*

This is implicit in the above considerations about the effectiveness of communicating indirectly. YOU notice it, and use it to help them, but making them aware of it can unnecessarily complicate and even compound the solidity of their problem. If they are made to feel self-conscious in a way that debilitates them, they feel exposed, not only with you, but with others, and may generate new limiting behaviors.

13) *Take your clients literally*

Listen to them carefully; they will tell you with their own imagery how they structure their internal experience:

> *"I went through the roof..." "That's interesting... would you mind explaining the physics behind that?"*

You might not challenge their symbology like this initially; it's more of an advanced practice for bringing them out of self-trance. Instead you would pace their language when the opportunity arises during the session to create imagery of like kind that sends the message..."you are understood."

For example:

> *"I feel like I'm getting bogged down at work..."*

In trance, take them to a bog, explore it , how to get around it or through it...how to get out if they get stuck...what happens if they don't...etc.

As you develop your appreciation of the creative nature of communication, <u>even communication about depressing problems</u>, you will always feel confident about having plenty of material to work with...*playfully*...to the clients advantage:

I once had a client who said, *"I feel like a can't stand on my own two feet..."*

I immediately became very interested with a naive passionate fascination for her ability to cripple herself instantaneously. We explored in detail how this might happen - she quickly became aware of the ridiculousness of taking her statement literally, but, at the same time, felt the poignancy that she takes it literally and acts it out in those situations that trigger it. Just this much insight into the hypnotic, ridiculous power and effect of a seemingly harmless cliché, made a dramatic shift of empowerment for her. She left that session never again to feel like *"she couldn't stand on her own two feet."*

Of course, she might have the feeling she was labeling, but with the <u>metaphorical</u> trance broken, she will have to experience it more directly for <u>what it is</u> and take more appropriate action. E.g., "I'm angry...I'm scared...what is making me feel this way and what can I do about it?" There is still a problem to deal with, but these new questions <u>presume the possibility of having the power to deal with it</u>, vs. the former strategy of getting lost in an image (internal trance display) that created an immediate surrender and belief in being powerless, and <u>an accompanying felt-sense of powerlessness</u>. (See Regression, Phase II)

14) *Use Models of Truth that carry great prestige*

I propose that, *"The Truth is the most powerful induction."*

This is an extension of pacing the client's reality, but relies on appealing to greater cultural, religious, and scientific <u>models of truth</u> that carry great weight with us even when we have been taking them for granted, i.e., assuming them unconsciously and therefore unnoticed. When a client is made to notice them, it can have a profound effect:

Once I had a client who was claiming to have no **faith,** and to be feeling so much anxiety and doubt that she thought hypnosis and therapy was really a waste of time. It didn't take great perceptual skills to notice that she also had a cold. I began talking to her about her cold, asking her how many times she had thought she would die from this cold:

> *"None!"*

> *"Of course not...you have had many colds and have taken for granted that your immune system can handle them. Think about that. You have so much faith in this inner intelligence to protect you and heal you...so much faith that you never give it a second thought...even to the point of forgetting to value it!"* (She is now focused on me, and her level of anxiety is noticeably diminished.)

> *"And by the way... how often do you go to bed worrying about waking up in the morning to find that the cells of your body have migrated to different parts of the room?"* (chuckles, what a silly thought...she's relaxing more and more as she makes friends again with this part of herself she had forgotten.)

> *"Or, how often do you worry that you'll wake up and not remember who you are, or what your problems are!...now wouldn't that be nice.."* (laughs)

> *"You see this mysterious power and intelligence that as you...think about it now...you realize you can never comprehend it with your conscious mind...but isn't it nice to know that it is inseparably a part of you...it is you so completely that you can take it for granted and forget it's there to the point that your conscious mind can complain about lack of faith and doubting and totally miss the fact that this greater mind is happily giving the conscious mind the very life and energy it needs to protest...just like a perfectly loving mother holding a crying, unhappy baby in her arms."* (She is now deeply relaxed into trance.)

This is an example of using scientific truth to awaken the client's perspective in such a way that they move into or out of trance -- depending on your point of view. An old-fashioned common sense way to talk about this point is that it was an indirect way to tell her to count her blessings, and, as she counted them, she relaxed and her dilemma dissolved. **You could say that helping people recapture the ability to count their blessings is the approach and goal of this hypnotherapy course in a nutshell.**

15) *Paternal, Technical, Maternal and Mutual Methods*

Paternal or prestige hypnosis was the initial method used to induce trance in Western European history. If you refer to the historical synopsis, you will note that the early hypnotists, starting with Mesmer, weren't really sure what the nature of the phenomena was, or what really caused it. Many theories were presented and refined over time. I encourage you to read some histories of hypnosis. They will provide insights, interesting contexts from which to view your endeavors, and a sense of connection to your precursors, including such good company as Ben Franklin (who wasn't a hypnotist, but he tested Mesmer, and decided it wasn't what Mesmer claimed it was). And, of course, they will provide you with material for stories and metaphors!

Paternal approach

Paternal, or prestige approach, refers to authority: the early hypnotists put people in trance by virtue of the power of their personality, either genuine or imagined by the client (a trance in itself) because of credentials, attire, confusion (weak-mindedness), cultural trances concerning roles, power, and inhibition (propriety!), or whatever! Thus, the power was considered to reside in the hypnotist.

This is the style most are familiar with from watching stage hypnotists. The subjects are told what to do and to experience. If you have a problem, you are told you don't have it anymore. If the impact of the authority is great enough, you don't have it anymore, **apparently!**

The problem with this approach is that, if genuine underlying needs aren't addressed, if the client isn't taught the skills of communication to satisfy those needs, the problem will come out in some other form of negative behavior, or eventually as the old behavior.

Paternalistic behaviors have a place in therapy if they are properly used in an overall ecological context. Some people are conditioned to be told what to do. It can be important to tell such people what to do - until you help them regain their own autonomy to make their own choices from awareness of their own true needs.

Technical approach

Emphasis on **technique** as repository of the power evolved as a natural egalitarian impulse, in my opinion. We feel a sense of insult thinking someone has a personal power beyond our ability. If we can find the map of the inner workings, the steps in the process, it can be taught to anyone, theoretically. Since even these paternal masters used technique, ritual, it follows that some would look to the ritual for the source of the effects.

Good technique plays an important part in the therapy process, but not as the source of power, rather as a tool to evoke power from its true source. Even though a large percentage of people may respond uniformly to a given technique, to rely on technique in the Newtonian stance of absolute separation between subject and object, therapist and client, is to fall into a limiting and perhaps dangerous area of manipulation without compassion. More on this throughout the course.

Maternal approach

The **maternalistic or evocative approach** starts from the premise of inherent purity and a natural tendency of the unconscious to reorganize energies in the direction of health and wakefulness, and relies on compassion. The maternalistic approach recognizes that we are always doing our best <u>in the context of our trance state which is dictating to us what is real and what our options are.</u> Anytime a trance state is modified or dissolved, the unconscious is ready to generate new and more resourceful awarenesses and choices, with the assistance of directive and evocative suggestion.

Mutual approach

One could be maternalistic and still hold a predominately unconscious Newtonian assumption regarding experience. Yes, they are evoking the client's inherent purity, but they still have a deep sense of separateness with regard to what they are experiencing in the presence of a client - they think they are a separate witness and facilitator. They miss the deep and subtle aspects of **mutuality,** of the responsiveness and dance of their energies as partners in communion, and they miss how this determines what arises in session, and when, and to what outcome.

An appreciation of this mutuality, this co-trance, if you will, is essential to transformative work. It is not so much a method, as an attitude and commitment to develop the sensitivity, clarity and honesty to experience relating as-it-is, without the support of fixed opaque notions of self and other. Thus, in this course, it goes beyond even the notion of cooperation, which requires a sense of self and other. (Do not read this as <u>discounting</u> cooperation. In most cases, going beyond cooperation requires an atmosphere of cooperation.) This furthest extension of method dissolves method altogether into reliance on grace, or what Buddhist doctrine terms No-Mind. The exploration and elucidation of this point is central to the on-going discussion of this course.

One key aspect of understanding this point is to recognize that it is not important to decide to take a paternalistic, technical or maternalistic approach to a session. It is important, *in the immediacy of being fully present with them.* moment by moment, word by word, phrase by phrase, to choose the right approach, ideally in an <u>atmosphere</u> of the largest No-Mind perspective, to assist the client to regain their own autonomy, which is marked by

    1) greater wakefulness,
    2) greater awareness of and honoring of genuine needs (i.e. true self needs),
    3) willingness to choose to exercise their own power to meet those needs and,
    4) to take responsibility for doing so.

Again, the meaning of this statement is central to our on-going discussion.

The **general emphasis** of this course in terms of **style** is evocative: maternalistic with a recognition of mutuality - honoring the client as having within themselves everything they need to wake up from limiting trance states. But the **emphasis in terms of your on-going attitude** is to maintain your own "beginner's mind." Stay free of prejudice regarding any particular approach or model so that you maintain the flexibility and awareness to be able to use anything that may be appropriate in the moment.

6. Structure of A Hypnotherapy Session

A) *Pre-induction talk*

Establishes rapport about hypnosis, per se, as an issue, and, in an on-going therapy relationship, provides you with valuable information to utilize in trance states, such as imagery unself-consciously conveyed by the client which the therapist then uses as trance imagery. The impact on the unconscious self of the client is: *"Ah...he understands me, he speaks my language."* It also gives you advance warnings of fears and hopes which you can then incorporate into suggestions to anticipate their arousal and thereby diffuse them, e.g. *"should your arm twitch as it did in the last session, it will cause you to relax in such a way that your unconscious mind will bring you into a new understanding of its message and purpose in supporting these beneficial changes now..."* [ambiguity re: the word "its" is intentional- the unconscious?, the twitching?]

B) *Induction*

As used in some schools, this term means the whole trance process. Used here, it refers to the initial step of getting eye closure, eye catalepsy, and the focus on the therapists suggestions leading deeper into trance.

C) *Relaxation*

Directing the client's focus of attention to relaxing the body and mind systematically from head to toe.

D) *Deepening*

Using theatrical devices and imagery to more fully involve the client's absorption of attention in the inner focus following the guidance of the therapist.

E) *Therapy Work*

Having "set the stage," doing therapy procedures of choice to address the given issues to move towards a favorable outcome.

F) *Contextualization of learnings*

1) <u>Past Re-evaluation and Future Pace</u> - once you have brought resources into a situation and changed the client's relationship to it, you instruct the unconscious mind to take these new learnings, resources, and perspectives into any and all other similar and relevant situations in their past to transform them into resources as well, releasing all frozen emotional energies and generating and preserving insights. The conscious mind may be aware that it is being allowed to participate as evidenced by its awareness of one or more memories being changed, but, at the unconscious level, *the unconscious has the power to change them all,* taking all the time it needs to do so. Since the unconscious isn't limited by the conscious space/time construct, it may take all the time it needs during 30 minutes

or 30 days of conscious time. You can suggest or ask what that conscious time marker could/should/might be.

2) Once past re-evaluation suggestions are in place, you instruct the unconscious mind to project the new resources into the future of the client. You engage the client in actively imagining being in future anticipated and future unanticipated situations remembering and being supported by these new learnings *and by the new resources of their transformed relationship to their entire past and all the power and insight that brings to them.* You are conditioning them, consciously and unconsciously, to be able *to remember*, consciously **and/or** unconsciously, the new perspectives and choices they have at their disposal, and *to recognize*, consciously **and/or** unconsciously, where they are appropriate, and *to experience* how it feels to do them in the future.

G) *Formless integration*

Always dissolve all the elements of the entire session into a golden white light surrounding the client. This light is pervaded with all the intelligence, learnings and transformative power gained in the session. Dissolve the light into the client's body, permeating every cell with these resources- living resources that will continue to grow and elaborate themselves in the client's life from this moment forward, forever.

H) *Count them out*

Assuring them that these new learnings are alive and growing within them from now on, forever, you instruct them to let it all be handed over to their unconscious mind for safe keeping as they easily and delightfully come back to normal waking consciousness.

◆ ◆ ◆

7. The Nature of the Egoic Mind

Three Examples

In India, they trap monkeys by placing a piece of fruit in a container with a neck that is large enough for the monkey to squeeze in his empty hand, but once he has grasped the fruit, his hand cannot pull out of the container. The monkey will desperately try to get free, but, even at the approach of his captors, his efforts are futile, because, the more afraid he becomes and the harder he tries, the more powerfully he grasps the fruit that is binding him.

◆

When I was nineteen, I was helping my father screen in our back porch. The 2x4 beams that would support the screening were approximately 3 feet apart, and we put up the screen section by section. It was June; nice weather and, of course flies flying around. For some reason, I was really impressed watching a fly repeatedly buzz up against the screen I was working on obviously trying to get free! It was the first section of screen, so there was space everywhere else in the direction he wanted to go- not to mention the space of going back the way he came. But he was willing to buzz against his obstacle to the point of exhaustion and death. I like to imagine that he was a fly philosopher or a fly psychologist - I like to listen to his discourses decrying our existential dilemma.(Or like me, when I'm complaining or feeling stuck.)

◆

If you put a bunch of fleas in an aquarium with a glass top, they will initially jump and bounce against the top. After a while, no more fleas will hit the top, having "learned" the boundary of their world. At that point, if you remove the top, very few fleas will escape the aquarium. They will bounce to their now self-imposed height limitation.

◆ ◆ ◆

8. Suggestibility Games

The following two demonstrations allow you to test people's initial affinity for suggestions, prior to any particular establishment of pacing, leading, or rapport. Personally, I have never used these with a client. But they could be effective and enjoyable ways of giving the client a taste of the power of the mind to create **kinesthetic** impact in surprising ways that will cause the skeptical client to pause and ponder.

They are also potentially useful in group settings to give people an enjoyable and quick taste of the power of the imagining factor of the mind. At the same time, they will provide you with information on the willingness of those in your audience to be hypnotized.

Script #1: Balloons and Telephone Books

Stand up and close your eyes. Keep your eyes closed until I tell you to open them. Just relax in a balanced way...and really allow yourself to vividly imagine the images I'm about to suggest to you. Now, raise your arms out in front of you horizontally. That's right. Now imagine a group of large *colorful* helium balloons being tied to your left wrist...look up and see them on the ends of the strings...*feel* them pulling your left wrist up...just *relax* your left arm *into* the sensation of *rising up...delightfully rising up...*that's right...surprisingly, the *more* you *relax* your left arm <u>*into the pull*</u> of those balloons, the *stronger* the *pull* becomes, the *brighter* the colors of the balloons seem...and the *higher* your arm goes...that's right...perhaps you notice the sounds of a fair or circus in the background...as you look at these *colorful* balloons and *feel the good feelings of having fun at a fair...as you feel your arm being lifted higher and higher...*That's right.**((Be dramatic and emphasize key words such as those indicated. Raise your tone of voice higher as you talk of going higher.))**

Now...as you experience this delightful sensation of your left arm being lifted effortlessly higher...a *thick, heavy* **((emphasize the heaviness with your voice -- make your voice heavy and emphatic))** phone book is being tied on to your right wrist in such a way that it won't fall off...so now you feel this *heavy weight <u>pushing</u>* your right arm *<u>down</u>...heavier and heavier...*this *heavy* phone book pushing your right arm down...feel it being pushed down...feel that *heavy* phone book *pushing* your arm *down...***((shift voice - lighten up))**even as your left arm is being *lifted <u>up</u>*. That's right...**((light voice))** your left arm is lifting up...*(heavy voice)* as your right arm is being *pushed down* by the *weight* of this *thick heavy* phone book. **((Pause a few seconds.))**

Now, open your eyes and see where your arms are.

NOTE: The degree to which they allowed their arms to be effected by the imagery is an indication to you of their initial level of susceptibility to suggestion. It's a delightful way of ascertaining this information and everyone generally enjoys the experience, and there are usually many interesting occurrences in their inner worlds that they will want to share.

Script #2 - Pushing back and Pulling forward

The first script relied on the sound of your voice and the successful generation of internal imagery to create the "power" to move the arms. This two part exercise is a little more complex in that it utilizes the relationships of spatial coordination-ordination that the mind is always engaged in to keep us properly situated and properly balanced in our environment. This process is totally outside our conscious awareness virtually 100% of the time. When it is made conscious, as this exercise does, it can be quite astonishing. A common example of this effect we can all probably identify is taking an extra step on stairs when there isn't one, or <u>not</u> taking step when there is one (i.e. expecting level ground to meet our next step).

Have the subject stand erect with their arms at their side, and their feet touching together. Stand behind them, place your hands lightly on their shoulder blades, and stand with your feet spread one behind the other to give you a strong supportive posture. Then ask:

"I want you to lean back, just let your self go, you can feel my hands on your shoulder blades. Just lean back and let me support you."

When they have complied, put them erect and ask them if they had to force themselves to lean back. There is no right answer — this is just for feed back, and it indicates their level of trust. Now have them stand again as before, and you resume your posture except that now your hands are a few inches away [just one or two]. Tell them:

"Now my hands are just off your shoulder blades. I want you to lean back again and I'll support you. Just lean back, that's right."

When they have complied, stand them erect again and ask if that was more difficult. Generally, it will be more difficult for a subject to let go without the feel of your hands on their back.

Now have them stand again as before. This time you stand beside them with one hand lightly on their back and the other hand about 8 inches from their face and about 3 or 4 inches above eye level, fisted with your thumb sticking out so they can see your thumbnail. Say:

"Keeping your head level, focus all your attention on my thumbnail...that's right...all your attention on my thumbnail...in a moment I'm going to ask you to close your eyes. When I do I'm going to move behind you and you will have the sensation of tipping back...just let it happen because you know I will support you. Just keep looking at my thumbnail...now...close your eyes (**(keeping your hand on the back, move quickly behind them , sliding the hand over so you can place your other hand on the back as well, <u>remembering to space your feet to give you a strong base, saying as you do:</u>)**), feel yourself coming back...coming back...that's right."

Put them erect and ask what their experience was when they closed their eyes. Many times, subjects will report that upon closing their eyes, the thumbnail came zooming at them and "pushed" them back. There are versions of this script where you imply that by suggesting they might see the thumbnail on the back of their eyelids when they close their eyes. I like to do it first with no such suggestions to see what their pure response will be.

If your not happy with your results, you can add a line about the thumbnail on the back of the eyelids and check the difference.

Now face them; they are standing in the same way; you have the same spread stance for support. Point to your eye and say:

"Look into my eye...focus all your attention on my eye...that's right ((**while they are looking into your eye, move your hands close to each side of their head like blinders used on horses. Your weight is in a forward position on your front foot. As you shift your weight to your back foot keeping your arms and body fixed so your whole body moves as a unit, saying:))**

"Focusing all your attention on my eye...coming forward...coming forward...((**catch them as necessary)).**

If you create the proper effect by the positioning of your hands, and the movement of your body as a single unit, the established focus of their attention will create for them the feeling of a "force" pulling them towards you. That force is the internal creation of their mind trying to maintain the status quo of the visually established anchors.

◆ ◆ ◆

9. Quick Inductions

In its initial stages, it was thought to take up to twenty minutes or more to induce a state of trance in clients through fixing visual attention in various ways. Tiring of the eyes seemed to have an important role to play in the shifting of states, and many techniques were developed to fixate eye attention in ways to tire the eyes. pendulums, candles, spots on the wall, swirling discs, etc. It was very tedious to take twenty minutes or more to induce trance, particularly if it made hypnosis impractical altogether because of time constraints. The desire to find faster more efficient means became an important task in this century where speed and improvement characterized the whole atmosphere of the scientific-industrial revolution.

Quick or rapid inductions were pioneered in many ways by Dave Ellman and others for specific purposes. They provide doctors and dentists with a fast means of getting clients into trance since their time with them was usually limited. Stage hypnotists also rely on them, not only because their time is limited with subjects, but because they are impressive for the audience to watch.

Our purpose in using them is in the context of therapy where they do save some time by facilitating eye closure and eye catalepsy which is the initial demonstration <u>clients make to themselves</u> that they can make or allow themselves to go into trance. But speed is not a primary concern at all with us. We can and should take the time we need to establish rapport and to understand the dynamics that are being presented and to determine how to address them.

Nevertheless these are interesting maneuvers to practice and to utilize in your formal trance work.

1) *The Magic Eye Closure Technique*

((Slowly bring your finger and thumb up to the client's eyes in such a way that they aren't disturbed, saying:))

I'm going to close your eyes with my finger and thumb.

((At this point a subject will almost always assist you by closing their eyes so you find that what you actually do is just rest your finger and thumb lightly on their lids, saying:))

That's right. Now I want you to pretend with your whole heart and soul that you cannot open your eyes...pretend with your whole heart and soul that you cannot open your eyes...that's right...make it happen...as long as you are pretending with your whole heart and soul that you cannot open your eyes...your eyes just won't open...now I'm taking my hand away as you continue to pretend that you cannot open your eyes...in a moment I'm going to ask you to try to open your eyes...but because you are pretending you cannot open them, they just won't open...want that to happen...and make it happen...when I ask you to try to open them...the more you try the more impossible it will become for them to open...in fact <u>the harder you try the more relaxed and closed they will become</u>...want that to happen and make it happen...now try to open your eyes and find that you cannot...***((wait just a few seconds))***...and stop trying...

> ***((In a session you would continue from this point with the rest of your trance work.))***

Pretense is a powerful tool important to utilize throughout the therapeutic process. This should not be surprising since our approach is based on the realization that all mental constructs, **including the clients' problems,** are imaginary. Imaginary and illusory, yes, but always remember that imaginary does not imply without substance. Even though they aren't <u>**real,**</u> they can be very powerful and a challenge to change.

2) Thumbnail With Eye Closure

> ***((Hold your closed hand with your thumb sticking out and your thumbnail about eight inches from the subject's eyes and about three inches above eye level, saying:))***

Focus on my thumbnail...focus on my thumbnail with all your attention...as I raise my thumbnail higher...follow it with your eyes <u>not</u> your head...that's right...following it with all your attention...your eyelids probably tiring now...just keep focused on my thumbnail...in a moment I'm going to drop my hand down...when I do...let your eyelids close and relax... loose and limp...releasing all the tension building in them now...***((drop hand))***...now eyes closing...that's right...loose and limp...so loose and limp that they just won't open now even if you try to open them.

((Eye catalepsy challenge could follow:)) Try to open them and find they just won't open...and stop trying...going even deeper into relaxation throughout your whole body...***((or, move into a progressive relaxation of the head and body.))***

3) Handshake With Eye Fixation -- A Coordinated Approach

This can be a very powerful inducement to trance because it combines 1) tiring of the eyes with 2) verbal cues punctuated by 3) kinesthetic enforcement. However, it takes some practice to master since it's somewhat like patting your head and rubbing your stomach at the same time.

> ***((Hold out your right hand and ask for the client's right hand. After you have their hand in yours, make sure they have relaxed it in your grasp, and <u>make sure you are standing to the side with your body out of their visual field.</u> Then place the edge of your left hand horizontally at their eye level about eight inches in front of them, saying:))***

Focus your attention on the edge of my left hand...focus all your attention on the edge of my left hand...as you do, I'm going to slowly raise it higher *((begin to raise it))*...follow it with your eyes but not with your head...that's right...keeping your head level and relaxed...follow the edge of my hand with your eyes...all your attention on the edge of my hand.

((Stop the hand about a foot above their eyes or at the point <u>before</u> they loose sight of it. Their eyes are now straining.))

In a moment I'm going to shake your hand 3 times...the first time I shake your hand, your eyes will feel very tired...the second time, they will want to close...let that happen...the third shake you feel will cause your eyes to be locked tight shut...want that to happen...experience it happening.

((As you shake their hand, coordinate the shakes with your other hand dropping <u>smoothly</u> so that it starts dropping on the first shake, is at eye level on the second, and is down to their abdomen on the third. The shake of the hand should have just the right amount of force to emphasize the bold word in each corresponding sentence of the script below.))

1) **Begin lowering the your left hand, as you raise the right hand to shake it, saying:**

Your eyes are feeling **tired**. *((raise their hand in preparation to shake on the words: "your eyes are feeling..." then, emphasize shake and voice on "tired."))*

2) **Left hand is brought to eye level as right hand is raising and ready to shake, saying:**

Your eyes are **closing**. *((raise their hand on "Your eyes are..." then, emphasizing shake and voice on "closing."))*

3) **Left hand all the way down, right hand raising and ready to shake, saying:**

Your eyes are **locked** tightly shut. *((again, raising their hand on, "Your eyes are..." then, emphasizing shake and voice on "locked."))* That's right...your eyes are so tired...so loose and limp...your eyelids are locked so tightly shut that they won't open even if you try to open them...try to open them now and find they just won't open...*((Wait about 2 seconds))*...and stop trying and relax even more completely...allowing that relaxation in your eyes to spread throughout your body...deepening more delightfully as it goes from the top of your head **down** to the tips of your toes...bringing you more and more pleasant feelings as it goes...that's right...

((Continue here with more induction of your choice.))

((Awaken to normal consciousness.)) And now I'm going to touch you on your right shoulder...when I do you will easily and effortlessly come back to normal waking consciousness...feeling clear headed and refreshed.

((Touch, wait & observe, continue to encourage as necessary.))

4) Arm Raising Induction

((Take the client's arm at the wrist and raise it out in front of them horizontally. Let go saying:))

Hold your arm there...that's right...now, close your eyes...very good, thank you...now hold your arm there and ***don't*** let it drop to your lap ***any faster than*** you align all your *energies, willingness, and attention* to *sliding eeeasily* into a *deep relaxing* trance...perfectly oriented in relationship to your unconscious mind and resources in such a way that it will be *delightfully easy now* to accomplish the most important learning you need to accomplish today...that's right...moving *deeper*...

((Just relax and encourage them every now and then, particularly when you get some kind of movement in the arm or any kind of responsiveness anywhere in the body. Remember to notice their breathing, and work with it.))

5) Simple eye closure with relaxation

The following induction is adapted from Dave Ellman's book, <u>Hypnotherapy</u>, (copyright 1964, Westwood Publishing Co., Glendale, Ca.). It demonstrates three interesting aspects of hypnosis developed by Mr. Elman:

First, it is a brief induction to induce somnambulism in about five minutes. As you remember, this level of trance is extremely valuable because of the enhanced capacities of the subject to remember virtually anything, to create anesthesia in the body, and to suggest amnesia, or have spontaneous amnesia.

Secondly, it demonstrates incremental deepening through the use of repeated eye opening and closing, which Mr. Elman developed on a hunch for a short cut to achieve a level of depth in one session equal to what normally took several. His hunch was that the significant "marker" between sessions was the opening and closing of the eyes. Therefore it might follow that, instead of waiting for a patient to come back for repeated inductions to build a well conditioned state, it would suffice to simply open and close their eyes several times accompanied by appropriate suggestions. He tried it and it worked!

Thirdly, it elucidates his recognition of the difference between **real somnambulism** and **apparent somnambulism**. This is very important to distinguish. For example with pain control procedures, real somnambulism gives the client the capacity to maintain a pain free state on their own for long periods of time -- with child birth for example. False somnambulism, which he calls artificial somnambulism, may not produce any anesthesia at all, or, at best, will require the constant monitoring and re-enforcement of the hypnotist. The distinction you need to watch for is the actual disappearance of the numbers (see script) which is a result of an **actual moment of amnesia**, which Mr. Elman states is the prerequisite occurrence for the development of somnambulism, versus the **apparent disappearance** of the numbers which is simply the clients unwillingness to speak because of relaxation -- what Mr. Elman terms **aphasia** which is quite different from **amnesia**. It's the difference between being unable to do something and being unwilling to do it, and in terms of the hypnotic state and capacities accessed, it is a dramatic difference.

Close your eyes...that's right...and *easily* and naturally begin to think about aligning all your energies towards the experience of *effortless, pleasant, deep* relaxation...that's right...think about that...as you now breathe in slowly and deeply...that's right...and now exhale slowly and easily...breathing out all tension...good...very good.

Now allow your attention to focus on your eye muscles and think about your eye muscles *relaxing* completely...your eye muscles, *becoming loose...limp...completely* letting go... easily and effortlessly into a wonderful sensation of complete restfulness...experience that happening now...your eye muscles becoming *so completely loose and limp now* that they just won't open your eyes...*even* if you tried...want that to happen...want your eye muscles to be *so relaxed*...enjoying that *loose, easy* feeling so much...they just won't open even if you try to open them...now when they are relaxed in this way...try to open them and find that they do not open...try to open them and find they do not open...***((wait about 2 seconds)).***

...Stop trying...good...Now imagine and experience that relaxation around your eyes *spreading* over your face...over the top of your head and down through your whole body...washing through *every cell* of your body as it goes...***((Sweep your hand over their body as you imagine the energy going from the top of their head to the tips of their toes. Have the attitude that the client, even with eyes closed, can see you. Given that, think about how to participate physically to emphasize your verbal instructions))***

...washing through and *releasing* every cell into a *deep* state of pleasant, refreshing restfulness from the top of your head...*((sweep))* to the tips of your toes...that's right...going 10 times more relaxed...that's right...let your body show you how good it feels to go *ten* times more relaxed...***((pause))***

Now I want you to open your eyes and then close them...and as you do you will experience *even deeper* relaxation...open your eyes...***((as they open, say:))*** now close them...close them and go *deeply* relaxed...very good. ***((pause))***

Now...open them again...and close them going completely relaxed...that's right *even deeper, wonderful, restful* feelings moving throughout your body...every muscle going limp now. ***((pause))***

Experience how *good* this feels...soon I'm going to ask you to open and close your eyes a third time...when you do this the third time you will *double* this restful state you are experiencing right now...every muscle and nerve...every cell *resting twice as deeply as before*...***((pause))***

Now...open your eyes...and close them again...that's right...doubling your relaxation throughout your body...***((pause))***

Now make sure that relaxation is enjoyed mentally as well as physically...this is how you can do it...[When I tell you to...start counting out loud backward from 100...counting out loud...hearing your own voice and feeling your mouth move will only *increase* your relaxation in a delightful way... so, as you count out loud backward from 100, each time you say a number, saying it will *double* your relaxation...and by the time you reach 98...having doubled your relaxation with each number...you will be *so relaxed* that you will *relax* those numbers right out of your mind...so *make that happen...want it to happen*...I can't make you *do it*...but you can *make it happen*]...

> *((repeat section in [brackets]))*

Count out loud, and as you count I will continue giving you suggestions...now start counting and make those numbers disappear as you relax..

((As they say 100, say:)) Now double your relaxation and watch the numbers begin disappearing...don't just say them...watch them disappear (**99**) that's right, watch them disappear (**98**)...now they are gone...make it happen make them vanish...relaxed right out of your mind...Are they gone? *((If not, keep going in the same manner, doubling on each number, encouraging them to vanish each time.))* Are they gone?

If they are truly gone you should have a somnambulistic state. Elman emphasizes that this whole process is a process of <u>consent</u>. If the client is blocking it, you can't force them. His approach is to try an innuendo of blame, treating the resistance as an obstacle to his agenda of getting somnambulism. He would say, "Some people are willing to do it the easy way, I guess you want to do it the hard way." expecting an apologetic, acquiescence in response that would make the client comply.

From a therapeutic standpoint, throughout the course I will be emphasizing a different approach. My approach is to throw out the whole notion of resistance. To do this you have to throw out fixed agendas — if you have no fixed agenda, how can there be resistance to anything? If so-called resistance comes up to something you are doing, <u>that very resistance becomes the focus of interest and exploration instead of being regarded as a nuisance.)</u>

Here is a device Elman uses if he has aphasia instead of somnambulism to turn aphasia into true somnambulism:

> I'm going to lift your arm (hand) and drop to your side (lap or whatever)...when it drops to your side the lights will go out and the numbers will be gone...*((drop hand))*...Are they gone?

Recognize this is just a <u>choice</u> of imagery used to effect a change...<u>you may have an idea of your own...go with it</u>...test it...this particular image is not the <u>magic, right</u> image...it's just a good image that he found worked a majority of the time for him.

◆ ◆ ◆

10. Progressive Relaxation

Some form of progressive relaxation should almost always be a part of an induction to facilitate the client's shift into more resourceful states of trance or, with luck -- out of egoic trance altogether, however briefly. The script below is not the only way to do it. Use it, memorize it if you like, but hopefully, it is only a stepping stone that supports you until you are skilled enough to enjoy creating your own effective scripts as you go along with each client.

I have incorporated some of the points of pre-induction material to demonstrate how this could be done as well.

Close your eyes. Take a deep breath...that's right...let it out slowly...take another slow easy deep breath...good...let it out slowly as you feel your whole body relax...

> *((pause))*

...think about your breathing...think about your breathing **relaxing** your body...each breath communicating to every cell of your body the wonderful sensations of restful **release** and **ease**...want it to happen...**remembering you are in control of this process...opening and trusting that deeper, wiser, more powerful part of your being we call the unconscious mind to manage this process for your benefit...***((pause))***

...as each breath carries this pleasant feeling of ease and relaxation to each cell with every breath...that's right...every breath you take carries oxygen to every cell of your body...and every cell of your body **effortlessly** responds to the presence of the oxygen...opening and absorbing the oxygen **deeply** into its being to support all life processes...*((pause))*

...in the same way **now**...imagine this relaxing energy being breathed in right along with the oxygen...this **relaxing** energy is being carried to every cell right along with the oxygen on **every** breath....and each and every cell recognizes the gift and healing power of this relaxing energy in the same way that they recognize and utilize the oxygen...accepting the gift of this relaxation right along with the oxygen **deep** into their being...to pervade the entire being with wonderful feelings of **ease and peacefulness.***((pause))*

Know that each cell of your body is listening and will go on accepting this relaxing healing energy on every breath ...even as I direct your ordinary attention to other areas...so relax into the awareness that every cell of your body is supporting you now in ways your conscious mind will never comprehend...anymore than your conscious mind can comprehend how your unconscious mind can create, coordinate, and sustain this breathing process without rest, unceasingly, every moment of your life...even when your conscious mind is paying no attention to it...even when your conscious mind is totally **unconscious** as it is in the sleep state...*((pause))*

...As you are now reminded of this powerful, mysterious, **loving** intelligence of your own unconscious mind...allow your appreciation of this loving power of your own being to **relax you effortlessly**...to make it possible for you to enjoy [[aligning all your energies in relationship to the true needs of your entire being in such a way that we can **easily accomplish** the learnings most appropriate for you to master today as revealed by this **deep** intelligence of your own being.]]

> *((Repeat section in brackets. Begin with: "Think about..." and continue with bracketed section "[[aligning...]]")) ((pause))*

As you relax now...even **more deeply** on every breath...prepare yourself to follow my suggestions to the letter for your highest benefit... as we move through a progressive attention to every part of your body...

As we begin, scan your whole body and assess your mental state and experience thus far...**if there is any way in which you sense that you need a suggestion or clarification that I have not yet given...recognize that you have the power now to experience those suggestions and clarifications taking full force and effect, just as if I had said them, causing you to go easily into a deeply relaxed state...**

> *((repeat all in bold -- pause))*

Now allow your attention to focus on your eye muscles...and relax your eyes so completely that they will not open...even if you try to open them...so completely relaxed they will not open...want it to happen...make it happen...your eye muscles so loose and limp and rested...they just don't want to open even if you try...*((pause))*

...now, try to open them and find you cannot...the more you try the more relaxed they become...the more you try...the more **relaxed** they become...good...stop trying and relax even more deeply...allowing that relaxation around your eyes to spread up over your forehead...relaxing the muscles of your forehead...up over your scalp...think about the muscles of your scalp relaxing...you probably rarely think about these muscles...think about them now...as this wonderful energy **flows** over your scalp...down the back of your head and into the base of your brain...the sleep center of your brain...being gently flooded with this relaxing energy...that's right...*((pause))*

Experience and imagine this wonderful relaxing energy flowing, now, throughout your brain...**caressing** and **enlivening,** and **purifying** every brain cell...as you realize that your brain is in communication with and controls the functioning of every cell in your body...experience your brain cells communicating this wonderful sensation to every cell of your body as you allow yourself to **relax completely** into this chair... accepting the willingness of this chair to support you completely...and the more you relax...the more you feel this support...and the more you relax...you appreciate the support of your unconscious mind...and the more you appreciate this support...the more you **let go completely now** into a beautiful state of physical and mental relaxation that floods even negative and fearful thoughts with the energy of ease and love and peacefulness...want that to happen ...experience that happening **now**...*((pause))*

Now feel the relaxing energy moving all around your jaw...relaxing your jaw muscles completely...it's fine if your jaw should droop slightly...feel this relaxation moving all around your lips...your cheeks...all around your face...as it flows **down** your throat...and the back of your neck...vertebrae by vertebrae radiating out all around your neck and throat...

Feel it moving into your shoulder muscles...relaxing them completely...feel it **flowing down** your arms...through your elbows...into your forearms...**down** into your wrists...into you hands...and out to the tips of your fingers...

((pause, repeat anything that seems appropriate))

Now experience your right arm becoming filled with this relaxing energy...imagine your right arm becoming so relaxed it feels like it has just dissolved into a feeling of being a liquid pool of peaceful energy that just **feels so good** it doesn't want to move...experience your right arm...now...so relaxed...like a pool of liquid energy...that it won't move even if you try to move it...that's right...*((pause))*

Now try to move your right arm and find that you cannot...try to and find that you cannot...the more you try the more relaxed it becomes...that's right...the more you try, the more **relaxed** it becomes...now stop trying and let that relaxation flow **even more deeply**...((option: *repeat with the left arm in the same way*))

((If there was movement, say:)) **"Good, now you have demonstrated you have the control to move your arm...now demonstrate to your self that you have the power and control to make your arm so relaxed it won't move even when you try to move it."**

((If you still get movement, you can repeat once more, but if there is still movement, this would be a point in a therapy session where you would address the issue. You might ask for their experience of what it is that is stopping them from letting themselves have this power over their own body and go from there. More on therapy approaches as we go.))

((Another option to deepen is to use the counting down method:))
"I'm going to count from 5 (or 7) down to one...as I do...you will
go deeper into relaxation on each beat of the count...

    5...going deeper and deeper into relaxation
    4...deeper and deeper down...just giving in and letting go
    3...even deeper...just giving in and letting go...that's right
    2...deeper still...very good...even deeper
    1...very deep now...very relaxed...ready to experience your arm so
       relaxed it just won't move..."

*((Note: Understand that this device of counting down can be interjected
anywhere and anytime you feel it would be useful, and that it can be
repeated two or three times in a row if it seems to be working -- is it
working? That's always the test for whether or not to keep doing
something.))*

...Now feel that relaxation moving into your chest...moving into your lungs and all
around your heart...**soothing** your heart...moving into your diaphragm...**relaxing**
your lungs and diaphragm so that your breathing becomes even **more peaceful
and easy**...that's right...feel it moving down your back, vertebrae by vertebrae,
radiating out into all the muscles of the back...*((pause))*

Now moving into your abdomen...washing through all your internal
organs...stomach...kidneys...intestines...liver and spleen...your genitals...your
buttocks...all around your hips...**deeply releasing and at ease**...as it flows down
into your thighs...**relaxing** the muscles of your thighs...flowing down into your
knees...through your knees into your calves...**relaxing** the muscles of your
calves...that's right...and down through your ankles into your feet...through your
feet out to the tips of your toes...*((pause))*

...good...*((option: test for catalepsy in the legs in the same way you did the
arms))*...feel this wonderful peaceful energy from the top of your head to the tips
of your toes...*((repeat))*...**flowing** through every cell of your body...**permeating
and relaxing** your mind and emotional energy...cleansing and rejuvenating your
entire being. *((pause))*

*((In a session we would move on to therapy at this point, but in this
exercise, we will give the client 5 minutes of silence to enjoy this
relaxation.))*

Now I will be silent for 5 minutes to give you the opportunity to **enjoy** and **deepen** and
explore this wonderful state you have created for yourself. Open up to it
completely...allow for the possibility that healing will take place...and new learnings and
resources generated for your own highest benefit and, by your sharing these benefits, for
the benefit of all beings.

((Five minutes of silence.))

In a moment, I'm going to count from 1 to 5, bringing you back to ordinary waking consciousness...you will come back effortlessly and delightfully... experiencing yourself clear-headed with your energies alert and balanced to carry on and have a wonderful day...[[all the learnings and resources and discoveries you have experienced today will stay with you **from now on forever**...radiating throughout your past...transforming your relationship to your past **in such a way** that your past will no longer limit you in harmful ways...*((repeat in brackets))*]]...sense that happening, **now**...*((pause))*

[[...radiating out into your future to support you with new perceptions, new choices, and new empowerments as you move into your future constantly discovering the expansion and purity of your own being...*((repeat))*]]...sense that happening, **now**...*((pause))*

...these new learnings, resources and discoveries are alive and full of intelligence, and therefore will continue to grow and generate new learnings, new resources, and new discoveries for your highest benefit, forever...*((pause))*

So now just relax into this wonderful new experience as it brings you back to a new normal waking consciousness

1...begin coming back...*((raising and enlivening your voice and energy as you go))*

2...coming back more and more...easily coming back...

3...coming back even more...wakeful energy moving through your arms and legs...move your fingers...wiggle your toes...that's right... move your fingers and toes...coming back...

4...breathe in deeply...breathe in wakeful energy...waking you up completely...clearing your head...filling your body with waking energy...and...

5...open your eyes...open your eyes...come fully back...fully back...breathe in wakeful energy...and come fully back.

◆ ◆ ◆

11. Progressive Relaxation

An Alternative

This script is less metaphysical, perhaps more simple and ordinary. It's presented to give you a sense of flexibility and contrast. Take your pick. Move between the "polarities" of style as it suits you, and as it suits your client.

Shift your body into a comfortable position. Let go of all your concerns...let yourself have these few moments to be at peace...nothing else has to be important during this time...just let it all go...knowing you can have it all back later **in any way you wish**...*((P))* now take a long slow deep breath...hold it for just a second...and then exhale slowly and easily...closing your eyes as you do...that's right...feel your whole body let go into a state of rest...Now breath deeply again...and let it out in the same way...experiencing your body respond pleasantly by going even deeper into a state of ease...that's right...good...*((P))*

Now think about your eye muscle relaxing...all those tiny muscles that move the eyes going loose and limp...into a state of rest and happy ease...think about the muscles of your eyelids easing into that same restful state, now...as your eye muscles relax your whole body also responds by following them **even deeper** into this wonderful gift of peaceful relaxation you are giving yourself now..*((P))*

Feel this energy of peace and rest moving all over your face now...relaxing the muscles in the cheeks...around the lips...all around the jaw...muscles releasing...letting go...moving pleasantly into a state of rest. *((P))*

Feel it spread up into your forehead...back over your scalp...releasing the muscles of your forehead and scalp...as it flows **eeasily** and effortlessly down the back of your head into the base of your brain...flooding your brain with wonderful peaceful relaxing energy...that your brain cells transmit to every cell of your body...experience that sensation of healing relaxation being transmitted from your brain to every cell in your body *((P))*

Now experience that flow of relaxing energy moving down the back of your neck into your shoulders...soothing and releasing your shoulder muscles in a delightful way as you notice now **just how eagerly** you anticipate and assist the spread of this wonderful relaxing energy as you listen to and follow my suggestions to the letter for your own enjoyment and benefit. *((P))* That's right.

Feel that release of tension in your upper arms now...in all the muscles of your upper arms as they too relax completely into this restful pleasurable state...good...just let it flow through your elbows now...into all the muscles of the forearms...down through the wrists and into the hands and out to the tips of your fingers...relaxing all the muscles there *((P))*

Focus your attention on your right arm now...and as you become aware of your right arm... that causes your right arm to become even more relaxed...want that to happen...imagine your right arm becoming so relaxed it just won't want to move even if you were to try to move it...experience that happening now...your right arm becoming so relaxed it just won't move even if you try to move it...*((P))* Now try to move your right arm and find that it just won't move...the more you try the more relaxed it becomes...the more you try the more relaxed it becomes...now stop trying and let that deep restful energy spread even more deeply throughout your body.*((P))*

> *((The same options apply as in the last script...do the other arm in the same way if you wish...do the same approaches if the arm does move))*

Now experience that relaxing energy flowing down your back vertebrae by vertebrae...radiating out into every muscle...pleasantly relaxing every muscle...as it spreads all around your rib cage and washes through all your internal organs...sense all your internal organs just giving in to this healing peaceful energy...allowing themselves to be washed through with this wonderful feeling...your heart...lungs...your diaphragm...liver kidneys... intestines...genitals... spleen...all your organs being released into this restful state...*((P))*

Feel this relaxation spreading now down into your hips and buttocks...flowing down into your legs...all the muscles in your thighs relaxing...flowing down through the knees relaxing all the muscles in the lower legs...*((P))* now flowing down through the ankles into the feet and out to the tips of your toes...*((P))*

Feel this wonderful pleasant relaxation now from the top of your head to the tips of your toes...*((P))* *((Watch the breath...on each exhale say,))* "Good, That's right...**even deeper**..." *((Do this two or three times on the exhale))*

> *((Option 1: Count down from 3, 5, or 7 several times to deepen. Perhaps start with a count down from 3, then 5, then 7, as the progression of the numbers themselves suggests deepening.*
>
> *((Option 2: Do leg catalepsy and challenge, in the same way you did with the arms and eyes.))*
>
> *((Example of count down:))* **I'm going to count from three down to one...as I do you will double your relaxation by the time I get to one...3...relaxation doubling...2...doubling even deeper...1 relaxation doubled.**
>
> *or*
>
> **I'm now going to count down 5 to 1 and this wonderful relaxation will triple...**((or ten times --whatever you want, just keep it believable))

5...relaxation tripling...that's it...4...deeper...even deeper...relaxation tripling...3...deeper still...your whole body letting go...2...that's right...even deeper...almost tripled...and...1 relaxation tripled. *((It generally has more impact to say the numbers on the exhale, as well as any cadence of "deepers" or whatever))*

I'm now going to be silent for five minutes so you can enjoy and intensify and explore this pleasant wonderful state with your whole body and mind.

((5 minutes silence))

Soon I will count you out from 1 to 5 coming to full normal waking consciousness on the count of five. When I reach 5 you will be clear-headed, wide awake...your energies will be balanced and alert and you'll be ready to carry on with the rest of your day.

Number 1...begin coming back...feel your energies begin to stir delightfully...moving greatly refreshed towards waking consciousness

Number 2...feel the energy in your limbs being energized...your breathing waking up...

Number 3...wiggle your toes and fingers...wiggle your toes and fingers...coming back *((your voice on each count getting more emphatic and perky))*

Number 4...breathe in wakeful energy...breathe it in...clearing your head...bringing you fully back...

Number 5...open your eyes...wide awake...fully back...come fully back...*((keep encouraging them as necessary))*

◆ ◆ ◆

12. Self Hypnosis Induction

Induction of choice, e.g.:

I want you to look at my thumbnail. Focus all your attention on my thumbnail...*((raise it))*...following it with your eyes not your head...that's right...as I raise it higher and higher...your eyes are becoming tired...your eyelids feeling heavier and heavier...more and more tired...wanting to close...in a moment, I'm going to lower my hand...when I do your eyes will eagerly close and relax causing you whole body to relax pleasantly as well...want that to happen...want to experience beautiful relaxation in your eyelids and your whole body when I lower my hand. *((lower hand))*

Now I'm going to count from 5 down to one...as I do, allow your body to relax even more totally on each count increasing *for yourself* these wonderful peaceful and healing feelings...

5...more and more *deeply* relaxed
4...even *deeper*...more and more *relaxed*...just letting it happen
3...gently scanning your body...*releasing*...*sinking* in this peaceful relaxation
2...*deeper* and *deeper*...that's right...*deeper* and *deeper* with every exhale
1...very *deep*...very at *ease*...wonderful sensations moving through your body and
    mind as the sound of my voice now causes you to *easily* go *deeply* into
    relaxation for your own benefit. Just the *sound* of my voice makes it easy for
    you to open in just the right way for you to experience a delightful trance state
    of relaxation...*just let it happen*...the more your body relaxes the more peaceful
    you feel...and the more peaceful you feel the more your body relaxes...really
    enjoying this special new learning you are developing *right now* for yourself as
    you discover just how easy it can be to...*let yourself go into a deep state of*
    ease and peace.

Now I'm going to lift your right wrist...*((Make sure they let you have it, i.e. that they exhibit no tension or anticipation of it dropping. Move it around gently to test for anticipation, encouraging them to let it go as they are feeling it while you test:* **"Just let that tension go...let me have your arm...that's right..."***))*

...I'm going to drop your hand gently on your lap ((*or,* by your side))...when I do let your body relax even more deeply *all by itself...want it to happen*...knowing the pleasant feelings you will enjoy...*((drop hand))*. *Deeply relaxed. Excellent.*

Now I'm going to do the same with your left hand...let me have it...that's right...when I drop let your body go even more deeply relaxed *all by itself. ((Drop hand))* *Deeply relaxed. That's great.*

Now I'm going to count *down* again...this time from 7 down to one...let your body go *deeper* with each count and let your mind relax into a *wonderful spacious peaceful experience*...as you just let go...letting your *deeper* mind take over completely for your own pleasure and benefit.

> 7...going deeper
>
> 6...sliding down...(like easing into a warm tub on a cold day)
>
> 5...sink down (into that warmth) and just relax
>
> 4...that's right...even deeper
>
> 3...it *feels so good*...just letting go
>
> 2...and *deeper*
>
> 1...*very* deep and *relaxed* now...*((option: count down again))* the state you are in now will cause you to *easily* understand the new learning I am about to give you that you can take home with you for your own benefit.

The instructions I'm going to give you now will enable you to enter this wonderful state any time you want to for your own benefit and enjoyment...so as you relax, listen with *easy* pleasant attention...[When I say the words **"Deeply relax"**, you will immediately and spontaneously relax, closing your eyes and allowing yourself to go right back to this wonderful state you are in right now, each time doing it more easily, going back more deeply, enjoying it more and more...each time learning more and more...each time developing this skill of benefiting yourself more and more...each time you do it.] *((Repeat [ ]))*

[Now I'm going to count from 1 to 3 and bring you back to normal waking consciousness on the count of 3.

> Number 1...easily coming back *((remember to enliven your voice))*
> Number 2...coming fully back...easily and effortlessly...coming fully back...and
> Number 3...open your eyes...fully back...wide awake...

Now...close you eyes and go **"Deeply relaxed"**. That's right, deeply relax, going right back to that wonderful state...just sliding right back in...wonderful feelings and sensations moving through your body and mind.] *((option: repeat a third time: [ ]))*

Now that you have learned to relax yourself...having done it twice *((or, 3 times))* with me speaking...you are going to exercise this new learning all by yourself so you can appreciate even more this wonderful capacity you now have to benefit yourself in this way.

There are special considerations you will want to establish every time you do this:

[First, it must be an appropriate time and place where you will be safe and at ease. This is required.

Second, you must set a time limit. This is also required. In a moment I'll ask you to do this from waking consciousness, and you will do it this time for 30 seconds. As you practice, you will go back more easily and more deeply and pleasantly each time you do it, and you will be able to set whatever time limit is uniquely appropriate.

Third, this is the way you will go "deeply relaxed" by yourself. Once you are safe and comfortable and have set your time limit, you will put your hand on your leg. You will raise the index finger. When you are ready, you will let the index finger drop. As soon as it touches your leg, you will go "deeply relaxed" just as if you heard me say "deeply relax"...going right back to this wonderful state as you have done twice today with my suggestions. You will spontaneously come back to normal waking consciousness when you have reached your preset time limit.]
((Repeat instructions []))

Now I will count from 1 to 3 bringing you back to normal waking consciousness, and you will do this on your own for 30 seconds as I have just instructed you.

　1...coming back...coming back easily and effortlessly...

　2...coming back...feeling light and refreshed in every way...

　3...open your eyes...take a deep breath...come fully back...good

((Now do it for 30 seconds))

◆ ◆ ◆

13. Self Hypnosis Format

This is an explicit outline of how to format a script for yourself or to teach to clients to create a hypnosis tape for personal use.

Step 1: Create eye fatigue and eye closure

Since you're alone, the best way is simply to focus on a spot above eye level until you get fatigue and closure. (Of course, you have the option to use "Deeply Relax," which you have now as a tool. You can also decide *where* to use it, not necessarily as step one. If you give "Deeply Relax" to your clients, remind them that they have the same flexibility.)

Step 2: Eye catalepsy testing

Give yourself instructions to relax your eyes so completely, they will not open. Then try to open them -- remember allow only a of couple seconds, then instruct to stop trying and let go even more.

Step 3: Do a progressive relaxation on yourself

Since you are more intimate with your body than a therapist is, use that to your advantage by focusing attention on particular blockages you know about that definitely need/want to be included, and any particular resources you're aware of about yourself -- like a particular kind of stroking that may really make it easy for you to release -- give it to yourself in the suggestions.

Before sending clients off to do tapes, make sure they have permission to recognize such resources about themselves, as opposed to having an attitude that they "have to go by the book." It's also important to help them construct <u>significant</u> well-formed suggestions that address the heart of matters instead of just skimming the surface.

Step 4: Deepen with countdowns

Use one or more countdowns -- 3 to 1, 5 to 1, or 7 to 1. I never go above 7, but if you want to try a higher number, do it and find out if it's useful. Remember to be focused with emphasis and energy at the same time your voice is being "metronomic:"

"deeper...deeper...deeper...down...down...down..."

Focus with "Beginner's Mind": each "deeper" and each "down" is the very first one and deserves your full attention. If you want, the countdowns can be situational, i.e. in a natural setting, down a hill to a beautiful meadow, or, in a magical setting of an ancient library or catacomb, down a staircase to a secret study or auditorium.

You are free to create here in accordance with whatever you sense will be conducive to a genuine inner opening and communion.

In my opinion, it is most beneficial to generate a sense of humility and honor for your own mysterious, benevolent being. Remember, your conscious mind is the newcomer in this area, and reverence and respect will have a definite effect on the nature and depth of what you access.

If it's to your liking, you can call on God, Guides or Masters, surround yourself with light, or anything else that gives meaning to this sense of invocation. "Ask and ye shall receive" has an important corollary, "Don't ask, and ye won't receive." I don't mean this to suggest withholding on the part of spiritual sources of aid, but to point out that, in the context of honoring our free will, they cannot generally intervene uninvited.

An image of light I would suggest would be something to the effect of:

"Imagine a stream of golden white light streaming into the top of your head from the superconscious level (or from the source of infinite loving, healing intelligence)...

...imagine it flowing down into your heart *((P))*...filling your heart with loving, healing energy *((R/P))*...that begins then to radiate out throughout your body...throughout your being...permeating every cell of your being with this infinite healing, loving energy *((P))*...**that recognizes your true needs even if you consciously haven't recognized them** *((P))*...relax into this light and allow it to lift these needs out of your being to present them into the loving intelligence of this light as offerings and requests for purification, healing, and enlightenment (i.e. powerful, genuine learnings of all kinds) *((P))*...for the sake of your highest benefit and the highest benefit of all beings...open to this...make an inner gesture with your whole heart and soul that this be so, now *((P))*...and relax into the light...feeling it permeating and surrounding your body in a protective and magnetic aura that draws these blessings to you."

((Naturally you would adapt this into first person. Any questions?))

Step 5: *Begin invocations, suggestions & therapy*

Once you have "arrived", following the relaxation and countdowns, begin with inner therapeutic methods or invocation of inner resources. This would be the time to read any pre-planned positive suggestions -- if you're doing therapy, they come <u>after</u> therapy work: after you've cleared the space.

Step 6: *Contextualize the learnings*

Give suggestions that all new learnings and benefits gained from the session will be taken, <u>*now*</u>, into your past by the unconscious mind to re-evaluate all appropriate relationships with your past to produce greater advantage for you, and then projected into your future, imagining yourself vividly in future anticipated and unanticipated situations with these resources activated and available to you.

Remember, make it vivid in all your sensory channels, and your unconscious mind accepts it as real and acts on in your behalf. "As ye think so shall ye be!"

Step 7: Count yourself out to normal waking consciousness.

◆ ◆ ◆

14. The Coma State

The coma state until very recently was considered dangerous and mysterious. Misconceptions included the fear that someone could go away, and never come back. Because a person in a coma state wouldn't respond to suggestion of any kind, it was assumed that they were in some kind of insentient state. Stage hypnotists who occasionally encountered people who would drop below their level of control over them, i.e., below the somnambulistic state, found them to be very disruptive to their act since their aura of power, knowledge, control, and prestige was paramount to their credibility.

The common denominator in these and virtually all other attitudes about this mysterious state was fear. *And fear always inhibits clear thinking, inquisitiveness, and honesty.* In your practice of hypnotherapy, this would be one of the most important lessons to learn -- how to go beyond fear and its allies. This information about the evolution of the understanding of the coma state, in my opinion, is more instructive as an <u>example</u> of this generalized problem of fear than as a story unto itself of a problem being overcome.

As you will read in the history material, James Esdaile, in the 1800's, was able to consistently produce this state using Mesmer's methods, without really understanding what worked about them (Mesmer never understood either). Taking advantage of the spontaneous anesthesia it produced, he performed hundreds of documented major and minor surgeries in India.

His methods were cumbersome, sometimes taking 1-2 hours to produce the state, and since he didn't understand why it worked, when he tried to share his discovery with the medical establishment of his day in England, he failed miserably. His is just another of the sad stories of fear, arrogance and prejudice confronting and suppressing innovation that occurs in every age throughout history.

It important to note, that people who were adventuresome enough to keep experimenting with his work "in the closet" achieved very little because they were afraid to talk to each other, and they were afraid to really investigate closely the inner experience of their clients through that dangerous and mystical process known as: <u>"Asking questions!"</u>

<u>Don't fall prey to this dilemma in your career or in this class. Experiment, test, ask questions, don't be afraid of making a mistake. Don't be afraid of appearing foolish!</u>

It wasn't until Dave Elman, in his fearlessness, inquisitiveness, and passion, came along that this "dangerous" state was divested of most of its mystery. Elman initially had the common prejudices. Coma was a non-suggestible accidental state that happened perhaps once in 15,000 instances of hypnosis, and there was nothing you could do with it, and there was no reliable way to bring someone out of it -- they had to sleep it off.

Curious, Elman decided to explore the subject. Since he was versed in hypnosis, and educated in all the misconceptions about coma, he made a radical approach to the problem -- HE ASKED THE SUBJECTS WHAT THEIR EXPERIENCE WAS LIKE!

He found in every case that the subject was sentient and alert, that he felt euphoric, and that he didn't respond to suggestion because he didn't want to be disturbed! From this

Elman made the first radical innovation in working with coma -- he devised a somewhat devious but reliable method of bring a subject out of coma. He would simply tell them that **if they didn't come out in response to his suggestion to awaken, they would never be able to be hypnotized again, and therefore, would never be able to enjoy this wonderful state again.** It worked infallibly.

Once he had solved the problem of control of the awakening procedure, and had discovered, as well, that coma subjects couldn't/wouldn't respond to physical suggestions, but could and would respond mentally, he challenged the notion that you couldn't intentionally induce the coma state.(I say couldn't/wouldn't because he can't respond physically at coma level, but he can bring himself up to somnambulism where he can move either through his own choice or in response to suggestion. So the line between can't/won't is thin.)

His method was very simple. As you remember, he had a reliable way of inducing somnambulism (disappearing the numbers). Not knowing what to expect, he took a subject to somnambulism, and then suggested to them to relax further. He used the image of three further deeper floors of relaxation, and *through his language and delivery made the prospect of achieving these deeper levels so desirably compelling that he immediately had incredible success.*

It's interesting to note that it was his open-mindedness that got him to this point, but, once he had a "technique" that worked, he tended to solidify his ideas around the technique as being THE way to do it.

One of his own students, thinking that he was doing something wrong and must be mistaken in some way, approached Elman apologetically in a seminar. He told him he had a subject who couldn't disappear the numbers to achieve somnambulism. As an experiment he had induced him without trying to achieve somnambulism. He just used progressive relaxation, then the three deeper levels, then the tests (see below), and he got anesthesia without suggestion which enabled him to perform dental work on the subject.

Elman's first reaction was disbelief, but after having several hundred other doctors do it that way and getting consistent results, he and his students proved it is possible to get coma state consistently by suggestion as quickly as within 5 minutes.

Note that "coma" for Elman includes catatonia and ultra depth. The characteristics of these two states are actually paramount qualities of the tests for coma. As we have discussed, it is somewhat rhetorical to try to decide if there is a meaningful difference. It's more important to be able to do it and use it.

This is his method for achieving coma in as little as 5 minutes, as adapted from his book, Hypnotherapy (Westwood Publishing Co., Glendale Ca.):

Get subject to somnambulism by disappearing the numbers (p. 51, or by progressive relaxation).

Talk to them about how relaxed they are feeling and explain to them that there is a deeper level of wonderful euphoric relaxation available to them. To make it compelling and to test that they are with you at the same time, question them in this manner, *"I'll bet you can sense this deeper capacity and your ability to achieve it ,now, can't you?"*

If they say yes, you know it's probably going to be easy. Their manner of response will let you know whether to proceed or if you need to make it more attractive, safe, or whatever. REMEMBER YOU CAN ASK THEM WHAT THEY MIGHT

NEED TO FEEL WHOLE HEARTED ABOUT DOING IT, IF YOU SENSE A RESERVATION.

Once you have a yes, explain to them that just as there is a maximum level of tension or contraction they could produce in their body (you could use the example of clenching the fist), there is a maximum level of total release and relaxation -- a bottom level, a basement of relaxation.

You're going to ride an imaginary elevator down to that basement of relaxation. There are three floors down to the basement. As you go down, I want you to stop at each level and let me know when you are there. When you reach each new level your relaxation will double from the floor before so that by the time you get to the basement you will be totally relaxed, and you will be showing signs that this is so.

But I'm not going to tell you right now what those signs are, because I want you to discover them as they occur. Everyone who has ever gone to the basement of relaxation has experienced these same signs, so I don't need to tell you them.

The first floor is floor A, the second is B, and the basement, the third, is C.

You're on the elevator now and on the count of three you will begin down to floor A. If you relax twice as much as you are now you will reach floor A. When you have reached floor A, let me know by saying "A" out loud. O.K. Let's go. 1...2...3...going down...doubling down to floor A...

((*Wait for a response.*))

Good. Now continue down to floor "B" on the count of three. If you double your relaxation you will reach "B." When you do, let me know by saying "B" out loud. It may be difficult to say "B" when you are so deeply, wonderfully relaxed, but I want you to do your best to say it out loud. Let's go...1...2...3...doubling down to "B"

((*Wait for response. If they can't respond, you should still see some indication of effort. This is a good sign.*))

Repeat the same suggestions to get to "C". At "C" they should not be able to speak and there should be no muscle movement. If they do, that could be an indication that for them there are (shall we say) 2 deeper levels of sub-basement to go to reach total relaxation. (Whatever it takes!)

Test 1: Once at "C", without any suggestion or explanation, you will test for spontaneous anesthesia by pinching their arm. If they have reached coma, there should be no response to the pinch.

Test 2: Ask them to move an arm or leg. Not try to move it etc. like the catalepsy tests, but more of an order to move the arm or leg. There might be a brief quiver, but the limb should not move.

Test 3: Order them to open their eyes. There should be no movement at all. If these three tests are passed, the 4th is to test for catatonia.

<u>Test 4:</u> If they are in coma, you should be able to lift their arm in to the air and they should hold it in place effortlessly and indefinitely.

If all 4 tests are passed, put the arm down and tell them you are going to let them enjoy this state for 5 more minutes, and then you will be asking them to come out on the count of 5, easily and effortlessly, feeling wonderful in every way.

((Wait 5 minutes. Count them out.))

And remember -- Elman's student did it with progressive relaxation, then the floors, then the tests. I personally did it with guided imagery alone, but since I didn't test, that's just my opinion based on the client's comments afterwards.

There is never only one right way.

APPENDIX I

Phase I

◆

History of Hypnosis

◆

◆ ◆ ◆

History of Hypnosis

One of the premier insights needed to facilitate quick, effective, lasting therapy is the comprehension of the importance of regaining choices of perspective on the contents of one's experience. Understanding the importance of taking various positions of perspective when interpreting and relating to experience saves one from becoming reactive, diminished and habitual. Relative to a knowledge and understanding of history, flexible perspectives save us from having to repeat history, personally as well as culturally. Knowing the historical roots of your trade is an important perceptual 'location' from which to gain a valuable perspective on therapeutic process.

It will help you demystify the hypnotic relationship for yourself and your clients at the same time that it helps you to honor the true mystery in healing communication. From the operating theorem of this course - *that conscious mind, as well as so-called unconscious mind, consists of a shifting of momentary trance-thought phenomena of false identity notions interspersed with moments of wakefulness to True Self, which generally go unnoticed and unappreciated*, one implication that arises is that understanding the cultural trance contexts of the precursors of modern hypnosis is a crucial element when interpreting their actions and beliefs regarding the nature of hypnosis and the formulation of its definition as a model of psychic function..

It also enhances our reflection on our own cultural trance bias, our own blind-spot presuppositions about the nature of reality and what is possible.

Some regard hypnosis as a science. Indeed in the current era, rational science carries the requisite mantle of prestige to confer Truth and Respectability upon questionable fields of endeavor, of which hypnosis has been one quite questionable field for the last 300 years. So it is important to approach it scientifically to avoid, as much as possible, the attacks of various forms of fear and prejudice, personal, social and political.

The effort to rely on an impartial fearless discipline of discrimination that only wants to see what is, is the best and truest aspect of what passes for a scientific method. In the study of hypnosis, and of any field of human endeavor, one will find that personal, social, and, political prejudice often pollute the function of pure discrimination. It is essential therefore, to cultivate and protect an open questioning mind that can live comfortably with a sense of not knowing with conceptual finality, in order to know in a deeper more comprehensive way.

From this perspective the "science" of hypnosis is as old as history. Its roots are the very beginning of man's questioning of his own nature, and, therefore, they mingle inseparably with his emerging sense of religion, spirituality and ritual. Awe, respect, and use of trance phenomena have played an invaluable part of every civilization we "moderns" have studied. As far as recent history is concerned, its use is evident among the Egyptians (3000 BC.), Mayans, Greeks, Native Americans, Africans, Aborigines - in short every culture on every continent where its understanding and use have been practiced and safe-guarded by the High Priests, Shamans, and Medicine men.

The fact that hypnosis is struggling currently to gain a new respectability is simply attributable to the ebb and flow of societal integrity and degradation. Our Western culture demonized the living spiritual heritage and the mysteries potentially available to each man in favor of centralized religious control over the course of the development of the Christian Church and its Imperialistic Political Sister - the spread of Western 'Rational' Civilization. From the 1500's Catholic edicts cut people off from whole continents of their psyche and declared that priestly service as intermediaries with these now distinct powers was an absolute necessity. People were robbed of their ownership of this natural aspect and capacity of their own being. This phenomena of territoriality, a primordial fear-based trance in itself, is very much a factor today in preventing people from gaining direct access to their own sacred inner territories.

One must fight fire with fire. Therefore, the development of the scientific method in relation to the exposition of hypnosis was and is crucial in such a cultural environment to preserve, to protect, and to foster the development of hypnosis as a respectable tool for relating, healing, and self-discovery.

Prior to the use of scientific method and analysis, explanations of the phenomena were held in ungrounded fantasy - fuzzy thinking about magic, magnetic fluids, spirits and Divine Power. These metaphorical approaches to understanding can have great power and value - as long as one can remain open minded to the fact that one is telling a story to explain the unknowable. (Quantum science has finally revealed that this is true of science as well - it too is just a metaphor.) These fuzzy thinkers can be traced back at least to Greece, and up through such men as Albertus Magnus, Roger Bacon, Raymond Lully, Pico Della Mirandola, Paracelsus, Holinotios, Robert Fludd, Maxwell, Father Kirchner, Burcq, and Father Hell.

Relative to more recent and somewhat scientific attitudes were Anton Mesmer, the Father of Hypnosis, Father Gassner, the Marquis de Puysegur, and James Martin Charcot.

Men who grounded the study more thoroughly in scientific method (the acceptable trance version of inquiry of their time) include Elliotson, Braid and Esdaile, Bernheim, Breuer, Liebault, and Freud. Many of Freud's disciples broke with him in their struggle to create a more comprehensive model of the human psyche and potential. One notable breakaway disciple relevant to the transpersonal approach of this course is Roberto Assagioli, the founder of Psychosynthesis. Assagioli wedded the genius of Freud's insights into the subconscious and unconscious with the insights about our Superconscious capacities which he studied as a esoteric spiritual student of the renegade Christian Adept and Renaissance Man, Rudolph Steiner.

Our current American century gave rise to the genius of such innovators and explorers as Walter Sichort, Henry Arons, David Elman, and Milton Erickson on the eve of the New Age emergence of exploration into the cybernetic, the synergistic, and the quantum nature of communication within and among living systems. This would include the founders of Neuro-Linguistic Programming, John Grinder and Richard Bandler, their esteemed yet lesser known mentors such as Gregory Bateson, and their myriad and talented students - a group in which I include myself.

What follows are brief synopses of important "recent" researchers. It would be very instructive for you to investigate their lives in detail - to contemplate the extraordinary nature of their procedures and results in consideration of the concepts of the psyche and prevailing sexual attitudes and societal roles of their time. These issues would be revealed in a more detailed reading of the anecdotes of their lives and research.

1) Frans Anton Mesmer

Although the term hypnosis was not even in use at the time, and it is questionable if he ever produced a hypnotic trance, per se, Mesmer is considered the "Father of Hypnosis" as the first man to attempt to explain scientifically the phenomena he created in clients, which was typically dramatically convulsive and many times created extraordinary healing results.

Born in Germany in 1734, Mesmer became a doctor and his interest turned to the use of magnets for cures. He was a contemporary of Father Hell and seems to have received instruction in their use from him. He effected some extraordinary results with clients, but soon came to believe that the magnets were superfluous. He posited the existence of an invisible magnetic fluid (fluidism) that permeated everywhere and that was influenced by the planets (planetism). Though it pervaded everywhere, some people, notably himself, had more than others. The theory of 'animal magnetism' spread and Mesmer indeed exhibited a strong influence over many. Mesmer was attacked as quack by the medical establishment and they eventually forced him out of Germany in 1781.

He became somewhat of a notorious showman in Paris, and had the allegiance of powerful people including the likes of Mozart. His practices at creating convulsions in people generated great controversy. Finally Louis XVI appointed a commission to investigate him headed by Benjamin Franklin. They concluded that it was all a fraud relying on the imagination of highly suggestible and gullible subjects. Mesmer was forced into retirement in 1795 and lived in Switzerland until his death at 1815.

2) Father Gassner

A Catholic priest, he was one of the first men to produce a calm trance state versus the convulsive states typical of Mesmer's methods. He was contemporary with Mesmer, living from 1727 to 1779. Whether he appreciated the true source of his power is doubtful. He utilized suggestion to put people in trance, but suggestion wrapped in the powerful prestige of religious ritual. He hypnotized people in the cathedral, circling them with a candle-lit crucifix, repeating 'sleep' in Latin. You can imagine the response he got from the devote, superstitious subjects at the touch of the cross!

When he succeeded at putting a woman into a deathlike trance, lowering her pulse and heart rate so profoundly that two invited physicians pronounced her dead, whereupon he revived her, his reputation as having special dispensation from heavenly domains was assured.

3) Marquis Chastenet De Puysegur

De Puysegur was a student of Mesmer and stumbled into unknown territories, for better or worse. He "magnetized" an elm tree in his home town of Buzancy, France where people could come and put themselves into convulsive trance without his needing to be there.

In 1784 he unintentionally produced a quiet trance in a young shepherd, by all indications somnambulism, since the boy lost his hearing, but seemed hyper-alert mentally. De Puysegur could only resort to supernatural assumptions to explain the phenomena and he proceeded to experiment with clairvoyance. He proposed medical diagnosis through communication with extrasensory awareness located in the stomach of his clients. He was generally incorrect, but is credited with being the first to induce somnambulism and to apply hypnotic technique to diagnosis of disease.

4) *Abbe Jose Castodi De Faria*

The first truly scientific researcher. Working in Paris in the early 1800's, he was the first to assert that trance induction required the subject's consent, and declared that expectation and psychological attitudes were crucial to trance inducement.

5) *John Elliotson*

An Englishman born in 1791, Elliotson was to become the greatest proponent of the scientific implementation of hypnotism and mesmerism to this point in European history. He was a professor of theory and a physician at the London University Hospital. He learned of Faria's work with magnetism and began practicing with trance to eliminate pain in the surgical setting.

The prevailing medical mind set of the day was that pain was essential to the healing process. He outraged the establishment with his success at eliminating pain during major surgical operations, trance diagnosis, and apparent cures through direct suggestion. His success spoke louder than his detractors, and he gained a huge following among younger more open-mined doctors.

Hospital authorities did in time succeed in forcing him to leave the university, and proceeded to eradicate all traces of his influence and the use of mesmerism and trance work. Elliotson continued his fight on his own, particularly through the publication of the "Zoist." However, his work was not greatly recognized and he died in 1868 without the appreciation his contributions merited.

6) *James Braid*

James Braid was a Scottish surgeon who lived from 1795 to 1869. He is the true father of hypnosis, although he shares the title with Mesmer and Ambroise Liebault.

Braid was a strict scientist and, as such, did his utmost to debunk the phenomena of mesmerism. Witnessing Elliotson's mesmerism in 1841, he saw that the subject was certainly under the influence of the "magnetizer," but he discounted completely the explanations of fluidism and planetism. Left with a powerful manifestation with no explanation, he determined there must be a physical explanation.

His theories were the first to posit the importance of eye strain and eye fatigue at inducing a sleep-like state. He successfully experimented on his wife and a friend, having them stare at a wine bottle. Within a few minutes he duplicated the signs of mesmeric sleep, thus refuting the theories of invisible forces. He was first to point out central elements, both physical and psychological, to the development of trance - eye fatigue plus willing belief and expectation. He named the phenomena "hypnotism" from the Greek "hypnos" for sleep. This term took hold and has persisted to today, even though he tried to change it to "monodiesm" when he realized the trance state had nothing to do with sleep.

A true pioneer, he also produced "waking hypnosis" in 1847, but as with Elliotson, his work was dismissed by his English peers. The French, however, were more open to his discoveries, notably a Professor Azam of Bordeaux who duplicated Braid's work with emphasis on anesthesia. He published a scientific paper verifying the truth of the principles of what he called "Braidism."

In 1848 Braid's interest turned to phrenology and other non-scientific areas and his further contributions to the field ended.

7) James Esdaile

Relying on the inspiration of the writings of Elliotson in the 'Zoist', this Scottish surgeon (1808-1859), stationed in India, documented the performance of several thousand minor and approximately 300 major operations, including amputations, by 1846. Pain-free surgery dramatically reduced the death rates from all causes, particularly those related to post-operative shock.

Since he was working in a "backward" country, motherland to all sorts of outlandish beliefs, the Medical Association had no trouble accepting that his peasant patients could be so influenced by the hocus-pocus of mesmerism. Esdaile didn't threaten the establishment on their own territory and thus escaped the attacks that fell to Elliotson and Braid.

8) Ambroise August Liebault & Hippolite Bernheim - The School of Nancy

A French country doctor practicing hypnotic cures for free in Nancy, France in 1864, Liebault is honored by many as the true "Father of Hypnosis" because he recognized and demonstrated that suggestion alone, even without eye fatigue, was all that was necessary to produce trance.

Learning of Liebault's work, Bernheim, a doctor at the Nancy School of Medicine , pronounced him a fraud. But upon investigation at Liebault's clinic he became a believer. Taking Liebault's methods to his own practice, he accomplished outstanding success. Bernheim kept careful documentation and records. His "Suggestive Therapeutics," published in 1886, is still used today as a reference for medical hypnosis.

Together Liebault and Bernheim founded the School of Nancy, the first institution to base therapeutic use of hypnosis on scientific principles.

Liebault would eventually become disillusioned with hypnosis because his cures did not last. History would have to wait for Josef Breuer to discover that prestige suggestion alone could not effect a permanent cure because, in that method, there was no understanding of underlying unconscious causes for conscious symptoms.

9) James Martin Charcot, The School of Salpetriere

A contemporary of Bernheim and Liebault, Charcot's contributions to the advancement of hypnosis are a mixed blessing. To his credit, he and his students were first to recognize and test distinct levels of trance states. In "On the Distinct Nororaphy of the Different Phases of Sciences Comprised under the Name of Hypnotism," he describes the three levels of trance states: lethargy, catalepsy, and somnambulism.

Because he was recognized and honored as a neurologist, his conclusions regarding the validity of hypnotic trance were generally accepted by his peers. Unfortunately, (this is the mixed part of the blessing), his misconceptions regarding hypnotism were also accepted. These most notably revolved around the conviction that hypnosis was a form of hysteria, and that only hysterics could be hypnotized. It would be interesting to evaluate the theories of hysteria of the time in the context of the unquestioned patriarchal social conditioning that lead to this phenomena almost exclusively in women, who were, of course, treated exclusively by men.

Nevertheless, Bernheim, Liebault, and Charcot caused the science of hypnosis to receive wide European acceptance. Definitely still crude in its understanding of psycho-dynamics, and hence relying on prestige suggestion (paternal overlay or displacement) it produced remarkable cures, at least for short periods (no extensive follow-up studies exist). Some practitioners of interest include: Oudet - treatment of skin problems, Landame - treatment of alcoholism, Forel - incorporation of hypnosis in a general medical practice, and Berillon - moral habit reconstruction in problem children.

10) Dr. Josef Breuer

Breuer made two major contributions to the field of hypnosis and psychology. He was a contemporary (1842-1925) of Freud, and is credited by Freud and others as the principle predecessor of modern psychoanalysis.

His discovery that unconscious, unresolved experiences are at the root of conscious symptoms, and that once the unconscious memory is re-made conscious the symptoms disappear, would transform the effectiveness of therapy and hypnosis. Until this point, hypnosis have been by prestige suggestion, which for a time could eliminate symptoms, but, because the root source of the symptom was never addressed, the symptoms would reappear. Now real transformation could occur.

Breuer also discovered the value of free association as a way to get at unconscious material. Breuer disclosed his treatment process to Sigmund Freud, and they co-wrote a paper on the case, *Studien liber Hysterie*. Breuer did not pursue clinical work, instead referring clients to Freud. Their cooperation soon ended over disagreements about basic theory.

11) Sigmund Freud

Considered the Father of modern psychoanalysis, Freud (1856-1939) built on the work of Breuer and many others. He was a student of hypnosis at both the School of Nancy and of Salpetriere. He subscribed to Charcot's mistaken theories, and was apparently bored by the monotony of hypnotic therapy and disillusioned that many were unresponsive to his authoritarian techniques. He threw the baby out with the bath water in concluding that, since his authoritarian methods didn't work, hypnosis didn't work.

Taking and building upon Breuer's key insights, he experienced better results with free association in the waking state. He was such an intellectual giant of his times that he practically single-handedly destroyed the field of hypnosis by 1900 claiming that psychoanalysis had rightly supplanted the inferior methods of hypnosis.

Read the works of Alice Miller, particularly **For Your Own Good**, for an analysis of Freud's intellectual dishonesty in misrepresenting his findings of wide-spread sexual abuse in German society. It was too explosive an issue to expose in the context of the cultural trance of the times, and he succumbed to a sense of self-preservation and relegated his client's stories to the realm of fantasy with his renowned theories of childhood development. A traditionally trained psychoanalyst of 40+ years, Miller has risked her own standing and reputation to present these views.

Thanks to Freud and the growing sophistication of drug therapies, it would take the First World War to create conditions for the re-emergence of hypnosis. The demand for treatment of large numbers of casualties, and the shortage of psychotherapists, forced the medical community to turn to hypnosis for the treatment of war related trauma illnesses. Between the Great Wars there was still little interest in the use of hypnosis to clear root causes of emotional symptoms because of the prestige of psychoanalysis.

J.G. Watkins book, <u>Hypnotherapy of War Neuroses</u>, (1949), describing his success using hypnosis to rapidly heal war trauma was an important milestone of renewed post-war interest in hypnosis. Watkins utilized the simple (to understand, yet requiring skill to accomplish) formula of regressing the client to the root experience of the symptom, and eliciting abreaction of repressed emotions, whereupon symptoms disappeared. (These techniques are covered in Phase II of this training.)

Others of note who brought hypnosis back to life include:

1) R.M. Linder, coined the term "hypnoanalysis," in 1944 to describe his work combining psychoanalysis and hypnosis.

2) L.R. Wolberg, promoted the use of hypnoanalysis in his book Medical Hypnosis to treat compulsive disorders.

3) B. Gindes, coined the term "hypnosynthesis" in 1951 in his book, New Concepts of Hypnosis, describing his approach of first accessing repressed material and then integrating change comprehensively throughout the personality.

4) Milton Erickson from the 1940's to the 1980's had a huge impact on all therapeutic philosophy and really single-handedly created a new respectability for hypnotherapy due to his respected position as a psychiatrist, and to his phenomenal genius in the creation of innovative approaches to the use of hypnosis as a therapeutic tool capable of creating rapid healing and psychic reorganization in clients. As a result of his work, both the AMA and the American Psychiatrical Association had endorsed hypnosis by the early 1960's. Erickson's insights and behavioral procedures with client's form the foundation of the relatively new and powerful discipline of Neuro-Linguistic Programming. The founders of NLP, John Grinder and Richard Bandler spent years studying with, and studying, Erickson.

5) Dave Elman, whose book, Hypnotherapy, (1964) is required reading for this course, advanced the use of hypnosis medically and dentally through his tireless training of thousands of dentists and doctors throughout the U.S. He was a great innovator in the field, creating rapid inductions, and demystifying the phenomena of hypnotic trance making its use less intimidating and more user friendly.

6) Walter Sichort, in the 1960's discovered and defined three additional trance depth levels below somnambulism: coma, catatonic, and ultradepth, which we have discussed in Phase I.

7) Leslie Lecron, a clinical psychologist, throughout the 50's and 60's advanced the use of hypnosis as a therapeutic tool and made it accessible to the layman with his book, Self-Hypnotism, in 1964. He furthered the use of "ideomotor responses" to communicate with the unconscious to learn the truth about critical repressed material even in light trance states, bringing memories to awareness back even to birth.

8) Gil Boyne, one of the foremost political advocates for the protection and validation of the profession of hypnotherapy in our lifetime. For over 5 decades Gil has been a dynamic educator certifying thousands of hypnotherapists in comprehensive trainings with high standards of competency to insure the benefit and protection of the public. He has also been a tireless clinician helping tens of thousands of people to improve their lives by tapping their own inner resources with hypnosis. Through his publishing company, Westwood Publishing, one of the largest publishers of hypnotism, hypnotherapy, mind power, and self-improvement products, he makes quality books and tapes about the profession available to a large audience. His methods are presented in his book: Transforming Therapy: A New Approach to Hypnotherapy.

9) Charles Tebbetts, one of many great and respected hypnotherapists originally trained by Gil Boyne, was esteemed by some until his passing as the grandfather of modern hypnosis . <u>Miracles on Demand, the Radical Short-Term Hypnotherapy</u>.

10) Ormond McGill, "the Dean of American Hypnotists." Respected by all for decades of teaching, clinical work and showmanship! Not only was he one of the first to research and present Eastern approaches to altered states work, but he was a master showman, entertaining thousands with stage hypnotism. <u>Hypnotism and Mysticism of India</u>, <u>The Encyclopedia of Satge Hypnotism</u>

And from the late 1960's - an explosion of good work:

John Grinder and Richard Bandler, founders of NLP, and Stephen Gilligan, disciple of Milton Erickson, contemporary and student of John Grinder continue to press the envelope of hypnotic communication theory. James Maynard created Transpersonal Hypnotherapy, fusing psychosynthesis models with the hypnotic training he received from Walter Sichort and Charles Tebbets. Many other bright minds and good hearts from the late 60's to the present, including myself, have synthesized the best of the insights from Western and Eastern thought, according to each one's unique experience and background, to make hypnotherapy the powerful holistic and spiritual discipline it is becoming today.

◆ ◆ ◆

Table of Contents
Phase II

◆ ◆ ◆

1. Models of the Psyche;
Concepts of Reality
The Three Malas

In the Vedic tradition of India, the name of the energy that underlies and controls all phenomenal reality is "Shakti." Since this energy gives birth to everything, it is considered female. She gives birth to everything out of her own being. She is everything, in no way separate from any phenomenon, yet remains untainted and exuberant in the play of her own energies. She is our own inherent pure being - we do not simply have a little piece of her inside us - we are entirely her.

The unmanifest reality out of which the Shakti arises is called Shiva. Shiva is the all-encompassing awareness of the play - the immovable, indestructible witness - the male consort (lover) of the Shakti. Locked in eternal embrace - the same, yet different, ecstatically merging and moving apart to merge again.

The Shakti has many facets, i.e., there are different kinds of Shakti. The most important for our purposes is called "Matrika Shakti." Matrika Shakti is the power of illusion, the power of "maya" as it is called in many eastern traditions. What is the root of this power? **Letters!** Therefore, **Words!**, **Language!**...The primordial hypnosis - the thinking mind.

In our approach, it is important to contemplate the significance of the dream creating power of our thinking minds. We have to access our "Shivahood" to do this - our awakened awareness. Otherwise, hypnotherapy becomes just the shifting of one trance for another, always within the realm of the most powerful most subtle underlying trance: **the egoic "minding."** I choose to call it "minding", not mind, because it is not a "thing," but a process. Until egoic minding is dissolved completely, awareness must be alert to its subterfuge - in yourself and your clients.

If this sounds intimidating, it doesn't have to be, because short-circuiting the egoic underpinnings of people's problems can make transformation much quicker, easier, and more delightful.

Yes, more delightful - the egoic minding doesn't have a true sense of humor-so humor is a powerful tool in breaking its spell.

Humor arises out of awareness. Awareness of what? Awareness of 1) not being the thinking; 2) not being an object being thought about; and 3) awareness of being the awareness without having to think about it.

Think about it! <u>While maintaining an awareness that thinking is occurring</u>, contemplate that: 1) people's problems are always about themselves as the <u>object</u> of the problem; 2) in order to be the object you have to be <u>something</u>; 3) that <u>something</u> is always an idea (or set of ideas), in other words, a *suggestion (hypnosis!)* of who and what you are, but never really what you are (what are you anyway?).

In other words, the problems are about a false self, an idea of self, a trance, an illusion, and could simply, in theory, be walked away from.

What makes it hard to walk away? <u>The subtlety and complexity of the shadowy (our blind spots) dualistic play of egoic minding.</u>

The Matrika's wheel of delusion

The core process of egoic minding is the dualistic play of thought. The seesaw, the polarity, the fixing to one side of a polarity to the exclusion (negative hallucination) of the other; overlooking the unity of the poles of hope & fear, good & bad, right & wrong, up & down, praise & blame which keeps the wheel turning. The wheel of delusion of letters and words tells you: 1) who you are, 2) where you are, 3) what is happening, and, 4) what you need to do. The master hypnotist, the master con-artist is your own egoic-minding.

Here's what it looks like:

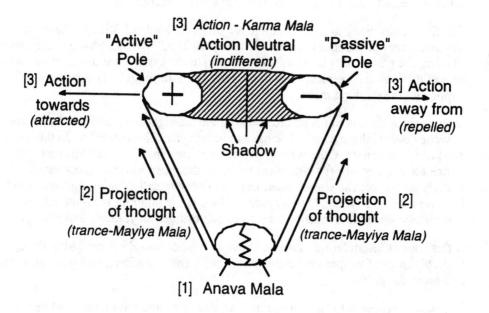

Figure 2.1: The processes that arise out of the Matrika Shakti.

Figure 2.1 represents what arises out of the Matrika Shakti: the three malas: 1) *anava mala* - the thought "I am imperfect" (cf. shame, Ph.IV); 2) *mayiya mala* - the rise of the knowledge of duality, the notion of differences, the notion of the inherent separateness (and therefore antipathy) between these differences, and the projection of thoughts based on this duality; 3) *karma mala* - the performance of good and bad actions based on the trance of the first two. *"We gotta do something about all these differences!"*

In the dualistic trance of the 3 malas, we focus (selectively attend) to one side of duality or the other. The other side becomes the shadow - the unseen dimension. But the more subtle shadow aspect is the space in between the polarities. We may briefly see the validity of the poles being flip sides of the same coin, but the hidden dynamics of their unity and their illusory manifestation as completely separate entities, keep putting us back into the trance struggle of having to choose between opposites or having to reconcile them. It's like seeing the tips of two icebergs and agreeing they are made of ice, but totally missing that under the surface, it's just all one iceberg.

Whatever we don't own consciously, whichever side or aspect of a dualistic split we imagine to be truly "other," we project on to the world, and in this sense we create our reality.

We draw into our lives people and situations that reflect our shadow parts, because, when all is said and done, **we are propelled to represent our wholeness**, either directly and simply, or in a dreamlike symbolic fashion of identifying with acceptable parts of our own wholeness and projecting their unacceptable polar parts outside of ourselves, making others the repositories of these undesirable aspects of ourselves.

This is the profound, powerful, elegant, and complex web of illusion of the Matrika Shakti - our own egoic minding.

Waking up from egoic trance

The notion of the possibility of waking up from this trance in relationship to self-improvement arises with the recognition of the flaw of the third mala - action. In other words, *trying to improve, trying to fix it,* is still **inside the circle** of the trance dilemma of self. Wakefulness is outside the circle, and *nothing you do in the circle to try to fix things in the circle gets you outside the circle!*

To the untrained entranced observer, it may seem that action or striving helps, but it doesn't. The only thing that gets you out, that wakes you up, is waking up - just do it! Waking up occurs as grace - from yourSelf to yourself, because you are inherently pure and perfect and that purity never goes away - in fact, our purity indulges us and supports the egoic play. The egoic play has no energy of its own.

There is only one energy source, and it (You) supports everything until it (You) decides that enough is enough. Within the play that may look like striving to improve, but there comes a point where one learns of the notion that the striving is **not** to create the goodness, the freedom, but to clean the perceptual and cognitive faculties to see the **already existing** perfection and freedom that one forgot one is (i.e., anava mala), and conversely, to see that the dilemma of self was an illusion.

Perhaps this is your first introduction to this notion of waking from the illusion of dilemma altogether vs. trying to fix things in the illusion. It is a very subtle shift that deserves contemplation, moment by moment, in an on-going fashion, taking care not to let the egoic process use this insight for its own ends -- primarily by creating black and white extreme conclusions to get you to discount the insight altogether, never learning how it is useful as an operating theory to foster waking up.

This course is intended to clarify this issue, and to make it a useful notion to help you become more and more sensitive to this beguilement of egoic thinking.

Waking up, rather than changing how you act, initially, is more akin to having been acting in a dark room, and, suddenly, the lights are turned on. From one perspective nothing has changed, but from another, everything has changed.

Becoming established in this perspective will enable you to use all the hypnotic and NLP techniques to much greater effectiveness. WHY? - *because you won't be playing unconsciously in the shadows with your clients!* You won't be caught in the serious and endless trance game of fixing things (although you delightfully may fix things as a skillful choice). You will be moving clients into the wakefulness that allows people to see that they don't have to fix their problems if they realize they can dissolve them. You help clients understand how to walk away from problems and experience them dissolve of their own accord because they are unreal (yet powerful) to begin with.

Walking away will require strength, but the strength is not developed in **opposition** to the strength of the trance. It *is* the very strength **of** the trance as you recognize it as your own strength, and that you are at cause over it.

So we have come back again to honoring the pure intent underlying the problem, embracing the problem so that the energy of the problem can change its patterning and expand the flexibility of energy utilization in the context of the wakeful recognition of the expansion of choice and meaning, i.e.: *"I don't have to do that anymore!" "I don't have to let that bother me anymore." "I can afford to take my time and learn new ways of living without fear of making mistakes. Its O.K. to make mistakes - the trance of shame (anava mala) is over."*

These last few pages may seem very dense, even obtuse. Again, the whole course is a discussion and exploration of the meaning of these statements.

Accessing the True Self

The first way we are going to apply these notions is by going into "trance" to access the inherently pure intelligence. People will generally come to you with a sense of it and a name for it: God, God-self, True Self, Higher Self, True Inner Self, etc. It is important to know their preference and to use it, incorporating it into the script. Later on we will discuss ways of exploring how to ascertain if and how their beliefs about the Higher Self actually inhibit the direct experience of the Higher Self, and what you can do to alleviate those problems.

In a sense, that is a statement of what this course is all about.

Before his death, Einstein said, "Everything has changed with the splitting of the atom except one thing - the way we think. We must change the way we think!"

- I would suggest to you that the new way we need to think is an old way we forgot about, and which we are going to remember and apply to hypnotherapy in this course.

◆ ◆ ◆

2. Accessing the True Self/ Inner Self/Higher Self

Do induction/relaxation + limb challenges, then:

As you enjoy this deeply relaxed state...allow the sound of my voice to guide you into just the right state of receptivity to EASILY become aware of the presence of your True Inner Self (or Higher self, etc.,)...scan your body with this relaxed awareness...notice any areas of tension and let them release...as you contemplate that what you are now doing for yourself is for your highest benefit...and your Higher Self is always present...whether or not you are consciously aware of it, now...to give you everything you need in the way of guidance and support to free you from those problems...those unnecessary limitations...that are getting ready to be released easily...in just the right way for you to keep whatever is of value for you, now...releasing, dissolving whatever needs to release the problems now...that's right...feel yourself breathing as you go even deeper into relaxation letting your unconscious mind handle the reevaluation of these problems in the healing, loving light of your Higher Self as you become aware of it now, in some way...or another...

Begin to have a sense...begin to become aware NOW...of your body being surrounded by a golden white light of pure loving energy...a golden white light surrounding your body now...becoming more apparent to you in many interesting ways...as breath by breath you FEEL GOOD as you picture and imagine this light all around you, and you begin to recognize in a surprising and secure way that this light is full of intelligence and healing power...and it is welcoming you into its presence, now...in such a way that you are learning to **remember,** that it is always surrounding you...that it has always surrounded you...and from now on you can *think about it* and that causes your experience of the presence of your Higher Self to be enhanced...as you learn to *listen to its guidance* with more and more trust, now...with each relaxed breath...opening deeper to its healing energy...that's right...deeper...and...deeper...more and more...learning to *trust your own true inner goodness*...your own true inner goodness...

((*Option:* "As you do so this light begins to lift you up...lifting you up higher and higher into the presence of your Higher Self"))...think about all the ways you *used to* think you weren't worthy of contacting this inner goodness as they dissolve into the light that is surrounding you ((*Option:* "as

you feel yourself being lifted higher and higher...opening more and more"))...offer any doubts or hesitations into this light in such a way that you sense them becoming obsolete and then dissolving as you breathe the light into your being to be carried to every cell of your body right along with the oxygen you breathe...being delivered effortlessly by your unconscious mind whether or not you *think about it* consciously NOW...*relax with the feeling of this goodness gently touching every part of your being*...bringing healing, rejuvenating energy everywhere that it is needed...**((*Option:* "as you move still higher almost up to the realm of your Higher Self...**")) and you get to share in this process by taking a wonderful breath as you imagine this light, this healing, loving energy spreading throughout your being, now...breath by... breath...deeper...easily...effortlessly...with each breath...deeper...that's right...**((*Option:* "it's spreading through you deeper and deeper as you rise higher and higher...")) dissolving whatever thoughts or feelings may arise, whether bad or good, into this healing light...allowing... offering all your thoughts... all your feelings into this light to be healed and transformed in just the right ways for your own highest benefit, now...that's right...**((*Option:* "completely ready now to arrive in the presence of your Higher Self on the count of three:...one...two ...three...there now...**"))

> *((Note: If you find that they have not sensed the light, in fact, if they tell you that your suggestions have caused them to experience a lot of doubtful or negative thoughts, tell them that that is good. Tell them: "The light has simply come to them as requested and highlighted these negativities that need to be seen through and released, and that they can gently shift their awareness to the background light now that they understand that they had simply been caught by a habit pattern of focusing on negativities, missing all the underlying goodness and power that they can experience now."))*

Imagine yourself standing easily erect and at ease in the presence of your Higher Self surrounded by this loving energy...recognize that this is the unconditional love of your own inner purity... the true integrity of your being that is so pure, so free that it is not tainted or diminished by anything you have ever thought or said or done...it is not tainted or diminished by anything that has been thought, said or done about you or to you by anyone else...as you *think about this now*... your unconscious mind, in the energizing aura of your Higher Self, completely and effortlessly reevaluates all your life experiences, beliefs, and attitudes in such a way that *you are released from whatever you need to be released from* in order to come into total alignment with the purity of your Higher Self in such a way that it flows unobstructed throughout your being, **now**...breathe that in...that's right... and again...**eeven** deeper...as your unconscious mind also keeps everything that is truly of value to you from your life experience and *learnings that make it easy for you*...**now**...to *come* *into full, open alignment with the presence and energy of your Higher Self...your true being...*

As you experience these wonderful, relaxed feelings...thinking whatever thoughts that are being exposed in the light of your Higher Self...you can now ask questions of your Higher Self...carrying on an inner dialogue and an inner communion in any way you wish...I will remain silent for 5 minutes or until you signal me that you are ready to go on by raising the index finger of your right hand...if you understand raise the index finger of your right hand now.

((Repeat if you get no response. It is possible to compose questions with the client before hand and state them for the client aloud, eliciting verbal responses from the client about the answers received.))

[In a moment I will count from 1 to 5 bringing you back to normal waking consciousness on the count of five...understand that all *you have learned and experienced in this session* will continue *to grow in beneficial ways* in your being, generating new and deeper bonds between your True Self and your ordinary waking consciousness, your dream consciousness, and your deep sleep state in such a way that *you are more and more awake to your own inner goodness,* expressing it more and more easily, joyfully and in all ways appropriately for the highest benefit of yourself and all beings *now and moment by moment, day by day into your future.*] *((Repeat section within brackets [ ]))*

((Count client out:))

One...beginning to come back...

Two...coming back more and more...all the energy and learnings of this experience being effortlessly, enjoyably absorbed into your being...being absorbed into every cell of your body...

Three...moving your fingers and toes...(repeat)...more and more awake.. coming back...carrying these new learnings and empowerments into your future...starting *now...*

Four...breathe in wakeful energy...that's right...breathe in wakeful energy...clearing your head...balancing your energies...feeling wonderful in every way...

Five...open your eyes...fully coming back...fully back...wide awake...that's right

Note regarding "rising up" options in script: There are certain archetypal precedents for relating "up" to Heaven and the superconscious level, and "down" to earth and the subconscious level. It can be intuitively compelling for our psyche, so, experiment using this rising up imagery for Higher Self access to see if you get different results. On the other hand, "As above, so below" - there is an equally compelling intuition to go deep inside to the

"Heart of hearts to find the True/Higher Self. I like to combine them: *Feeling this light shining down on you from high above you...as you feel it radiating out from deep inside you...shining down from high above...radiating from deep inside...permeating your whole being.*

3. Regression/Past Life Therapy

Our waking trances, the bundle of learned behaviors, <u>both resourceful and unresourceful</u>, that largely define us, that we are used to, that make us feel at home with ourselves, are established in our past. They solidify as "us," and become "fixed" according to the same mental/emotional dynamics that we enlist from the hypnosis basics of Phase I to impress the unconscious mind to create traditional trance: repetition and vividness or emotional impact.

Similar experiences that embody the same learnings or messages "string" themselves out like pearls on a necklace. There comes a point, *not necessarily the first experience,* at which a critical mass is reached, and the unconscious mind "fixes" the message and the learnings and the emotional dynamics around this class of experiences, in such a way, that we go on automatic pilot in relationship to them as memories, *and* to similar on-going experiences. Two important characteristics of this occurrence are:

1) We stop learning anything new from on-going similar, *yet still unique,* experiences, <u>except to the extent that our fixed focus scans for information to more solidly confirm the conclusions (i.e. beliefs) fixed at critical mass</u>, and

2) We stop looking for new choices because in fixing at critical mass, *an integral part of the fixation is <u>the conclusion that no new choices will ever exist.</u>*

Thus, a fixed belief about the nature of reality is created!

The critical mass point, the point of origination of the problem or trance, is the point to which you must regress the client in order to clear the problem. The suitable metaphor would be that to remove a weed, you have to pull it up by the roots, not break off the leaves or flowers. Traditional therapeutic approaches, including most hypnotherapeutic approaches, recognize this. The regression approach of hypnosis is held within the model of:

1) putting the client into trance, and, then,

2) taking him "back" to the problem time in the past, and

3) reevaluating with an adult perspective.

This approach is workable, and we will practice it. But our approach also includes recognizing that the client is already instantaneously in the regressed trance state when the problem behavior is active. They are projecting their inner "true" reality from the past on to the present time circumstance, translating present time things-as-they-are into symbolic representations of the "real" past event/meaning where they are stuck. In this approach, since we recognize that they are already in trance, no formal trance work is necessary to "get" them there. The techniques involved build on the standard approach, but also enhance it. The crucial understanding to become familiar with, in order to relax with these processes, is that *hypnosis is redundant* - the client is already "there" - *there is no question of getting there, only the challenge of bringing "there" into awareness.* Working with that challenge can bring all sorts of useful changes and insights into view - even more important issues or insights than the presenting issue that you and/or the client thought was so important. (Especially watch for the hinting elucidation of the dualistic, polar. shadow side of the issue.)

Example: Client complaining of the nasty treatment by her teenagers. "I've trained them to treat me badly, in the same way my father treated me." Therapist (me). "Oh. you miss your father!(who we know is dead) Immediately the client moves into tears and this is the "opening" to unravel and release a lot of pent up feeling. Since the client was "selectively attending" to her trance of complaint about the teenagers she was negatively hallucinating the feelings (i.e., they're not there) about the loss of father.

So, develop the confidence that you don't have to struggle to "get there." They are already there - you are just playing with their perceptions, beliefs, and fear dynamics to allow a healing shift, either with "conscious" participation, or with only "unconscious" participation.

Remember the importance of theater (it's <u>all</u> theater), and the importance of theatrical devices to accomplish the regression/past life regression. For example, some tried and true devices that make time travel "feasible":

- TIME machine,
- a tunnel of time,
- a raft floating laaazily down a river, witnessing scenes along the bank, if you wish, as you go back to just the right place where you will disembark on the bank,
- fly there - float above the body and then back, coming down at right time (how to fly? Just fly, or use a magic carpet, be carried by a guiding spirit eagle... Remember, theater - what do you think will do it? Ask the client!),
- Repeating a significant phrase that encapsulates the issue, attended with suggestions that, as it is repeated, takes you back to the origin of the issue ("I'm afraid, I'm afraid"...*that's right, keep saying it...keep feeling it...the feeling has all the knowledge within it of where it was born...say it, and allow the feeling to carry you back...*),
- a subway or lightrail.

You get the idea...

Once you're there, you may have to assist in establishing an experience. Clients commonly won't be anywhere, or may feel dizzy, or spinning in space, or have a vague sense of dread. I usually get the sense that, rather than this being a *failure*, it is an example of touching the feelings, but maintaining a negative hallucination(repression) of the facts of the situation. You need to:

1) Explore and encourage their engagement with what they <u>are</u> experiencing, no matter how vague.

2) Move back or forward in time to find a foothold.

3) Chunk down: have them look at their feet, then up their legs, or out from their feet to where they're standing. Keep building the experience, always

suggesting that the piece they get makes it easier to get more (cause and effect-remember?).

4) Watch for opportunities to use polarity shifts, e.g. *"How are you dressed?" "I don't know." "Are you naked?"* Suddenly they have something! *"I'm wearing a pink dress..."* and you're on your way!, or *"I can't see anything." "What don't you want to see?"*

5) Counting devices - *on the count of three you ...(whatever), when I say a,b,c, you'll....*

6) Move back and forward in time, this time to gather significant experiences and meaning to make sense of why you are where you are.

7) Combine devices, e.g. on the count of three you'll be at the next significant event....

8) Remember to make it vivid- emphasize seeing, hearing, feeling, moving, smelling, tasting.

As you'll see in the scripts, it is recommended to put the experience and new learnings in a greater context from the level of the higher self, and in the case of past life work, to move through the death experience to the after death state, then to the higher self perspective to integrate and overview.

Clients will have varying degrees of sophistication with the concepts of regression and past life work. Some will be totally in your hands for guidance, others may have a lot of experience accessing, and have preferred ways of doing it that you should inquire about.

Almost no one will have thought about the concept of already being "there" in trance right now, disguising it by projecting it on to present time reality, and that the point is not necessarily to "go back there," but to "WAKE UP!" When you think about it, do you see that all this potentially elaborate theater is to get them to wake up, anyway, when all is said and done?

UNFORTUNATELY, IF THIS IS NOT UNDERSTOOD, THE CONSEQUENCE CAN BE THAT PEOPLE "GO BACK" AND USE THE INFORMATION GATHERED FOR FURTHER ELABORATING THEIR TRANCES. "I WAS A THIS...I DID THAT...AND THAT'S WHY I CAN'T...ETC."

Likewise, most will have an overlay (trance) about how it "has to be done" and how having it or healing it is a part of the dream of who they are (and of course watch out for the therapist's dream about what's going on and how it has to happen). You need to be aware of these beliefs and pace and utilize them. If it doesn't happen the way they want it to, **they might not allow it to happen** - obviously this can make the change work difficult.

If they can drop preconceptions, if you can drop preconceptions, the work can be fast. For example, if they will play, make whatever issue coming up *superfluous* and ask what their life would be like now (after all the past is over! - WAKE UP CALL!) For example:

"I have a problem X."

"Pretend this problem and all of its related dynamics are totally released; pretend all these ideas and feelings about this problem are totally superfluous to your life. Imagine they are as light and insubstantial as helium and you are injecting them into colorful balloons and releasing them to float away into the distant stratosphere - gone, dissolved forever (because you know what happens to helium balloons when they get really high - they burst! And the helium dissolves into the atmosphere). Imagine what your life is like now if this is the case."

◆ ◆ ◆

4. Regression Script

Induction/Relaxation + limb challenges (include counting backward procedures to achieve somnambulism, at times, and compare the results. What other ways could you check effectiveness at varying "depth" levels? Something to think about as you learn more.

Experience yourself gradually becoming aware of the presence of the energy of your pure inner being...recognize it as the *relaxation you feel* caressing every part of your body, now...feel it surrounding your body...gently touching your skin...communicating in some way...a feeling of love and intelligence and secure power...protective loving power...the power and intelligence that operates and sustains your body even when you are totally unconscious...*think about that*...think about how all your life you have on a daily basis *surrendered yourself* to this inner loving power and intelligence...without even thinking about it...without a second thought...*easily drifting* into sleep every night... in some way knowing...outside or...under...or behind...your conscious mind...in some way *knowing you can* completely trust this inner awareness and power to care for you...consciously and unconsciously...

...And isn't it good to know that you can ask its assistance in this trance simply by *relaxing now*...following these suggestions to the letter... guiding you into just the right state to allow this inner power, your unconscious mind, to take these suggestions and to *act on them, now,* for your highest benefit...so...*feel* your breath now...that's right breathe as you become more aware of this aura of loving power surrounding your body...and, breathe this loving healing energy into your body right along with the oxygen...carried right along with the oxygen to every cell of your body...every cell being bathed *effortlessly* by this healing power of your unconscious mind, your true pure inner being...

...Breathe it in...every breath *going deeper...and deeper ...gently... easily...* every heartbeat now...*effortlessly...deeply relaxing...opening...opening* to the guidance of this power and intelligence that knows you completely...and completely...lovingly supports you...feel this power...imagine it as a gentle golden white light permeating every cell of your body...radiating throughout your being...aligning the focus of awareness of every cell of your being in such a way that it will be *easy for you* to access the experience in your past that is the root of this problem you came with today.

Every experience you have ever had is recorded in your memory...and your unconscious mind can easily access whatever you need to access to contact the root of this problem...so that you can experience it in such a way that you will be free of all the ways in which it had been limiting you until you *release it now*...experiencing it in such a way that all the emotional energy that has been held in a harmful way in your body can *be released*...released and healed and freed to flow back into the pool of your pure inner energy where it can be freely accessed for your own highest benefit...

[...As you experience this past experience...<u>in such a way that all limitations are released</u>...you will keep whatever learnings are important and valuable to you...*keeping the learnings that give you power*...noticing that you are learning to keep the learnings that give you power and *let the old held emotions be released* as you simply keep the learnings that give you power in just the appropriate ways...and freeing the living energy that *used to be trapped* by that old problem in those old held emotions in your body.] *((Repeat text within brackets [ ], if appropriate.))*

In a moment I am going to count from one to three...As I count from one to three...you will feel yourself *effortlessly drifting back* in time... guided by the power and knowing of your unconscious mind, your pure inner being...just relax into the light and energy that is permeating your being and surrounding your body as you *feel yourself carried back in time*...back to the origin of this problem...to experience it again in a new way with whatever resources you need...to *experience it and be freed completely from this problem.*

Number one...going back...drifting back...relaxing into the protective aura of your pure inner being...

Number two...farther back...protected and strengthened by this aura of light...on the count of three, you'll be there...fully aware of the root experience of this problem in such a way that you will easily be freed from this problem...

Number three...now there, fully aware...go with your first impression of what you are experiencing.

((As necessary, assist client to orient into the experience. Do emotional clearing (PII,#7) as appropriate, remember you have the flexibility to go forward and backward in time to gather resources and to process as required. Remember to chunk the experience into small pieces to help them build up their awareness of where they are and what is happening.))

((For very traumatic memories, it may be necessary and advisable to approach them first by floating up above their life stream and move back in time at a height that allows them to perceive the events without getting pulled into them. The vantage point for this will generally be from <u>behind</u> the event, i.e. they have floated towards it from its future, over it in its present, and moved behind it to a position prior to its occurrence where they can see it as a future event in the context of all other future events stretching out in the life stream. See PII,#7, & PIV,#4.))

Share with me what you are experiencing...

((Assist them with input on whatever resources they need, e.g. inner guidance, their adult self to come in as an ally. Find a way to make it safe for them to see new choices of action to take, and to let themselves see new perspectives on the situation that release blame, shame, guilt, resentment, bitterness, etc. and <u>then to relive, reenact the situation with these new resources</u>. See Emotional Clearing Guidelines, PII,#7.))

Experience yourself as you were then *((or, if they are observing from above:* "See the you down there"*...etc.))*, but with these new understandings and resources, acting and expressing in such a way that this whole experience is being transformed into an affirmation of your inner purity, freedom, and worthiness to be just who you are, simply and effortlessly, without needing to justify yourself or your feelings...completely protected and free to say and do whatever is necessary to affirm your inner power and truth...share with me what you are experiencing...

> *((Interact throughout the experience keeping them encouraged and focused and* active *in releasing the limitations and seeing with greater clarity. If they are above seeing themselves down there...see what effect you get if you have them run the old experience in black and white, and then the "new" reality, with resources and choices, in color. When that one down there really "gets it," have them jump into the scene and fully associate into the experience of this new power. If they need further "back up," try pointing out to them that they can maintain dual awareness, i.e., jump in, yet still be above as present time self, or come down as ally into the scene to support the past self relearning its right to hold on to its dignity as an inherently pure spiritual being. See Emotional Clearing Guidelines, PII #7.))*

Good...now experience your unconscious mind taking these new resources, insights, and capacities that you have just created for yourself into the rest of your past...into every experience that needs to be reevaluated and released in the same way...give your wholehearted permission for your unconscious mind to *do this, now*...imagine it radiating the power of these new resources... seeking out and reevaluating all these experiences...transforming them now in the same way into resources for you as new learnings and new affirmations of your inner purity and inner strength and capacity to *take care of yourself appropriately...now, relax into it... sense it in some way...*

((Depending on your calibration of their state, you may ask for them to share to see if they need assistance. Also, when it seems appropriate, feel free to repeat phrases and/or elaborate for effectiveness.)) You may notice that your conscious awareness is participating by *remembering something in a new way, now*...as you sense in some way your unconscious mind *directing the completion of this process throughout your past, now... Experience yourself moving into your future, now...moving into anticipated familiar future situations and entirely new future situations with these new resources and this transformed past that is full of brilliant, joyful, peaceful, exuberant affirmations of you as a pure innocent being capable of enjoying life for your own highest benefit* which includes the highest benefit of all beings*...imagine that...imagine walking into your future with these resources and attitudes....see yourself doing things free of the fear of being judged...feel yourself there...hear yourself...experience how all your sensory channels seem vibrant and vivid...*((**Pause for processing, possibly asking for sharing**...encouraging appropriately.))** Now slowly bring your awareness back to this room...relax and reflect on all you have given yourself in this experience...with gratitude, affirm the on-going transformation your unconscious mind is going to continue for your highest benefit even when you come back to waking consciousness... yes...that's right... with every breath you take... with every step you take, from now on, these new resources and insights are going to grow and elaborate more and more powerfully throughout

your being for your highest benefit, now and forever...*want it to be happening now forever*...give your wholehearted grateful acknowledgment to this pure loving transformative power of your own being...understanding that you will effortlessly be keeping everything that is truly of value to you and releasing everything that is limiting you unnecessarily...now allow this whole experience to dissolve into the light of your pure inner being...experience the whole experience dissolving into the light surrounding your body...now feel this light dissolving into your body...carrying it into every cell...permeating your whole being with the power and blessings of the resources and insights you have generated for yourself today...that's right...*((Pause a moment or so...calibrate...then end the session.))*
Now I'm going to count from one to five...when I reach five you'll be fully back in waking consciousness feeling light, refreshed, and awake...

One...coming back...begin coming back...
Two...more and more...easily coming back...feeling new energies flowing through you...
Three...wiggle your fingers and toes...that's right...wiggle them...more and more awake...
Four ...breathe in deeply now...breathe in wakeful energy...clearing your head...coming back...
Five...eyes open now...wide awake...fully back...feeling refreshed and awake...that's right.

◆ ◆ ◆

5. Regression Script
Preliminary Practice Version

Do Induction/Relaxation and limb challenges (include counting backward procedures to achieve somnambulism, at times, and compare the results.) What other ways could you check effectiveness at varying "depth" levels?

Experience yourself gradually becoming aware of the presence of the energy of your pure inner being...recognize it as the *relaxation you feel* caressing every part of your body, now...feel it surrounding your body...gently touching your skin...communicating in some way...a feeling of love and intelligence and power...protective loving power...the power and intelligence that operates and sustains your body even when you are totally unconscious...*think about that*...think about how all your life you have on a daily basis *surrendered yourself* to this inner loving power and intelligence...without even thinking about it...without a second thought...*easily drifting* into sleep every night... in some way knowing...outside or...under...or behind...your conscious mind...in some way *knowing you can* completely trust this inner awareness and power to care for you...consciously and unconsciously.

...And isn't it good to know that you can ask its assistance in this trance simply by *relaxing now*...following these suggestions to the letter... guiding you into just the right state to allow this inner power, your unconscious mind, to take these suggestions and to *act on them, now,* for your highest benefit...so...*feel* your breath now...that's right breathe as you become more aware of this aura of loving power surrounding your body now...and, breathe this loving healing energy into your body right along with the oxygen...carried right along with the oxygen to every cell of your body.

...Every cell being bathed *effortlessly* by this healing power of your unconscious mind, your true pure inner being...breathe it in...every breath *going deeper...and deeper...gently...easily...*every heartbeat now...*effortlessly...deeply relaxing...opening...opening* to the guidance of this power and intelligence that knows you completely...and completely...lovingly supports you...feel this power...imagine it as a gentle golden white light permeating every cell of your body...radiating throughout your being now...aligning the focus of awareness of every cell of your being <u>in such a way</u> that it will be *easy for you* to access the experience in your past that is the root of this problem you came with today.

Every experience you have ever had is recorded in your memory...and your unconscious mind can easily access whatever you need to access to contact the root of this problem...so that you can remember and experience it <u>in such a way</u> that you will be free of all the ways in which it had been limiting you until you *release it now*...remembering and experiencing it <u>in such a way</u> that all the emotional energy that has been held in a harmful way in your body can *be released now*... released and healed and freed to flow back into the pool of your pure inner energy where it can be freely accessed for your own highest benefit.

...As you remember and experience this past experience...in such a way that all limitations are released...you will keep whatever learnings are important and valuable to you...*keeping the learnings that give you power*...noticing that you are learning to keep the learnings that give you power and *let the old held emotions be released* as you simply keep the learnings that give you power in just the appropriate ways...and free the energy of old held emotions that *used to be trapped* by that old problem in your body .

In a moment I am going to count from one to three...As I count from one to three...you will feel yourself *effortlessly drifting back* in time... guided by the power and knowing of your unconscious mind, your pure inner being...just relax into the light and energy that is permeating your being and surrounding your body as you *feel yourself carried back in time*...back to the origin of this problem...to remember and experience it again in a new way with whatever resources you need to...*remember and experience it and be freed completely from this problem.*

Number one...going back...drifting back...relaxing into the protective aura of your pure inner being...

Number two...farther back...protected and strengthened by this aura of light...on the count of three, you'll be there...fully aware of the root experience of this problem in such a way that you will easily be freed from this problem...

Number three...now there, fully aware...go with your first impression of what you are experiencing.

((As necessary, assist client to orient into the experience. Remember you have the flexibility to go forward and backward in time to gather resources and to process as required. Remember to chunk the experience into small pieces to help them build up their awareness of where they are and what is happening.))

Share with me what you are experiencing...

((Assist them with input on whatever resources they need, basically finding a way to make it safe for them to see new choices of action to take, and to let themselves see new perspectives on the situation that release blame, shame, guilt, resentment, bitterness, etc. This can be accomplished by having them float up above (e.g. **"On the count of three...floating up...etc."***) to a safe objective distance, even to the level of the Higher Self, to reevaluate the beliefs, choices, and ideas about self that were locked in at the time. Emphasize:* **"It's over,"** *and* **"they survived it,"** *and* **"they are not that person down there who they used to be."***))*

Experience yourself as you were then *((or, if they are observing from above:* "See the you down there...etc."*))*, but with these new understandings and resources, acting and expressing in such a way that this whole experience is being transformed into an affirmation of your inner purity, freedom, and worthiness to be without needing to justify anything...completely protected and free to say and do whatever is necessary to affirm your inner power and truth...share with me what you are experiencing...

((Interact throughout the experience keeping them encouraged and focused and <u>active</u> in releasing the limitations and seeing with greater clarity.))

Good...now experience your unconscious mind taking these new resources, insights, and capacities that you have just created for yourself into the rest of your past...into every experience that needs to be reevaluated and released in the same way...give your wholehearted permission for your unconscious mind to do this, now...imagine it radiating the power of these new resources...seeking out and reevaluating all these experiences...transforming them now in the same way into resources for you as new learnings and new affirmations of your inner purity and inner strength and capacity to take care of yourself appropriately, now...relax into it...sense it in some way...

((Depending on your calibration of their state, you may ask for them to share to see if they need assistance, also, where and when it seems appropriate, feel free to repeat phrases and/or elaborate for effectiveness))

...You may notice that your conscious awareness is participating by *remembering something in a new way, now*...as you sense <u>*in some way*</u> your unconscious mind *directing the completion of this process throughout your past, now...*

Experience yourself moving into your future now...moving into anticipated familiar future situations and entirely new future situations with these new resources and this transformed past that is full of brilliant, joyful, peaceful, exuberant affirmations of you as a pure innocent being capable of enjoying life for your own highest benefit <u>which includes the highest benefit of all beings</u>...imagine that...imagine walking into your future with these resources and attitudes...see yourself doing things free of the fear of being judged...feel yourself there...hear yourself...experience how all your sensory channels seem vibrant and vivid...

((Pause for processing, possibly asking for sharing ...encouraging appropriately))

Now slowly bring your awareness back to this room...relax and reflect on all you have given yourself in this experience...with gratitude, affirm the on-going transformation your unconscious mind is going to continue for your highest benefit even when you come back to waking consciousness...yes...that's right...with every breath you take... with every step you take from now on these new resources and insights are going to grow and elaborate more and more powerfully throughout your being for your highest benefit, now and forever...*want it to happen, now and forever*...give your wholehearted grateful acknowledgment to this pure loving transformative power of your own being...understanding that you effortlessly will be keeping everything that is truly of value to you and releasing everything that is limiting you unnecessarily...*((pause))* Now allow this whole experience to dissolve into the light of your pure inner being...experience the whole experience dissolving into the light surrounding your body...now feel this light dissolving into your body...carrying it into every cell...permeating your whole being with the power and blessings of the resources and insights you have generated for yourself today...that's right...

((Pause a moment or so...calibrate...then end the session))

Now I'm going to count from one to five...when I reach five you'll be fully back in waking consciousness feeling light, refreshed, and awake...

One...coming back...begin coming back...

Two...more and more...easily coming back...feeling new energies flowing through you...

Three...wiggle your fingers and toes...that's right...wiggle them...more and more awake...

Four ...breathe in deeply now...breathe in wakeful energy...clearing your head...coming back...

Five...eyes open now...wide awake...fully back...feeling refreshed and awake...that's right.

◆ ◆ ◆

6. Models and Concepts
The 5 Skandhas, 6 Realms, and NLP

The 5 Skandhas of Buddhism

In Buddhism, the model for understanding the evolution of the egoic mind's reactive thinking process is referred to as the five *skandhas* or "heaps." They are:

1) Form/Ignorance-Birth of "I"

Initially, there is open space/open mind. Then a blackout (trance) occurs, a disruption, causing identification to arise, e.g. the shock of birth. We wake up perceiving form, not recognizing we make it. We ignore our position as creator. "Ignore-ance" is not stupidity-it is very intelligent, but reactive. The perceiver wants to possess the space, the openness now perceived through trance as form, as possessable. Since space is space, at the root, this whole endeavor is futile (therefore, suffering is unavoidable). There are 3 aspects of ignorance, simultaneous and inseparable: 1) separateness/birth; 2) a sense of 'always so', this is the real state of affairs (positive hallucination) therefore perceiver must maintain it, which brings about the birth of a sense of awkwardness; 3) self-observing ignorance: Perceiver sees the self as "other," thereby beginning a relationship with an external world.

2) Feeling

Perceiver wonders about its relationship to form. Space is not bare space, it's full of color and energy. Since we're ignoring the openness of space, these qualities are a tremendous threat to our trance. We are trying to fix, to capture the color and energy of space, to make it solid and manageable. Because such fixation is an illusion, there is a great sense of insecurity about the reality of form. Feeling is a very efficient antidote to that insecurity: it feels real, therefore it is - ignore evidence to the contrary.

3) Perception/Impulse (P/I)

Perception = receiving information, Impulse = responding to information. This is a rudimentary sorting process of perceived forms. After deciding if an object is positive (+), negative (-), or neutral(0), the perceiver reacts accordingly. There are only 3 choices: towards (desire); away from (threat/hatred); or neutral (stupid).

4) Concept

Perceiver categorizes the objects of perception into either positive (+), negative (-), or neutral (0).

Perceiver develops names, rules, and evaluation mechanisms (past/present/future). Perception/Impulse is an auto-reaction to intuitive feeling. But, it's not a good enough defense of ignorance and insecurity. Intellect is needed to do a good job: the ability to name and categorize. Egoic mind goes beyond mere reaction and becomes more sophisticated. Intellectual speculation arises. Intellect creates *I/I am* to encompass all the stuff of ego into solid mass, confirming and interpreting self: putting self into logical situations, with natural tendency towards a positive condition to affirm one's existence (i.e., one's ignorance).

5) Consciousness

The intuitive intelligence of the 2nd skandha, plus the energy of the 3rd, plus the intellect of the 4th combine to produce thoughts and emotions. A hallucinatory quality arises as we project our version of reality on to the world.

NOTE: Skandhas 1-4 develop very simply and predictably. The 5th skandha is wild and irregular- creating unpredictable thought patterns - our normal state.

Concepts mix w/impulse energy to create **fully developed emotions**: mixture of energy and conceptual storyline (vivid trance!). Since the "real world" doesn't fit our storylines, our stories and energies are constantly thrown into conflict with themselves and worldly events. Confusion!! Rambling thought arises in the effort to maintain the validity of the trance, even when we're alone. Therefore, we're always alone with ourselves. Reading things into the world, one becomes completely immersed in one's trance. The power of the hallucination has a life of its own. It is called the Wheel of Life, the Six Realms of Existence:

1) Heaven/God Realm - full of (conditional) goodness, beauty, and freedom. Pride.

2) Jealous God Realm - having tasted or imagined heaven, one must defend it (the quivers of fear begin, the intimations of insubstantiality)- jealousy and envy arise

3) Human Realm - jealousy makes things get heavier, earth bound. Instead of alternating between jealousy and pride(they are too intense), one gets a more solid "homey" feeling - regular ordinary mundane life satisfying mundane desires.

4) Animal Realm - pursuing desire makes one get dull, heavier, more stupid, lazy. One would just crawl around and moo or bark, rather than make the effort to enjoy the pleasure of pride or envy.

5) Hungry Ghosts Realm - the heaviness gets oppressive, one remembers the God-realm, and wants to get back but doesn't know how. This generates great hunger and thirst, unquenchable/claustrophobic -and it builds.

6) Hell Realm -the continuing frustration results in loss of faith, great doubt arises, hopelessness, & violent reaction arises: Hatred for this nightmare and for oneself.

(My eternal gratitude to my teacher, Chogyam Trungpa, Rinpoche, for presenting this material in a vivid, loving, and humorous way)

The Reactive Model Diagram

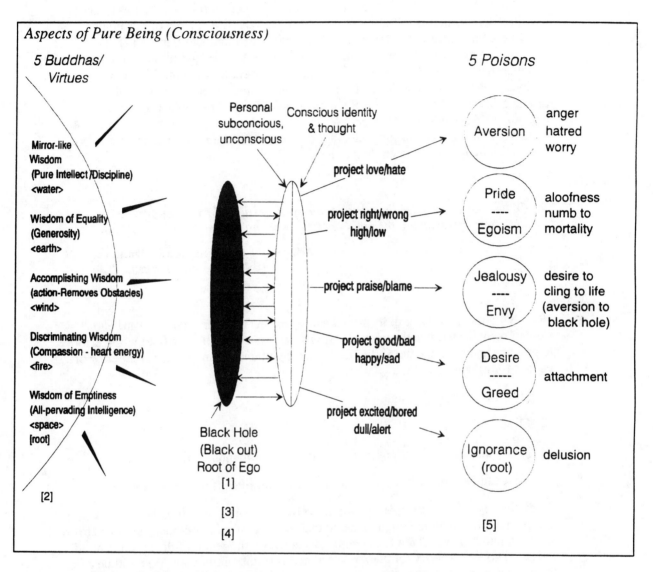

Figure 2-6a: A Model of the structure of Reactive Thinking

1] Awareness of the Black Hole.

We feel the Black Hole back there; sometimes we turn around and look at it (EcK!). We react to it aversively. The belief is that it is the end of the line, the deep dark secret badness/deficiency at the root of our being. We naturally bounce off of it constantly, fantasizing incessantly the hallucinations of the 6 realms. The irony is that <u>the driving force for all of this is an intuition of Pure Being</u>. But we separate from it (egoic trance/1st Skandha), make it an object to be attained, an "other," then project it outward. We read this most desperately needed "other" into all sorts of surrogate things, people, and situations, again according to our propensities within the 6 realms.

Instead of settling into the real thing as a given, and moving out into the world with our own true Fullness which then makes life a creative, enjoyable sharing adventure with nothing at stake, effortless and free of fear, we believe and <u>convincingly feel</u> we are separate from "It." We become a somebody, a doer(3rd mala), who has to get the missing piece or pieces to find peace. We run from the Black Hole of our inner emptiness (of a different order than True Emptiness which is Fullness). Life is experienced as a fearful struggle where there is a lot to lose, and it's an open question whether there is enough to share. We find ourselves endlessly running after our various projects and solutions to a problem that assumes an achievable goal, a produceable goal. But the goal is not a createable, producable object. It is pre-existing, self-existing, ever present. We have to learn to stop contracting into egoic endeavors to create it, and just relax into this presence. We need to learn to trust its support and guidance moment by moment:

> *"When these obstacles have been reduced to vestigial form, they can be destroyed by resolving the mind back to its primal cause."*

Aphorism 10, Section II: Yoga and Practice
<u>The Yoga Aphorisms of Patanjali.</u>

"Resolving the mind back to its primal cause" means to reverse the outward egoic flow of mental energy and awareness. It is much easier to put your faith in the effort to practice and cultivate the ability to do this if you understand the inherent error of egoic assumptions, i.e., that:

[1] something is missing,

[2] it's out there,

[3] it's an object, either physical or emotional, or mental, and

[4] it can be captured by either passive or aggressive effort.

Study this egoic mishap's operation moment by moment in your life. The more you comprehend it, the more you understand that the goal of transpersonal therapy is to wake up into "OKness," not to solve problems within the realm of the reactive mind theater. This will affect your therapy work in a very important way. You will be able to truly honor the real person as opposed to honoring their egoic notions of what they "should" achieve, fix, or self-improve. In an absolutely real way, "honoring" a client's agenda, to the degree that it is egoic, reinforces the on-going egoic dishonoring of their True Self and Its ability to shine through. You must have a deep understanding of the egoic process <u>in yourself and your client</u> in order to avoid the self-improvement trap.

2] The Sun of Pure Being is bigger than the Black Hole.

Although we focus on it and only sense it in egoic states, all egoic activity actually happens inside the Sun. Everything is always pervaded by purity; we never left the garden; we just fell asleep (into trance) in it. Since even our problems are supported by the energy of our purity, cultivating an on-going moment by moment remembrance to count ones' blessings (what are they?) can be a powerful yet simple antidote to reactive thought processes.

3] Challenge to cultivate faith.

Can you cultivate faith to renounce dilemma/seeking thinking for celebration/creative thinking? Not blind faith, which is a front for resentment and mistrust, but faith that is rational - because it is rooted in an understanding of the futile nature of egoic thought. Can you confront all the small secret voices and powerfully seductive feelings of doubt and fear as they arise moment by moment trying to put you in trance? <u>This faith is an active process of confrontation of fear-based thought forms.</u> ("Thank you for sharing, but what are you trying to accomplish by telling me this (fear based thought)?"). Renunciation of egoic thought does not mean a dead mind. You keep and hone your discrimination and capacity to criticize, but it is bathed in a spacious atmosphere of a priori gratitude, love, humor and compassion. It can be a subtle challenge to notice and own the atmosphere out of which ones' criticisms arise.

4] Duality of Egoic Mind.

Cut off from grace of source/always-present-fullness (5 Buddhas), mind seeks fullness in its reflection/projection (5 poisons). The fearful hope of finding 'It' outside to fill Black Hole inside is driven by the intuition of Pure Being.

5] The Purity behind the Poison.

Each Wisdom Aspect is the seed of goodness/awakeness of the poison across from it on the chart. Strip away the egoic aspect of anger/hatred and you have Mirror-like Wisdom, perfectly reflecting the reality of the situation, etc. This "flip" happens in an instant. Even in "ordinary" untrained people it happens, but goes mostly unnoticed. Thus, these moments are not seized upon and cultivated through: *(1) grateful contemplation* and, *(2) invitation to increase.* Core purity is the reason we diffuse client hatred of any of their 'stuff." ***Core purity instantly bursts forth when ego-trance is punctured***. A good example is humor diffusing anger/rage. Humor embodies a shift of perspective out of oneself; one suddenly sees the rageful one "over there" and the mirror-like clarity reflects the irony/absurdity inherent in the occurrence. Suddenly space and a breath of fresh air enters (literally in the release of contraction on the breath). **This course is an exploration of egoic trance-bursting theatrical devices.**

Words create delusions, they can also create consciousness. Good words, good concepts are most important in providing us with our tools: **the kinds of questions we can ask if we have interesting working models.** We can broaden our repertoire of working models and tools by drawing from both the world's ancient philosophical teachings and from modern therapeutic techniques.

Modified Psychosynthesis Model of the Psyche

(refer to audio tapes, Phase II & What We May Be, Piero Ferrucci)

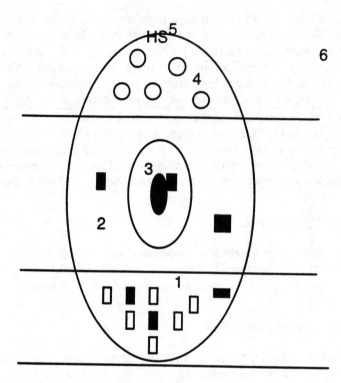

1 = Lower unconscious; subconscious

     white boxes = subpersonalities (see Phase I)

     black boxes = outer influences (see Phase VI)

2 = Middle unconscious; waking intuitions & gut feelings

3 = Personal self (black circle) and field of consciousness.

     black box = attachment by outer influence (see Phase VI)

4 = Superconscious: level of Higher Self and Archetypes (see Phase V)

     circles = Archetype

     no outer influences at Superconscious level

5 = HS: strictly speaking, Higher Self pervades entire psyche

6 = Collective Unconscious (Jungian conception)

Model of the Psyche

The following diagram illustrates how and where the theater of experience arises. It correlates an NLP model of the Psyche with the Five Skandhas of Buddhism:

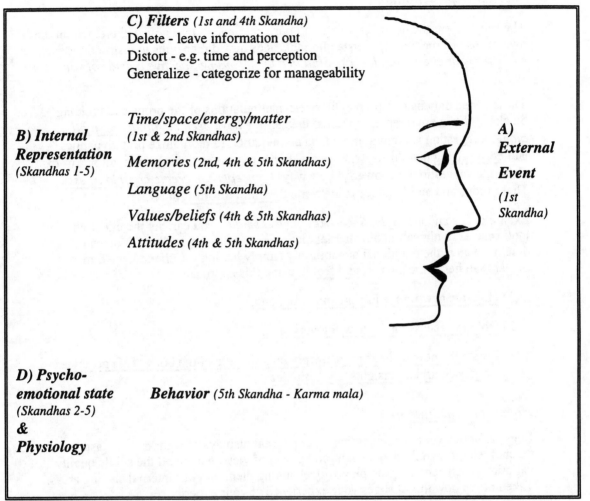

C) Filters (1st and 4th Skandha)
Delete - leave information out
Distort - e.g. time and perception
Generalize - categorize for manageability

B) Internal Representation (Skandhas 1-5)

Time/space/energy/matter (1st & 2nd Skandhas)

Memories (2nd, 4th & 5th Skandhas)

Language (5th Skandha)

Values/beliefs (4th & 5th Skandhas)

Attitudes (4th & 5th Skandhas)

A) External Event (1st Skandha)

D) Psycho-emotional state (Skandhas 2-5) & Physiology

Behavior (5th Skandha - Karma mala)

Figure 2-6b: The theater of experience. An NLP model of the psyche correlated with the 5 Skandhas of Buddhism.

A)"External" events

The so-called "objective reality," processed through various mental filters gives rise to *Internal Representations (B)* of the external events. We live in the internal representations, which are facsimiles of the events themselves. We contact, we touch, we experience an internal representation, not the event itself. This is what is meant by saying, *"We think we live in the world, but we live in our minds."*

External events, strictly speaking, include internal events. From the most subtle perspective, all events, all experiences are 'other' - not Self, occurring in the field of 'No-Self' awareness which is our True Self: Always-the-Seer-Never-the-Seen-TrueSelf. External events are built of all 5 skandhas, but, in this diagram, the 1st Skandha (concept of "I" as separate) is highlighted as the root from which the rest are born.

B) Internal Representation

The stage of our theater; everything - all our experience - takes place there, within the awareness of True Self. Understanding this adds new dimensions to instructions such as, *'Take your client literally,'* or, *'Shift to a humorous perspective outside of your self.'*

These added dimensions are playful overt manipulations of the props and building blocks of the internal representational theater. *We have been manipulating it all along.* Suggestion is nothing more than an invitation to reorganize prop dynamics. But **recognizing** that this is what we are doing, in its most literal sense, allows us to elaborate suggestions in powerful new ways (*concepts can create consciousness*). These props and building blocks are termed **'submodalities'** in NLP.

Example: If someone says, *"She makes me feel small,"* you can bet the client will look smaller to himself in his internal picture in comparison to "her." You can quickly change the emotional dynamics by simply having the client make himself bigger than her in the picture, and feel it, using this approach:

(1) Hold the new **image** in contemplation, and,

(2) Hold awareness on the new **feelings,** and,

(3) Breath the new feelings more deeply into all parts of the body. This generates new consciousness, insights, and attitudes.

Homework (*invitation*):

Begin to notice your submodalities, your internal displays of sight, sound, taste, touch, feeling, spatial relationships, and points of view. Notice all the subtle quality variations each contains, and play with changing them on your internal staging areas. Take note of how this changes your experience of your experience.

C) Filters

'Inside' the head, our mental systems and functions create the world of the skandhas: our ordinary, potentially effortless, experience. All five skandhas are present and interdependent, but those of the 4th skandha are highlighted as *filters*. A *filter* is anything created as and supported by concept.

If the 4th Skandha filters were **transparent**, *letting the Light of TrueSelf shine through, our experience of the world would be effortless and delightful.*

Opaque: 4th Skandha concepts - egoic concepts, twist our natural perception and create prejudice - solidified notions that separate and generate perceived needs for violence and hypocrisy. The opacity of these concepts simply blocks the Light of TrueSelf.

Thus, the Empty(Full of Light) "stuff" of the Formless Manifest passes through our filters and gives ***threatening*** form to many Internal Representations, the ***interpreted world*** in which we live. Studying the diagram, when we distinguish between the external world, and our internal thoughts, pictures, etc., the most natural conclusion ***seems to be*** to consider only our internal world the world of the Internal Representation. However, the external world is also an internal representation:

Our most Subtle Awareness knows everything as 'other' and recognizes that It *contains* all experience internally as representation, as Dream. In a truly awake state, we recognize the 'other' paradoxically as Self also, but we remain free of identification with the self/other of experience. We maintain Supreme Subjectivity in the midst of the awareness of being the substance of all the 'other'. **We can know ourselves as the substance of the Dream**, as life force itself, *even as we take on experience as a "separate" personality*. Thus, we remain unaffected by the drama of the Dream. We live free of support as Indestructible Awareness/Substance. As Christ said: *"Be in the world, but not of the world."*

Our bodies are in our Mind (our most Subtle Awareness), the world is in our Mind, and our little egoic thinking mind seems to be in our body. One can and should ***practice*** this subtle awareness of being the *Seer* (i.e., associated with our true essence), not the *Seen* (i.e., thoughts, feelings, body, etc.), until it becomes one's natural orientation.

"Be in the world...": When the 4th Skandha filters are *transparent*, letting in the Light of Self, of this Subtle Awareness, we can and must trust the natural intelligence of the skandhas, of the psycho-physical being, that creates and relates to the subjective world of the five senses, even though it is illusory (i.e., illusory because temporary). The 'real' illusion of the ordinary world, potentially free of prejudice, is our playground - even the Garden, if you will. It is a place to be at ease with clear-seeing impartiality based on the sanity (i.e., operative but *transparent* 4th Skandha) of an open-hearted, shame-free, body-mind synchronization: No hypocrisy, no fragmentation of false self-trances. We "walk our talk" and live by the Golden Rule and Ahimsa (non-violence)*"...but not of the world."*: Awake in the Subtle Awareness as Substance of All, what is there to be violent with or fearful of?

As stated above, we can trust the natural 'external' world. It's O.K. that it is illusory. Our body-mind is part of the illusion and, therefore, within the illusion, everything is real and has a real integrity with everything else in the illusion: Respect the Natural World.

We lose that Respect when we get lost in the mind-**in**-our-body, lost in the prejudice of ***opaque*** 4th Skandha concepts/filters which give rise to the 5th Skandha melodrama of: look-out-for-fearful-shamed-number-one's-survival-and-to-Hell-with-anyone-else!

Thus, ***prejudiced*** Internal Representations comprised of all the Skandhas, determine our Fearful State.

D) *Psycho-emotional state, physiology, & behavior*

Our **state**, our attitudes and emotional posture, profoundly affects our **physiology**, and our state creates, sustains, and ends our **behaviors**. Our behaviors, physiology, and changing state are locked in a feedback loop that affects the on-going generation of our Internal Representations. And when prejudiced, creates our on-going compulsively circular feedback loop world: the Six Realms of Existence.

This may all seem incredibly complex, but it is effortlessly comprehended by a humble, unbiased heart.

The submodality characteristics (how small, how fast, how hot, where located, etc.) and dynamics (the characteristic interactions) give the Internal Representation life and power. *When you make the right changes on this internal stage, you can quickly and profoundly effect change in the state, physiology, and behavior of the subject.*

The NLP Milton Meta Model

The NLP Milton Meta Model explains how the filters of distortions, deletions, and generalizations, the impactful vagaries of language, the Matrika Shakti, create and support the "mishap" of egoic minding. The following material, which elucidates the mental processes of distortion, deletion, and generalization, is adapted from Milton Erickson's Meta Model. Most of the category terminology is original to the founders of NLP.

Distortions

1) Mind reading: We are all famous for going into trance in this way. It is a pervasive form of sloganeering- and not just at election time. You need to be watchful of your own tendency to do it, and learn how to stop doing it. Developing the sensitivity to stop your own mind reading is a direct determinant of your ability to bring your clients out of their trance of doing it.

For example, a client might say: *"They don't like me."* To initiate self-inquiry, ask the question: *"How do you know they don't like you?"* The fruit of such self-inquiry identifies the source of the information.

2) Lost Subject (Actor/Performer). Statements of value judgments that leave out the initiator of the judgment.

For example: *"It's wrong to swear."* Question to initiate self-inquiry: *"How do you know..., who says...,according to whom? "* The fruit: the client identifies the source (of the belief), the subject (as source), or the logic(or prestige) that sustains the belief.

3) Cause-Effect Relationship. This is most important, not only to identify wrongly held views of particular cause/effect (*c/e*) relationships, but to put clients "at cause," completely, regarding how they respond to their experience.

For example: *"He makes me mad, sad, happy...etc."* Question to initiate self-inquiry: *"How does what he does cause you to **decide (to choose)** to feel bad?" "how specifically...?"* The fruit: the client regains an awareness of choice of how to respond, and of having the power to choose - the first step back to being **at cause** in one's life.

4) Complex Equivalence. Making things the same or equal, but missing that the c/e relationship is arbitrary (i.e., they made it up!).

For example, *"Whenever he sees me, he looks away; he doesn't like me."* Question: *"How does his looking away mean...(examine cause/effect)...have you ever looked away when you saw someone you liked?* (note: counter examples broaden awareness of perspectives beyond simply the counter example itself. If there are two ways to interpret something, there generally are more than two.) The fruit: the client breaks the fixation, and destroys the arbitrary "truth."

5) Presuppositions. The axioms upon which our beliefs about cause/effect are based. They are the unquestioned c/e relationships that underlie all our concepts of reality, and, they all are grounded in an all encompassing world view, whether the client is aware of it or not. In other words, *moment by moment,* we proceed in our thought processes from our theory of the origins of the universe (1st Skandha).

For example, *"If you knew how much that bothered me, you wouldn't do it."* (Presupposes: you are bothered...I am doing something...I don't know you are bothered.) Questions: *"How do you choose to feel bothered?"* The fruit: 1) Puts the client at cause over response: *"What am I doing?"* or, *"How does what I am doing cause...?"* 2) Clarifies action, *"How do you know I don't know?"* 3) Requires elucidation of their internal reality (i.e., representation of the events), and exposes the complex equivalence dynamics.

Generalizations

1) Universal Quantifiers: all, every, never, always, everyone, no one...For example: *"They always forget..."* Questions: 1) *"Always?"* Fruit: dissolves the absolute. 2) *"What would happen if they didn't?"* Fruit: elicits shadow presuppositions.

2) Modal Operators...of necessity; of possibility.

a) *Of necessity:* should, shouldn't, have to, must, etc. For example: *"I have to stay at this job."* Question: *"What would happen if you didn't?"* Fruit: client focuses on outcome, elucidates beliefs, cause/effect, presuppositions, internal representations - the whole trance/theater!

b) *Of possibility:* may/may not, can/can't, possible/impossible, etc. For example: *"I can't quit this job."* Question: *"What stops you?"* Fruit: recovers choice and cause, *"What would happen if you did?* Fruit: same as (a) above.

Deletions

1) Nominalizations. Changing processes into things (grammatically - changing verbs into nouns). For example: "We need to work on our relationship." Question: "How are you relating that you don't like." Fruit: changes "it" back into a process, elucidates the

"players," their actions, the presuppositions, etc...exposes the whole trance/drama.

Test for a nominalization: "Will it fit in a wheelbarrow?"

2) Unspecified Verbs. Leave out functional dynamics in a statement. For example: *"She hurt me."* Question: *"How exactly (specifically) did she hurt you?* Fruit: cause/effect dynamics, etc.

3) Simple deletions. Something is left out of the statement, such as a person, a thing, or a process (i.e., the referential index is missing). For example:
"You're silly." Q: *"How exactly?"*
"I'm unhappy." Q: *"About what?"*

"They won't answer." Q: *"Who, exactly?"*

"You're the best/worst!" Q: *"Compared to what/whom?"* (Note: in this case, the dynamics of comparison are left out: comparative deletion). Fruit in each case: recovery of deletion.

Fragmentation and shadow structures

From these examples, I'd like to propose to you that **all thoughts are incomplete**. They are either *fragmented* as those above, leaving out crucial aspects by their lack of comprehensive logic or perspective, or they have *"shadow" aspects*, implications intended to be left out. This is generally an unconscious intent on our part because we are not trained to be sensitive to the first four skandhas of the origination of our thoughts. We only recognize the fifth skandha tip of the iceberg. Thus, statements may be both fragmented and hiding shadow aspects, and generally are both.

The fragmentation keeps people going round and round in their trances of dilemma because, by nature, the fragmented logic and view of the thoughts denies them access to alternative choices of feeling and action. Fragmentation reinforces the felt sense of finality: the world view our thoughts describe is fixed and true. We become so used to these thought forms, individually and culturally, that we stop noticing the fragmentation, and, hence, rarely challenge it. We don't do enough self-inquiry.

Example - fragmentation: *"I can't do X."* This is a fixed thought, which leaves out time and process, and generates an aura of finality. Also, it is a strongly structured suggestion, concise and easily repeatable. Repetition creates conviction. As a therapist (and for therapist's own benefit) respond by adding the tag, "Yet!" Fruit: opens time flow, process, and recognition of possibility of change - everything changes! One word dissolves the fixation, restores fluidity, and initiates self-inquiry. *"I can't do X, yet."*

Example - shadow aspect: A prospective student discussing options for taking the course by intensive or weekend format. Strictly discussing logistics of learning, but body language and voice tone belie a deeper concern. Instead of responding to the issues presented, I say, *"First of all, you shouldn't worry at all about failing this course."* Student immediately relaxes, confesses that indeed *fear of failure* was the main concern, not deciding *the best way to learn*.

Flip side of wanting is fear of not getting: success/failure duality. One aspect of the incompleteness of thought is that we always express one side of a thought. Thoughts like coins have two sides, minimum. What is left unsaid is the shadow, and many times, as in this case, we leave it unsaid because it carries a truer statement about our state, about our hopes and fears, that we wish to deny or hide.

Example - shadow aspect: Phase I story - Woman who is tortured by her children. She trained them to treat her like her father treated her. Flip side of complaint about his treatment of her, treatment which she went to great lengths to replicate, is longing for his presence. Recognition of this dictated my response: *"Oh, you miss your Dad!"* Fruit: Immediate tears, restoration of capacity to feel the held true feelings.

Example - fragmentation: A student in class objected to my use of the word, *"Fuck."* I pointed out to her that the word had no power of its own, that we give power to words, suggesting to her that she examine how she has given this word power over her. For the benefit of the whole class, I went into a discussion of inherent qualities of words vs. inherent qualities of objects. As an example, I chose water. Wetness is an inherent quality of water. No matter who you are, no matter what you think, water will get you wet. Words, unlike water, do no have this inherent power - *we must invest them with power.*

Another student interrupted with great conviction that *"When a word is said, it has great power."* She started to go on and on about the power of words to affect people individually and in cultural groups, always using the linguistic form, *"When a word is said..."*

I pointed out to her that she was giving an example of the meta model category of **Lost Performer and Deleted Referential Index.** She was leaving out the subject, the doer: **Who** said the word. She was also leaving out the object, the listener: **who** heard the word. Without these crucial parts of the puzzle her emphatic pronouncements seemed very weighty to some, given the prestige, the passion, carried in her voice. She was persuading them, hypnotizing them with emotional impact, <u>vividness</u>.

But when these missing pieces were pointed out, it became obvious to her and to everyone that the "power of the word" was totally a function of the investment, by their attitudes, of the speaker and listener.

Used purposefully as linguistic devices and deceptions, these fragmentary and shadow structures are the means for creating vagueness, and large "chunks" of information conducive to hypnosis. They facilitate trance. **Specifying** creates clarity and smaller "chunks" that enable one to see the dynamics at play. *Neither is inherently better than the other:*

We use shadows and fragments inappropriately to make and maintain problem states; we can use them appropriately to unravel problem states and enhance desirable states.

As a therapist, you will generally be specifying (chunking down) to break the client's problem state through self-inquiry, and then generalizing, etc., to produce and maintain resourceful states. In other words, "chunking" activates their unconscious capacities to reevaluate and change relational processes beneficially over a wide range of interrelated data and experience.

Your ability to do this will be greatly enhanced by studying and comprehending the meta model, and by refining your competency at the art and skill of self-inquiry by practicing with clients and **with your own internal dialogue.**

Understanding the nature of incomplete thought is essential to waking up and staying awake yourself, and it is essential to working with clients' trances. The point is not to be able to explain it, but to be able to <u>recognize incomplete thinking as it occurs, moment by moment, and to know how to then utilize it to lead clients to more resourceful trance states and to wakefulness.</u>

Summary and Exercise:

Practice relaxing your body/mind and then listening and observing with the understanding that what someone says to you, or what you say to yourself, is the minimal exposure of information involved in the complex and deluded evolution of any thought to the extent that it is egoic in nature.

Moment by moment, pure bubbles of delightful energy/consciousness rise into awareness of being on their way to normal waking consciousness. When and to the extent that egoic guardian is present, at a certain level of awareness of being (still unconscious with respect to waking consciousness) the energy/consciousness is grasped and contracted into separate identity felt-sense(1st Skandha). As it continues to rise towards waking consciousness, it is further contracted as it is clothed with beliefs (fixed and fragmentary prejudices about experiences of being alive formed through the devices of deletion, distortion, and generalization)(2nd-4th Skandhas) These beliefs further contract the energy as they determine how the basically unlimited creative bubble will be allowed to squeeze out some of its "juice" in the form of capabilities or the lack thereof. These capabilities are relational - the notion of a capability can only have meaning **in relation to an 'other'** whether it be a person, thing, or situation. Therefore, the storyline opinion of self, public and private personality(5th Skandha), arises in the moment by moment assessment of how this separate entity is **doing** in this egoically defined waking world. In moments of love, joy, inspiration, pure anger, or pure any feeling, the bubble has shot straight to the surface without interruption or contraction, but such moments are quickly followed by contractions in thought that must pigeonhole such bursts into the storyline of self. This takes time, energy, and seriousness and, thus, makes these bursts few and far between for those of us deeply entranced in egoic minding.

If you understand this process of the emergence of conscious egoic thought, you understand that all problems have their root in the person's deepest relationship to Source, i.e., all problems are at their root problems of Faith and Remembrance of Pure Being. You can help the client, through exploring, curiously examining questioning(refer to meta-model and also to Phase III, self-inquiry processes), to trace back and to unravel the binding thought structures that are restricting and blocking their natural effortless experience of Pure Free Being. As you do this, it may look like a simple conversation, but if you are clear about the target and the process, and maintain rapport, the results can be quickly marvelous.

◆ ◆ ◆

7. Emotions:
Freeing the Energy of Life

The word "emotion" has been analyzed usefully in the following way: "E" - stands for energy, "motion" stands for movement.

Emotions are movements of energy, shakti, life force. Emotions are ***temporary*** ***"patternings"*** of our inherently pure and dynamically formless life force energy, swirling and playing, responding and communicating with all the "other" energy patternings it encounters.

Our life force is not separate from our intelligence, and, while it is supremely intelligent at a certain level, it is extremely gullible at another level - a real sucker for the trance forming logic of the thinking mind (thinking mind, both conscious and unconscious). This gullibility begins at the first skandha with the quality of ignorance.

The consequence is the arousal of fear as the primordial response (and in its context, an intelligent one) to the misperception of separate existence and the "instinctual" drive for survival.

As we move through the skandhas, building up the storyline of 'who we are,' and 'what is going on," we learn to "freeze" the energy of our being as a *best-effort-at-the-time-given- our-understanding-and-choices*. This freezing technique happens at the physical level. We learn we can "hold" our energy motions by holding our musculature (and, many times, we learn this holding technique under duress: *"Stop crying or I'll give you something to cry about!"*) This supremely <u>intelligent and powerful</u> capacity to modulate and coordinate the breath, the muscles, the posture, perceptions, and emotions, for most of us, to varying degrees, is habituated to inhibiting the movement of life-force-itself-freely-as-itself. Out of fear for its (our) survival as a separate entity and fear of pain, it (we) relinquishes the right and freedom to use this intelligent and powerful capacity to nourish its (our) own joyful, spontaneous expression of just-being-its (our)-I-don't-know-who-I-am-self (but that's O.K. because I feel so good).

Generally, therapy of any kind only produces dynamic results to the degree that the client remembers and relives the experience where freezing of emotions occurred, releasing the spontaneous flow of emotions from the holding patterns, and building enough faith and self-trust to redirect beneficially the habitual use of their own power.

Our energy is the energy of the universe, it is <u>**very**</u> powerful! In the trance of being a limited being, we feel we have only a little of it. We have much more than we think. In fact, the illusion of having "no energy" of our depressions is just the skillful ruse of our internal holding patterns. It's not that we have "no" energy. It's that unconsciously we are using most of our energy to hold our energy restricted to such a degree that the "conscious" self thinks and feels that no energy exists. It exists; it's just not available to play or enjoy, or to work or study, or anything else - it has it's hands full holding onto itself!

In fact, this holding task is so demanding that, if we had to stay conscious of it, we wouldn't and couldn't do it! We can manage to hold energy frozen for 5,10,20 years or a lifetime (or more) at a time only by handing the task over to the part of us that never tires and never runs out of energy, our unconscious mind.

In therapy, we use this fact to our advantage. If we bring a holding pattern to consciousness, it's too hard to hold, so, the client lets go. The energy is freed: they are freed! Remember, this metaphorical terminology about "bringing stuff to consciousness" is really about bringing the client out of the deep trance that allows this holding dynamic to go on with the so-called "conscious" mind floating on top of it.

Guidelines for Letting Go

A key factor in this holding process is the ability we have to <u>associate or dissociate</u>. We simply give ourselves the suggestion, *"this is me"* to associate, or, *"this isn't me"* to dissociate. Obviously, if you have put feelings out of consciousness, you have told yourself they aren't you. The signs of this dissociation are expressed linguistically and physically. Simply put, <u>in order to assist a client to wake up and free their emotional energy, you must get them to associate with what they are habitually dissociating from, and to dissociate from what they are habitually associating with (in all ways that such things are inappropriate)</u>.

Here are some guidelines to accomplish this:

1) Trust and rapport are the essential foundation. The client must feel safe, supported, and honored by you, which means you have to be free of being threatened by their issues, even if you have the same issues. This is a great challenge, <u>the great challenge</u> for a therapist: not to get lost with the client in the shadows of their mutual unconscious trances and, not even know it because the therapist is caught in the trance of being the therapist with all the agendas and taboos such a trance can entail, including the notion of the resistant client! You need to communicate, <u>primarily in a non-verbal way</u>, **genuineness**, <u>not necessarily caring</u>, and a fearless permission to the client that it is O.K. to feel, to speak, and to release their stuff from the shadows of trance denial.

2) Help them recognize that they are not their emotions, their stuff, the *temporary patterns* **of their energy.** This is the first stage of reorganization - helping them to dissociate from the *patterns* which they have been chronically associating with ("It's me, it's bad - that's why I have to hide it."). Help them to contemplate that *they are the energy itself, not simply and superficially the pattern.* They are the energy, the life force, which is inherently pure and good: <u>the kind of absolute goodness that is unaffected by anything they have ever thought or said or done, and unaffected by anything that has ever been thought or said about them, or done to them</u>. And they are not the body, or the personality. These are merely patterns as well. Thus, you help them to associate with what they have dissociated from: *a felt-sense* of their true sense of being, including the intuition/conviction of the right to be and express without fear or fearful pretense. *"We are not human beings having a spiritual experience. We are spiritual beings having a human experience."* Teilhard de Chardin.

3) Have them open up their posture as a first step. Notice holding expressions physically such as crossed limbs, slumped posture, knitted brows, clenched jaws, controlled breathing, etc. Gently and unobtrusively open some of those up by pacing and leading, or by simply asking: *"Would you please sit up straight with your feet on the floor and your hands on your knees and take a slow deep breath...that's right...good...thank you... that should help you think more clearly, now...in ways that are beneficial..."*

4) Notice if they are dissociating from their feeling in their verbal expression and get them to associate. For example:

   a) Are they using second or third person to talk about themselves? "You know how you don't like it when...." Respond with *"No...don't you like it when..."* or *"please use 'I' when you talk about yourself."*

   b) Are they maintaining a flat conversational tone of voice when the content is obviously charged? Also, are they using an incongruent tone or response such as a laugh or a smile when talking about something painful like being spanked as a child?

   - Ask: *"How does that make you feel?"*

   - Ask them to repeat over and over: "I feel angry" *"Again!"* "I feel angry" etc., associating them into the feeling.

   - Ask them to repeat that they don't feel: "I don't hate him" etc.

   - Say *"Let me hear the sadness (anger, fear)...let the sadness speak...let the energy of the sadness take control of your vocal cords and speak..."*

   - Role play. Feed back to them the insults as the insulter, but be sure you are in rapport to do this.

   - Exaggerate the expression, physical holding, or symptom. Instruct them to intensify the tightening symptom. **This associates them into the <u>energy</u> of the <u>pattern</u> and awakens the sense of being at cause over it.** (E.g., have a client tighten their whole body and do a *progressive <u>tightening</u> instruction* as they do, then instruct to stop abruptly and let go. This is an effective relaxation induction. Or triple the frequency of an habitual pattern. Go into it fiercely, rather than trying pathetically to back away from it.)

   - Have them use present tense in describing their feelings: *"that really scared me..."* have them say in present tense (and repeat) *"That really scares me..."* This can initiate regression all by itself. Do you see how it causes them to associate into the trance of the regressed state? They don't have to "go anywhere" to do it; they brought it with them!

   - More comprehensively, ask them to imagine being <u>the person they were then</u>, while keeping a dual awareness anchor of being in present time with you: *"AS you maintain your awareness of sitting across from me looking at my face, constantly aware of seeing my face, allow yourself to become that little girl there... then..."* This mixes the states and brings the adult resources to the aid of the trance child.

   - Tell them to see or hear the other person in the situation as they describe it, again more wakefully accessing the regression trance.

5) Ask where in the body they feel a block or the emotion. Either have them apply pressure gently there or, with their permission, you do it (generally with your hand over theirs)...simultaneously suggesting that this will allow/cause the emotion to move, to express, that this pressure will allow them to let it go...let it go...let it speak...

6) Get them to access the worst case scenario which they are unconsciously assuming and warding off with this behavior/holding.. This is to bring into awareness the root consequence/belief that holds the pattern together.

Once someone is associated strongly into the energy of their feelings, there are some important guidelines to assist this in such a way that the emotion is **cleared,** as opposed to simply expressed but not resolved. In my experience, there are many people with the experience of releasing and expressing emotions without any resolution, without any learning, without any alteration of their awareness. They understandably feel that expressing emotions is a futile endeavor - *"It doesn't do any good!"*

I have also encountered people who have opened up to feeling with a therapist, individually or in a group, only to be made to feel that their performance wasn't satisfactory. They didn't do it right or go far enough. This type of insult, in my opinion, is a result of the therapist's denial and fear of their own unresolved issues clouding their capacity to truly support the client. You must be able to fearlessly see these things arise in your consciousness. Yes, fearlessly feel your fear and admit to yourself that it's there, and refrain from projecting it on to your client.

Guidelines for supporting emotional release

You must remain non-judgmental and act in the manner of a mid-wife, nursing the expression and release of the emotion the way a midwife assists a birth. Once they are into it, just like a birth, you can trust the intelligence of the organism to take over, so:

1) Don't interrupt the flow of feeling. When in doubt be silent or occasionally encourage with a word or two: *"good...keep going...you're doing great...that's right...etc."* In general, it is always best to encourage them to increase the feeling, to intensify it, until they are fully associated into it and being carried by its energy. If they seem to get stuck in a feeling or become afraid of its persistence, still suggest, *"Stay with it, stay with it, experience it fully...until it changes to something else..."* (Note the pacing, leading, and imbedded command in this suggestion.)

2) Don't distract them by: a) intellectualizing about the data, or b) letting it trigger a sharing of your own similar stuff.

3) If they get lost, or the discharge slows, return them to the point that it began. It can be like riding a river rapids that has its rushes and becalmed spots. Just keep them in the flow of it. You'll learn to trust this process as you see it repeat itself in client after client. True discharge will move from anger to hurt to sadness to acceptance to peace to compassion. When they can take a perspective on the perpetrator as a victim of his/her own trance, you'll know they are really free. To take such a perspective, they have to be completely released from their own perspective as the victim.

4) Give them the resources they need to access and release the holding.
Remember:

a) Rely on the inherent purity of the releasing process. When you help them release a block, the energy goes in the direction of healthy reorganization, even though it may pass through the expression of extreme negativity for a time. **Don't let them get stuck in the negativity and fixate that.**

b) We are always doing our best, i.e., making the best choices, in the context of our trance, which dictates what meaning is present and what our options for choice are. This follows from inherent purity,

c) We, therefore, will easily change our choices and behaviors once we have the resources we need to understand that better choices are truly available,

d) It follows, therefore, that change should never be a struggle, should never be forced. Struggle is an indication of trying to get a change of choice without doing the groundwork of educating the "unconscious mind" as to the validity, safety, and ecology of the new choice(s),

e) Don't try to make them change. **Pace their understanding** regarding the trance/issue/situation/problem and **lead them into new perspectives** that embody the sanity (intelligence, congruence, and enhancement of power) of new choices. The choices of suggestion and direction you need to make will be apparent to you if you don't let the poignancy or intensity of their experience cause you to forget that you are witnessing an **internal theatrical construct** that the client has the power and right to reconstruct. Your job is to give them the *rememberance and experience* of this power by helping them play with the elements of the staging and the roles, the submodalities of their experience. Make it safe for them to act and express within the situation in new empowering ways, at the same time that you suggest to them to have the dual awareness that the situation is over with; they survived it and can be free of the limitations fixated in it.

Guidelines for resolving past situations

Emotional clearing will always involve memories of unresolved past situations, the trance "scenes" where their energy is frozen in its dilemma of past woundedness. There are several ways to give them new perspectives that imply new power and choice, especially with your encouragement:

1) Change their location in space - taking a new perspective, literally, in a spatial sense. Have them, for example: float out of their body to a point behind their abuser, looking over the abuser's shoulder at themselves. Or rise above to a safe objective level. For example, with an emotional abreaction, count them up above it, from 1 to 3, to regroup, or to stop the feelings altogether. Stopping the feeling would be a *last resort* in this approach. Remember you are *eliciting* emotions in clearing work. Take the learnings and strength gained from the higher perspective back into the trance scene and experience the changes that can be made with them.

2)Add identity mixing. Have them be there as their adult self defending their child self. Play the scene out in whatever way appropriate. For example:

a) Adult self says what needs to be said on behalf of the child.

b) Adult self's presence provides the safety and permission necessary for the child to say and do whatever is necessary, with the mutual awareness of each other's presence building new bonds of support that carry over into similar situations.

c) Call in other appropriate people as aids, (e.g., Ideal mother or father, Inner guides, angels, even characters from plays or movies) that the client can identify with as having the resources they need to play the scene out to a beneficial result.

d) Regarding parents - since most of the time they will be significant in these matters - create some form of ceremonial initiation that marks the independence of the client. Create a mutual acknowledgment that marks the client's movement into maturity and empowerment (while dissolving the bonds of immaturity and dependence), which releases the parents from bonds of responsibility. These bonds can be literal, e.g., ropes or chains. This will reverberate through every aspect of their being.

3) Create a time search for resources. Move back before anything bad ever happened, and, after firmly anchoring the resources there, move forward at the right speed that allows entry into the issue with the resources active. Also, go to past life situations where the client had relevant resources states available to them, and gather them up and bring them into the current issue.

Clearing is a natural process which you will begin to trust with experience. It will be marked by the spontaneous evolution of feeling states from the surface "held" emotion, (e.g., fear or anger) through underlying "softer" emotions of sadness and grief through to peace, compassion and genuine understanding, if it has unfolded completely. Once you have cleared the situation, and have created a new **empowered person/memory** through suggesting, guiding the reconstruction of the situation with the client feeling *their power precipitating the changes that dissolve shame, blame, and confusion and open the well-springs of healing feeling movement*, instruct their unconscious mind to take these new learnings and powers into every situation in their past where they are relevant to free up the frozen energy that has been holding their wounds hostage, denying entry to healing forces of clarity, perspective, and love . Then, sensing this new wave of momentum of resources flowing towards them from their healed past, have them experience themselves moving into the future, applying these new resources for their highest benefit in all appropriate ways and situations (see scripts).

Don't expect this to quickly wipe out all soreness or tenderness in the areas of their wounds. The shame, fear, anger, and blame may be released. The grieving, the loss, that accompanies any wounding may now be in the process of healthy integration. Understand that soreness, tenderness, is part of this process. The contemplation of the hurt feeling, free of storyline shame, is a rich quiet resting in dark fertile psychic space from which an abundance of rebirths will arise. Associating into feelings, *feeling feelings with a sustained uninterrupted awareness,* allows the natural goodness and intelligence of *The Flow of being/feeling energy* to carry one's awareness to the problem's source wound that will be healed with *presence, understanding, and love.*

◆ ◆ ◆

8. Past Life Regression Script

Do Induction/Relaxation + limb challenges (include counting backward procedures to achieve somnambulism, at times, and compare the results. What other ways could you check effectiveness at varying "depth" levels?)

Experience yourself gradually becoming aware of the presence of the energy of your pure inner being...recognize it as the *relaxation you feel* caressing every part of your body...*feel* it surrounding your body...gently touching your skin...communicating in some way...a feeling of love and intelligence and power...protective loving power...the power and intelligence that operates and sustains your body even when you are totally unconscious...think about that...think about how all your life you have on a daily basis surrendered yourself to this inner loving power and intelligence...without even thinking about it...without a second thought...*easily* drifting into sleep every night... in some way knowing...outside your mind, or...under...or behind...your conscious mind...in some way *knowing you can* completely trust this inner awareness and power to care for you...consciously and unconsciously...and isn't it good to know that you can *ask its assistance in this trance simply by relaxing now*...following these suggestions to the letter... guiding you into just the right state to allow this inner power, your unconscious mind, to take these suggestions and to act on them, now, for your highest benefit...so...*feel your breath*...that's right, breathe as you become more aware of this aura of loving power surrounding your body now...and, breathe this loving healing energy into your body right along with the oxygen...carried right along with the oxygen to every cell of your body...every cell being bathed effortlessly by this healing power of your unconscious mind, your true pure inner being...breathe it in...every breath going deeper...and deeper...gently...easily...every heartbeat...[...effortlessly...deeply relaxing...opening...opening to the guidance of this power and intelligence that knows you completely...and completely...lovingly supports you...feel this power...imagine it as a gentle golden white light permeating every cell of your body...radiating throughout your being...aligning the focus of awareness of every cell of your being in such a way that it will be *easy for you* to access the experience in your past that is the root of this problem you came with today.]

((Repeat section within brackets [ ] from: "...effortlessly...""))

Every experience you have ever had is recorded in your memory...and your unconscious mind can *easily access* whatever you need to access to *contact the past life root of this problem now*...so that you can experience it in such a way that you will be free of all the ways in which it used to limit you until *you release it now*...experiencing it in such a way that all the emotional energy that has been held in a harmful way in your body can *be released now*... released and healed and freed to flow back into the pool of your pure inner energy where it can be freely accessed for your own highest benefit...your unconscious mind can bring you this past life experience...in such a way that all limitations are released...your unconscious mind can *keep whatever learnings are important and valuable to you...keeping the learnings...noticing that you are learning to keep the learnings and can let the emotions be released, as you simply ask and allow your unconscious mind to keep the learnings in just the appropriate ways that free the emotional energy that used to be trapped in your body by that old problem.*

In a moment I am going to count from one to three...As I count from one to three...you will feel yourself effortlessly drifting back in time... guided by the power and knowing of your unconscious mind, your pure inner being...just relax into the light and energy that is permeating your being and surrounding your body as you feel yourself carried back in time...back to the past life origin of this problem...to experience it again in a new way with whatever resources you need to...*experience it and be freed completely from this problem.*

Number one...going back...drifting back...relaxing into the protective aura of your pure inner being...

Number two...farther back...protected and strengthened by this aura of light...relaxing your conscious mind, letting your unconscious mind do the work...on the count of three, you'll be there...fully aware of the past life root experience of this problem in such a way that you will easily be freed from this problem...

Number three...now there, fully aware...go with your first impression of what you are experiencing.

((As necessary, assist client to orient into the experience. Do emotional clearing as appropriate, remember you have the flexibility to go forward and backward in time, to gather resources and to process as required. Remember to chunk the experience into small pieces to help them build up their awareness of where they are and what is happening.))

((For very traumatic memories, it may be necessary and advisable to approach them first by floating up above their life stream and move back in time at a height that allows them to perceive the events without getting pulled into them. The vantage point for this will generally be from <u>behind</u> the event, i.e. they have floated towards it from its future, over it in its present, and moved behind it to a position prior to its occurrence where they can see it as a future event in the context of all other future events stretching out in the life stream. Find out what results you get by taking them back before the origin of their entire life stream[of all lives] to a point where they feel their unity with an infinite source of healing, loving energy, flowing down through them and out their heart as a beam of healing, loving energy washing through their entire life stream from its origin, through the present and out into the future, healing and reevaluating and transforming into beneficial resources all the events of their lives.))

Share with me what you are experiencing...

((Assist them with input on whatever resources they need, e.g. inner guidance, their adult self to come in as an ally - basically finding a way to make it safe for them to see new choices of action to take, and to let themselves see new perspectives on the situation that release blame, shame, guilt, resentment, bitterness, etc. and <u>then to relive, reenact the situation with these new resources.</u>))

Experience yourself as you were then *((or, if they are observing from above: "See the you down there...etc."))*,but with these new understandings and resources, acting and expressing in such a way that this whole experience is being transformed into an affirmation of your inner purity and freedom...completely protected and free to say and do whatever is necessary to affirm your inner power and truth, releasing all the limitations this experience used to have for you...share with me what you are experiencing...

((Interact throughout the experience keeping them encouraged and focused and <u>active</u> in releasing the limitations and seeing with greater clarity...if they are above seeing themselves "down there"...see what effect you get if you have them run the old experience in black and white, and then the "new" reality, with resources and choices, in color. When that one "down there" really "gets it," have them jump into the scene and fully associate into the experience of this new power.))

((If they need further "back up" try pointing out to them that they can maintain dual awareness, i.e., jump in, yet still be above as present time self, or come down as ally into the scene to support the past self

relearning its right to hold onto its dignity as an inherently pure spiritual being.))

Good...now, as you focus on how good it feels to be in touch with these new resources, insights, and capacities that you have just created for yourself...experience your unconscious mind taking them into the rest of your past life...into every experience that needs to be reevaluated and released in the same way... focus on your state, and sense its power and learnings being transmitted by your unconscious mind wherever they are needed...give your wholehearted permission for your unconscious mind to do this, now...imagine it radiating the power of these new resources...seeking out and reevaluating all these experiences... transforming them now in the same way into resources for who you were then as new learnings and new affirmations of your inner purity and inner strength and capacity to take care of yourself appropriately, now...relax into it... sense it in some way...

((Depending on your calibration of their state, you may ask for them to share to see if they need assistance. Also, where and when it seems appropriate, feel free to repeat phrases and/or elaborate for effectiveness.))

You may notice that your conscious awareness is participating by *remembering something in a new way, now*...as you sense <u>in some way</u> your unconscious mind *directing the completion of this process throughout your past life, now*...experience yourself moving through this past life to the last day of your life there ...experience your death...

((Assist as necessary, particularly with association/dissociation perspectives to allow them to move through it to the after death state.))

Now you are in the after death state...it is like waking up from a dream...the body has died but you are still alive...feel how easy it is to sense the light and love of your higher self in this state...rise up into this light...feeling more connected to an infinite source of loving, healing energy as you rise up...look back over that past life from this perspective...established in the awareness of your eternal being and experience all the experiences of that life being reevaluated and transformed into resources for you, now...to carry with you into your present life and forever...*((Elicit sharing appropriately.))*

Now experience yourself moving back into present time...acknowledge all the learnings you have generated in this experience...Experience them integrating into your being to be available in all appropriate ways as you move into your future from this moment forward...moving into anticipated familiar future situations...and entirely new future situations with these new resources and this transformed past life that is full of brilliant, joyful, peaceful, and exuberant recognitions of you as a pure innocent being capable of enjoying life for your own highest benefit which includes the highest benefit of all beings...imagine that...imagine walking into your future with these resources and attitudes...see yourself doing things...feel yourself there...hear yourself...experience how all your sensory channels seem vibrant and vivid...

((Pause for processing, possibly asking for sharing...encouraging appropriately.))

Now slowly bring your awareness back to this room...relax and reflect on all you have given yourself in this experience...with gratitude, affirm the on-going transformation your unconscious mind is going to continue for your highest benefit even when you come back to waking consciousness...yes...that's right...with every breath you take... with every step you take from now on these new resources and insights are going to grow and elaborate more and more powerfully throughout your being for your highest benefit, now and forever...want it to happen, now...give your wholehearted grateful acknowledgment to this pure loving transformative power of your own being...understanding that you will effortlessly be keeping everything that is truly of value to you and releasing everything that is limiting you unnecessarily...now allow this whole experience to dissolve into the light of your pure inner being...experience the whole experience dissolving into the light surrounding your body...now feel this light dissolving into your body...carrying it into every cell...permeating your whole being with the power and blessings of the resources and insights you have generated for yourself today...that's right...

((Pause a moment or so...calibrate...then end the session.))

Now I'm going to count from one to five...when I reach five you'll be fully back in waking consciousness feeling light, refreshed, and awake...

One...coming back...begin coming back...
Two...more and more...easily coming back...feeling new energies flowing through you...
Three...wiggle your fingers and toes...that's right...wiggle them...more and more awake...
Four ...breath in deeply now...breath in wakeful energy...clearing your head...coming back...
Five...eyes open now...wide awake...fully back...feeling refreshed and awake...that's right.

◆ ◆ ◆

9. Anchoring:
Taking Advantage of the Reactivity
of the Egoic Mind

Ironically, sometimes something is so obvious that it needs to be pointed out in order for it not to be missed. It needs to be contemplated and explored to penetrate beyond the first impression of its simplicity and obviousness. If that is done, a whole expanse of insights and applications may arise.

Anchors, stimulus-response reaction patterns (a la Pavlov), are an example of those simple obvious all-pervasive processes that layperson and therapist alike have been aware of "forever," but unappreciative of their full potential for assisting change work. Upon being inspired by noticing Milton Erickson naturally anchoring clients, the founders of NLP structured and codified steps to consciously tailor and install these processes to produce consistent predictable results.

The anchoring process is very simple in principal, yet can be very subtle, complex, elegant, and artful in application. (It can also be brutish and rude and intrusive when applied with wrong intent.) **It is not something that has to be taught, strictly speaking, because we are truly "anchoring machines," constantly creating, maintaining, and dissolving anchors. However, for most of us, it is predominantly an unconscious process, both in its beneficial and harmful aspects.**

Anchoring is a built-in capacity that we are constantly relying upon to navigate through the world psychically and physiologically, and, even more significantly, this function was and is central to the formation of our identity trances from our birth [and before].

We touched on its illusion creating power in Phase I when the feeling of being pulled was created by the movement of the therapist in the "Coming forward, coming forward," exercise.

Anchors provide us with an internal shorthand, instantly bringing resources on-line to meet situations on a moment by moment basis.

The problem with this natural function is the way in which we hand it over inappropriately to unconscious operation where it, to the extent that it is inappropriate, misfires, bringing on line instantaneous misperceptions. Limiting feelings are unnecessarily stimulated, *along with the feeling of the feelings that they are the right and only feelings one could have in the situation*, thereby dictating the only choices of behavior and resolution one may have in such a situation. Thus, many of our anchors support the limited fixations we habitually, *and without noticing*, use to give up our **right to choose** how to respond, and what to feel in a situation. For most of us, this is so ingrained that this notion of **always** having the right to choose what to feel will seem somehow blasphemous.

Anchoring techniques allow us to consciously reeducate ourselves and implant more beneficial and *flexible* anchored loops into our unconscious operation. Contemplating the anchoring phenomenon also wakes us up to a whole new/old perspective on human interaction that greatly enhances our ability to communicate beneficially.

Anchoring is simply the associative capacity of the mind to link a given stimulus to a given response, and to bring this stimulus/response unit on-line instantly in consciously and/or unconsciously perceived similar situations.

Pavlov's familiar experiment is almost folklore: teaching dogs to salivate at the sound of a bell, after having linked feeding to the sound of the bell. Then, even after the food has been withheld, the dogs continue to salivate at the sound of the bell.

The application of this insight in therapy is obvious. All projection of the anticipation of the repetition of past experience on to the present, for better or worse, is a stimulus/response mechanism that, person by person, to varying degrees, *inhibits actual contact with the living uniqueness of each moment, moment by moment.*

The whole creation and structuring of identity is recognized by object-relations theory as depending on the capacity of the mind to relate object (i.e., "other" - 2nd skandha) experience to internal response (i.e., self - 1st skandha) and to hold it in [un]consciousness to form boundaries of self and body image/identity trance states. (They might not describe it in this language, however.)

*Remember, we are calling them trance states because they are **mental constructs**, not our **real self**. They are **ideas of self** which, in various ways we tell ourselves we <u>are</u> and <u>are not</u> (splitting the acceptable from the unacceptable - duality within duality) in the same way essentially that under so-called "hypnosis" you could experience the belief that you are Elvis.*

The implications of this are immense. If this is the "glue" that holds together the sense of self, then by proper conscious application of anchoring principles, you could recreate a new self/body image/identity trance - and it is true! It has been applied successfully to alter even auto-immune responses such as allergy alleviation.

*The way in which our approach is unique is that we recognize the possibility, **<u>truly the necessity</u>**, to go beyond self-improvement (i.e. constructing "better" identity trances) to True Self discovery beyond any concept/construct. This can be a fearful process because the egoic mind, **<u>including the egoic mind of the therapist</u>**, assumes that these constructs of self are **<u>absolutely necessary for existing and functioning</u>**. There has not been in Western psychological dogma, until a recent dawning - in large part because of the influence of Eastern insights, of the notion that there is an **autonomous whole being capable of more powerfully and appropriately fulfilling the functions of the fragmented self-constructs that comprise the egoic mind/identity trance.***

THIS CAN NOT BE TOO STRONGLY EMPHASIZED AND MUST BE REALIZED THROUGH ON-GOING MINDFULNESS AND CONTEMPLATION: *One's model of the world, consciously and unconsciously, <u>profoundly determines what one can perceive as so-called "objective reality."</u> Without the notion of the existence of this Inherently Pure <u>Unconstructed</u> Self, Its perception constantly would be unrecognized. It would be a confusing anomaly, denied and repressed by the egoic mind in order to maintain egoic world. But the therapeutic process of self-improvement may make egoic constructs more and more transparent. This transparency allows the True Self's brilliance to shine through* *more and more. Without the knowledge of Awake Mind/True Self's existence, and without understanding Its possibilities of manifesting as experience, both pleasant and frightening, Its emergence at some point could be too threatening and the egoic mind would then shut down and stabilize the self-improvement process to protect egoic models of reality - the heaven realm being the highest possible expression of this inherent denial and refusal of True Self discovery beyond egoic models and egoic self-improvement! The simple brilliance of True self would go unrecognized, and unvalued; and devalued. Its experiential qualities relegated to the dumpster of aberrant neurological misfirings and chemical imbalances (e.g., Freud's attitude towards transcendent experience as fantasy compensation.).*

One of my favorite NLP quotes: **"The most profoundly anchored state is the human personality."**

Reflect on the fundamental requirements to induce a hypnotic state, or to imprint a "learning": **repetition and emotional impact**. These are the requirements for creating a stimulus response loop. *We have always been talking about anchoring!*

All the techniques of this course could be seen as ways of resorting and creating new anchored trance state building blocks of identity, hopefully more beneficial and more free [i.e. more transparent] than the old ones.

Anchoring Requirements and Procedures

At this point we are going to present the requirements and procedures that apply at the most simple and overt level. Then you need to contemplate these understandings and extrapolate their applications at more subtle levels. Remember, you can ask your unconscious mind and your True Self for help! To repeat - that is what we have been doing and will be doing for the rest of this course, although not necessarily using this terminology, so you get to make the correlation yourself! (Homework!)

To tailor anchored responses, there are some subtleties that have to be appreciated. Anchors can be established through each sensory channel. We will start with overtly placing physical anchors. This means you create a stimulus/response loop by touching the client appropriately.

Requirements for Physical Anchoring

There are three basic requirements for (physically) anchoring a suggestion. If you keep in mind that we are constantly moving among the anchored states of our multi-selved identities, these requirements can easily be recognized as self evident:

1) **Uniqueness of the (touch) stimulus.** Anchors exist all over our body, in fact our sense and image of body identity is a composite anchored state. It stands to reason, therefore, that the spot touched, and the manner of touching have to specified by their delivery to access what you want accessed.

2) **The intensity of the anchored state.** In order to prevent it from dissolving into the sea of anchored responses, it has to be specified to avoid generalization into vagueness and non-existence. Therefore, you ask for a specific event that embodies the client experiencing the resource, issue, or state you want, not a series of events. This is just another facet of the essential "thing" we identified in (1) as uniqueness.

3) Timing. Again, just another aspect of the essential "thingness" - the aspects of uniqueness. The further emphasis of uniqueness is to touch them [since in this case we are talking about physical anchoring] when they are experiencing the state most intensely, when they are fully there, not just entering or leaving the trance of it.

If you do this successfully, anytime you touch the anchor, it will put them into the state. Remember the buttons of the 60's, the triggers of the 70's - I wonder what they called them before they had buttons and triggers - slings and arrows!?!

Stacking, Merging and Collapsing Anchors

1) Since you will primarily be attempting to install resources, it is important to appreciate that you can stack anchors. You can associate various positive resource states to the same anchor. The uniqueness requirement doesn't exclude this possibility. E.g., you stack a peaceful balanced state on a confident state, on a happy state, on a motivated state to accomplish a task in an ecological way.

2) You can merge or collapse different anchors which requires an internal reorganization. The nice thing about this is that if the anchors being merged, one "good", one "bad", are of the same relative intensity, or if the good one is stronger than the bad, **the mind reorganizes in the direction of greater resourcefulness!** We place great reliance on this quality, which is rooted in the inherent goodness and intelligence of our True Self. It makes a lot of change work delightfully simple.

3) Words and images of all kinds impact us daily and stimulate internal states without our conscious intervention. The world of advertising, "our" song, "Love," "God and Country," "Mother." Most of us take such influences for granted more than we think, and give up a significant portion of our power to discriminate and filter these messages and the ways they manipulate our internal states.

Anchoring Procedure

Here is a physical anchoring procedure used to collapse a positive and negative state:

1) Pick a resource. Ask the client to think of a specific time when they felt an appropriate resource. You can have an initial discussion of the problem situation with no anchoring in order to reference what an appropriate resource would be. Have them fully associate into the experience in such a way that they relive the feeling of the resource. **When they are there, anchor it.** Knowing if they "are there" will be a function of your observational skills in reading their non-verbal signs, but you can also ask them to tell you or nod when they are strongly in the experience of the resource.

2) Create a boundary, a "partition," between the anchor and what follows. Distract the client for a few seconds with small talk about this or that.

3) Test the anchor. Without saying anything, after having broken the state with step #2, touch the anchor and observe if it triggers the resource. You can verify by asking them, and if it doesn't seem especially strong, make them aware that they can intensify it **now,** as you are touching them.

4) Break state. Same as [2] above.

5) Anchor the problem situation. In the same way as #1, have them associate with the problem, resourceless state. **When they are fully in it, anchor it.**

6) Break state.

7) Test as in #3.

8) Trigger the resource state and then the resourceless state saying, "Now take this resource *((touch))* into this situation *((touch))* and experience how it changes it for you. Experience yourself perceiving, moving, speaking and acting more appropriately with this new resourcefulness. Relive the whole situation with this new resource and the new choices it gives you, and come out when you're done."
((Remove your hands from the anchors and watch and wait.))

9) Break state.

10) Test by touching the old negative anchor and watch their response. If it has been successful, they will not remember the problem situation in the same way, and the emotional charge will have shifted.

11) If desired you could add and stack additional resources by accessing them and using the same anchor "spot."

Anchoring Applications

1) *"Deeply Relax"* from Phase I is an example of anchoring a resourceful state by Auditory, (*Hear the words, "Deeply Relax"*) and Kinesthetic means, (*"When your finger touches your thigh you will go right back to this deeply relaxed state"*).

2) Remember that any post-hypnotic suggestion is an anchored response state:

"When you get home, the instant your hand touches the front door knob you will relax and feel this good feeling moving through you, enabling you to organize your office with inspiration and zeal."

"As soon as your feet touch the floor in the morning, your jaw will begin to become numb, and, by the time you arrive at the dentist's office, your jaw and gum will be completely numb and prepared in every way for a successful pleasant experience of having your tooth fixed."

3) Anchor resourceful states at any time in trance work to use later on in the session or later sessions. E.g., touch the client's arm when they are happy and laughing. Later in session, for example, in a regressed situation when they are feeling a resistance to some material coming up, just touch the spot as you encourage them to let the difficulty into their awareness. Anchor a beneficial trance depth so it can be accessed at any later date.

4) Respect natural anchors that arise from repetition and emotional charge. The therapy chair, the process of going to the therapist's office. This could start as soon as they wake up, or before. One important reason we future pace is to "unglue" the learnings gained "in the chair" from the chair so they can take them with them.

5) Strategic times to anchor a shift: bedtime, wake-up time, before and after meals. Saying grace is an anchor that actually accesses beneficial and healing energies to transform the act of eating and digesting your food. Other times include: entering any familiar situation (walking into work), arriving home, getting in or out of your car, beginning or ending any task or project. The anchored response could be the simple cultivation of Self Remembrance: take a deep breath, relax, notice where you are (notice the storyline of where you are and what is going on), notice where you <u>really</u>

are (in the midst of The Great Mystery, i.e. relax into faith in and reliance upon your True Self, even if you don't feel it, just do your best to breathe and relax with conceptual support!), then proceed to relate to the situation at hand.

6) Anchoring strategic negative situations. Focus on anticipated situations of stress or challenge and, as in [5] above, pick the spot, the moment, to install an anchor *(a remembrance as a felt sense)* of an appropriate resource that will create a beneficial shift in the situation.

7) Anchoring strategic positive situations. Don't fall into the trap of only fixing problems. Enhance your resources and good times, as well. In fact, put more emphasis on appreciating and enhancing, and invoking the appreciation of your magnificence as an honorable part of the Magnificent Mystery of Life. (Egoic response: dullness, cynicism, fear, "Yeah, yeah, sure...")

8) Anchoring strategic objects. Your bed, bedroom, dining table, dining room, kitchen, bath, favorite chair, driver's seat of the car, articles of clothes, tools, your glasses, etc. Notice if just reaching for some familiar object in your life stirs a subtle sense of self, positive or negative, and re-anchor appropriately.

9) Anchors and ritual. Perhaps from the above you have already gotten a sense that following these suggestions could ritualize your life. By the same token you can reflect on the purpose of rituals in general as being the systematized chaining of anchors to elicit empowered and beneficial resource states. It is important to note that anchors can be polluted if they aren't done with focus and renewed intent, **because you will be anchoring whatever state is present.**

This is how rituals lose their power and meaning. It is not simply because they are repetitious (rigid). **It's because the insight is lost that they are functional, not moralistic.** *Functional in that they are something you do as an activity to break the activity of egoic mind in the moment, letting in the light of True Self. Therefore when you do it,* **you have to do it** *- you have to mean it - you have to put the focus and energy into accessing the appropriate states. If you can't -* **better not to do it at all.**

This is where morality becomes a problem. If you are coerced by some sense of morality - that you have to do it, then you go through the motions, but what is being accessed and anchored to the activity of the ritual is your resentment, apathy, dullness, and whatever. Thus, the feeling of sacredness of the ritual is lost.

10) Anchoring the anchors themselves. Touching fingers together, stepping into a power circle, visualizing yourself surrounded by light that lets in all beneficial communication, but keeps out any harm (emphasize, regulate or initiate with a secondary anchor, e.g. finger touch). Mentally rehearse making any stimulus an anchor, e.g., rehearse having that compulsive feeling arise, but, instead of it generating the feel bad judgment that used to drive you into acting out - running to the fridge, reaching for a smoke, etc., it now shifts in to an inspired remembrance of your new power and choices...and...without thinking...you step forward into them...look around...evaluate and move on in appropriate behavior to truly meet the real underlying needs free of judgment.

11) Anchoring insight to transform habitual thought pattern anchors around comparing and judging. If you notice that you put yourself, or others down, in reference to beliefs about standards of behavior or achievement, for example, if you see them judging you in your mind's eye; if you are small and they are big (note your sub modalities - the construction of your internal representations), think about this insight: **The way you know if you, or anyone else, has achieved something truly worth achieving is that you (they) will want to share it with everyone, will want everyone to be uplifted by it.** So, look at the picture, look at the judge (or listen - whatever is the mode) *holding in your awareness the understanding that if they have something truly valuable, they won't be withholding it and looking down on you - they will be holding it out to you, inviting you to partake of it!* On the basis of this insight/perspective, evaluate the judge's position, and the grounds upon which you used to buy into it. If they are judging, if you are comparing, your criteria are bogus. Anchor the insight, and experience the changes in your internal representations and feeling state.

12) Anchoring fun and playfulness. Think of a type of situation, such as a party, that makes you feel less than resourceful. Take some time to anchor and stack some appropriate resources, e.g. a sense of ease, confidence, playfulness, a time when you experienced the joy of a good conversation. (Have the anchor be easy and unobtrusive, like pressing your thumb and forefinger together.) Practice strengthening the anchor. Go to a party and do it! Guess what! -- after a few parties, you won't need to do it anymore, *because your anchoring mechanism will associate the party itself with those feelings as an anchor!*

10. Visual Accessing Cues

The recognition of the possible universality of visual accessing cues is one of the most significant contributions of the originators of NLP.

It makes establishing and maintaining rapport much easier, and it can reveal the sequencing of internal strategies for triggering states, without the need for explanation from the subject.

There are important applications for this insight in the educational field that are beyond the scope of this class. But you are encouraged to investigate it further as you wish. (e.g., spelling strategy, remembering strategies.)

For our purposes, at this level of your training, it is enough to recognize a person's eye movement cues as *indications of their momentary accessing process*. It is very helpful to notice and verify it through correlation with their language patterns, specifically their grammatical predicates, i.e., verb phrases, which describe the character of activity: seeing, hearing, feeling, etc.

This allows you to "mind read" representation systems allowing you to pace their experience and to lead them. (e.g., a client is talking about a problem with their spouse and they are looking up to their left trying to figure out how to say something, and you say, *"How does it look to you?"* or *"Maybe you could clarify what you see happening there,"* or *"Can you remember what that looked like?"* (their left is memory - See Figure 2-10)

People learning about this phenomena have a tendency to get performance anxiety about watching every little eye movement, needing to know what great import it has. They can become very obnoxious as people notice that they are being watched as if they were prey of some kind. My goal is for you to have a much more casual approach to this. Eye accessing cues give you signposts you can check in with, but you don't have to watch them every second, like a hawk, or be self-conscious about your own.

Remember that the eyes are not indicating only representational cues. Someone may be looking in any direction and visualizing, for instance, something located in that area of their inner space. So don't exclude common sense correlation with other verbal/non verbal information you are getting that they are looking at something down there in the corner vs. for example, just talking to themselves (their lower left- see chart, following page). People can have a different predominate accessing channel (visual, auditory, and kinesthetic) at each of the three levels of consciousness - conscious, subconscious, and unconscious. Recognizing these is a powerful assest in facillitating learning.

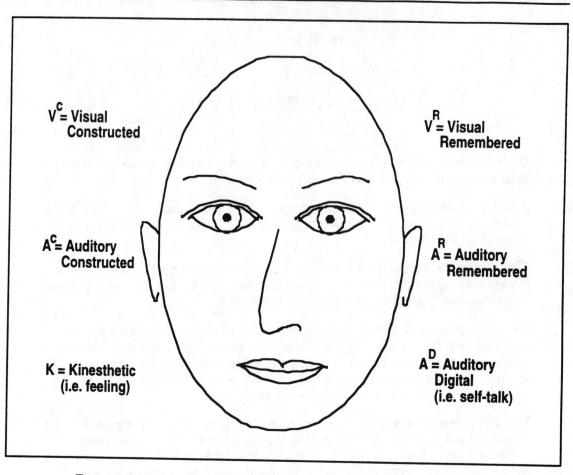

Figure 2-10: Eye Accessing Cues Chart (for normally organized right-handed subject)

Predicates and predicate phrases indicating sensory channels:

Auditory: listen, sounds, harmonize, silence, unhearing, resonate, hear, all ears, overtones, deafening, tone, buzz, thunderous, audible, etc.

Auditory phrases: clear as a bell, blabber mouth, call on, hear voices, telling message, give an account of, an earful, loudly expressed, describe in detail, inquire into, voice an opinion, tell the truth, tongue tied, outspoken, fast talk, manner of speaking, humming a tune, etc.

Visual: look, see, appear, reveal, clear, foggy, flash, illuminate, envision, sparkle, picture, visualize, brighten, show, watch, glimpse, etc.

Visual phrases: in light of, naked truth, show off, staring into the blue, out of the blue, right in front of you, pretty as a picture, picture this, short sighted, far-sighted, near-sighted, flashed on it, hazy notion, catch a glimpse, bird's eye view, in the shadows, etc.

Kinesthetic: touch, feel, hold, grab, grasp, bump, scrape, hit, solid, stand, throw, catch, trip, stumble, balance, spin, slip, freeze, melt, etc.

Kinesthetic phrases: come to grips with, get a handle on it, stumble into, jump on it, flew through my mind, getting in touch with, cool, calm, collected, hot head, he's a softy, laying your cards on the table, slipped my mind, stuffed shirt, light headed, heavy heart, handling it, caressing it, firmly rooted, leaning into it, etc.

Unspecified: sense, experience [our old faithful unspecified question: "What are you experiencing now?"], understand [although could be suggestive of kinesthetic], change, distinct, exact, know, perceive [leans toward visual], decide [leans toward digital auditory], process, learn, think, believe, etc.

◆ ◆ ◆

Table of Contents
Phase III

◆ ◆ ◆

1. Subpersonality or "Parts" Therapy

Subpersonality "parts" therapy is a very useful model for approaching the therapeutic task of enhancing a client's intrapersonal communication. Most of us already are relating inwardly according to this model..."*part of me wants to, part of me doesn't...*""*I'd like to go to Hawaii, BUT I don't think it would be wise...*" (whenever you hear "but", you'll usually also hear a tonal shift, which together indicate another part has finished the sentence.)

"Subpersonalities" or "parts" are semi-autonomous energy systems, **learnings and skills packages**, that are triggered into action at an appropriate stimulus. They are the response, attempting to comprehensively resolve the situation. They are basically finished products, **belief system containers**. They have made up their mind about what is going on and what means what. Each 'part' is ensnared in egoic logic (see Phase II); the 'whole' person is the composite of these parts; his 'ego' is the cluster of the parts' egoic processes. In other words, *they are trance states that project meaning on to present time situations based on similitude to the past situations that created and solidified them, as opposed to relating to the uniqueness of present experience moment by moment.*

As such they are more or less effective in dealing with the uniqueness of present experience. The parts that are less effective generally let us know through pain, physical and/or emotional. These less effective 'subs.' we call problems.

In the context of Phase II egoic structure model:

*The Subpersonality therapeutic process is a way to reverse the flow of the egoic logic. It is a self-inquiry process that has ancient roots in almost every living spiritual **practice** tradition.(i.e., practice as in putting teaching into practice vs. simply advocating a belief system.)*

Egoic logic experiences life as dilemma because awareness of **being** Inherent Purity is lost. All its projects in life are futile struggles to recapture its **projection of *its version*** of Inherent Purity generally giving emphasis to one of its perverted aspects. (See Phase II, 5 Buddha families/5 poisons) The presumption is that there is a **cause and effect relationship** between actions and creating Inherent Purity. Since Inherent Purity is *self-existing*, independent of cause and effect, such endeavors are bound to fail.

The Therapeutic Process

The subpersonality process is designed to break the amnesia/negative hallucination blocking awareness of **already existing** fullness, presence, love, being, and power.

We assist a given part, which compulsively is running an agenda to create some notion of fulfillment, to recognize it already has the goal of *essential* fulfillment, indeed, **already is the goal** it is desperately seeking. Relative to the Phase II chart, the self-inquiry process:

1) withdraws the energy from outward projections,

2) turns the energy back upon oneself (itself). This immediately begins to strengthen a sense of being and spaciousness, however slight, and begins to focus the energy as clarity of awareness regarding the integrity of desire and motivation,

3) pushes the consciousness through the black hole of egoic ignorance and confusion into the experience of the light of Pure Being, if carried through with persistence and perseverance.

The process is elegantly simple:

1) One simply inquires - asks the part what they are trying to accomplish by their behavior.

2) Whatever the answer, the therapist asks them to imagine having it totally. He/She takes the time to help the client associate into the achieved goal and feel what it feels like to have it, to make it real. Do you see the similarity to worst case scenario? Best case scenario also relieves the dualistic polar charge of egoic blind compulsivity. Settling into best case relaxes the psycho-physical state, providing energy for deeper focus and contemplation.

3) Ask what deeper desire having this goal puts them in touch with.

4) Whatever the answer repeat (2).

5) Repeat (3), then (2).

6) Continue this process, ideally, until their inquiry into desire and motivation takes them to some aspect of Inherent Purity. This will typically be expressed as Love, Peace, Fullness, Bliss, Clarity. There are two ways of knowing they have made it: a) they will tell you there is nothing more, and b) they will **be** the goal: "I am Love", or "Love" vs., "I feel loved."

7) Starting with this richness, the subpersonality can then reevaluate its projects, goals, and desires. Starting with Fullness shifts life from dilemma/seeking activity to creative, expressive celebration of pre-existing fullness. Nothing is at stake, therefore effortless joy and generosity arise naturally. We discover it is this state that is the true source and nature of Abundance, the "Abundance of the Universe" so many are striving for monetarily, (but with a New Age attitude that is supposed to make it spiritual). The therapist takes the client back, desire by desire, motivation by motivation, up through the steps of the inquiry they just completed, asking the client

to stop, experience, and share how already being (not simply having) the Inherent Purity changes the situation and dynamics of that desire and motivation.

Steps 1-7 would be a wonderful session if completed as is. There is more to the process, however:

8) Having completed the journey back to the original desire, motivation, behavior - all of which will be drastically transformed, you check in with the part and ask it to notice how old it is. Remember, all parts are chronically regressed learnings and skills packages. While the part, at this point, may be very awake, it may still be "young."

9) Regress to the part to point of origin, its "birth," with the part established in this new state of being and all its wakeful resources, to clear that situation. Then grow the part up through time, through all the client's past, generating a sense of having grown through a past always having been a strong state of Genuine Being and Resources (i.e., no shame, more on this in Phase IV).

Working with the Individual Parts

Since we experience subps. as having a mind of their own: *"I don't know what got into me...""I just wasn't myself when I did that,"* it can be very effective to relate to them in trance therapy work as independent beings, on a tentative basis. We are careful **not** to fixate and solidify them in their separateness. That would only serve to facilitate the fragmentation of the personality.

Since they are parts, and more or less confused, **yet powerful**, and because this is *client centered, evocative work*, we invite them to "appear" in whatever form is **most appropriate for them to communicate in a mutually beneficial way**, or, simply, in the **best way for them to manifest a full representation symbolically of who/what they are and what they are about.**

The following scripts will be self explanatory in indicating process and dialogue. Some important highlights and reminders:

1) As is implied by the above process description, positive intent underlies the problem behavior. Bring the positive intent into awareness, **phrased positively at root level,** or as close as possible to root level. In real life, you may not have an ideal step by step adventure in session. You can settle for reorganization at any clearer level of positive intent than what you started with in a given session. In practice, within time constraints, you may only get to some intermediate level, but intent at its root always comes down to some aspect and expression of the five Virtues (Phase II): love, peace, joy, being/presence, full expression of true self, etc. Knowing that positive intent is always present, and how to get to it, is tremendously relaxing and empowering for the therapist. Now you always know where you're going!

2) Separate the positive intent from the problematic behavior so they both can be viewed dissociatively with discrimination. This allows innate awake intelligence (that knows what makes sense) to begin to reevaluate the fixed beliefs and choices of the trance/part/subp. in the context of an awareness of: a) a larger context, b)varied

perspectives (interpretations of meaning and consequence), and c)greater freedom of choice.

3) Mediate on the basis of the insights in (2) and come to a higher resolution of being for the part that gives it more power and better choices, vs. attempting to complete the 9 step process above. The 9 step process can be a very powerful integrative process, but for people with a lot of fragmentation or 'distance' between parts, it may not go smoothly. They may get distracted or resist. Such distractions simply indicate other parts coming on line. If this happens, you may have to mix approaches, (e.g. regression, emotional clearing,) to clear obstacles and gather their energies to get back on track with contacting an experience of root intent(see 5 Virtues, PII) at some other time. Once you have it, take the client, anchored in that experience of Virtue, up through the levels of motivation. Don't be afraid of experimenting with a somewhat less than Virtue-level intent as the anchored basis for moving up through an evaluation of the levels of motivation. See what you get with what you use! Learn!

4) Always end a trance dissolving all the energies and manifestations of the parts into the light of the pure greater being and dissolve this into the physical body. We don't want to be creating a tendency towards multiple personalities anymore than the client is already doing it! Fixation on inner symbols is a powerful trap. Having the experience of a powerful inner symbol is a double-edged sword. It can be powerfully moving and meaningful in the moment, but then become a golden shackle if fixated. I have had several people come to me with powerful inner symbols that arose in the course of various forms of inner work, including rebirthing, soul retrieval, breathwork, voice dialogue, psycho-drama, and hypnotherapy. In each case, the images enhanced growth, insight, and shifts at the time, but since the time of arising had not evolved, had not engaged in any new communication with other parts. Thus, they had become part of the status quo.

Example: One client in the course of soul retrieval had "retrieved" a caged rageful tiger, and an elegant self-righteous crane. At the time, they both resonated powerfully as recaptured soul aspects, but they were competing parts. In the several years since the retrieval, they had been regarded as 'these parts of myself', i.e. fixed parts. Therefore, they had simply been held and reinforced in their stand-off. It hadn't occured to the client that they could attempt a reconciliation or integration. We did parts mediation. The caged tiger became strength and freedom; the crane became nurturing. I asked them to notice the complementary nature of these qualities, and that they arose from the same golden heart. On the basis of this recognition and appreciation of each other, they joined in the unity of a positive shared intent and complementary supporting aspects of True Being., Then we dissolved them into the client's being. Dramatic change, and a shift to an on-going fluidity of movement and learning.

5) Always remember the client is one whole being, therefore, with antagonistic or competing parts, *you can always reduce their motivation to the same inherently pure goal, or to* __*complementary aspects*__ *of Pure Being as in the example above. Then reach agreement on blending energies and skills to accomplish the shared goal, and for* __*continued evolving growth*__. Obviously, it is crucial that you study the aspects of Pure Being(PII) and can recall them in various terms: Wisdom, Compassion Power, Clarity, Strength, Freedom, Brilliance, Space, Nurturance, Love, Joy, Bliss, Merging, Peace, Oceanic Fullness, Non-Conceptual Openness, Kindness, Patience, Fearless Humility, etc. Get the idea? These are __*distinct yet inseparable*__ aspects of Pure Being,

therefore, as soon as parts recognise their particular aspect of Pure Being, they can easily merge.

6) Always address issues of ecology and secondary gains. <u>Distractions and resistance are simply the client's unconscious wisdom demanding this.</u> Respect distractions and resistance, and listen to them!

7) Always be respectful of the parts; always ask the client to be respectful of the parts. Acknowledge and thank them for sharing every time they do share.

It has been said regarding the profession of acting:

"Acting is living truthfully under imaginary circumstances."

Do you see how this describes what we do all day long in our trance personality states as they shift and dance? The difference is that an actor is **at cause** and **always knows (hopefully) that it is just a role.**

As mentioned earlier, hypnosis is theater and you are helping the client remember that. They are scriptwriter, director, and cast of characters.

Regression therapy rituals create the prestige necessary to allow clients to remember *already present* past events. The subp./parts model creates the prestige necessary to enable communication with the egoic process as it has compartmentalized itself into *"the little people."* **(Prestige being nothing more than convincing theatrical elements.)**

Why *"the little people?"* Remember from Phase II: **chronically regressed states.** Each part, which we defined as a 'learning and skills package' became fixed, made up its mind, **when it was the mind of the child at the critical choice point.** This becomes very important for enhanced integration of parts through the use of a combination of the regression process with the subpersonality process. This is laid out in the last script of this phase. As outlined above, once you have taken a part through the reevaluation process of the Subs. Script, you make it aware of its origin, which in all likelihood is still its current age. You 'go back there,' i.e., bring it into awareness and then 'grow it up' to full present-time participation. (See script.)

◆ ◆ ◆

2. Dialogue with a Subpersonality

Identify with the client a "part" that runs a behavior they want to address. Make sure the client can relate to this model, i.e., thinking about themselves as having parts that run their behaviors. Remember, parts run their resource behaviors, too, so balance that insight in their awareness so they don't develop a subtle attitude against parts as bad. If they have more than one subp. identified, decide which to address first, or get their agreement to let their unconscious decide what is most important to communicate with at this time. (Note: Many times, this is what happens anyway. Even if you get agreement from the client on the issue, once you do trance, something else pops up. Don't be so fixed in your agenda that you can't make the shift, and take the client with you. Think about how to interpret and relate to "resistance" from this perspective. Comment or ask questions in class.)

Do induction, relaxation, testing, and deepening. *[Utilize information, images, concerns, anticipate distractions based on discussions with client to build rapport (it lets their unconscious mind know you were listening - it humanizes the technique.)]*

Now that you are in this deeply relaxed state...allow your awareness to sense the energy of this problem...think about your experiences of it manifesting...it may be helpful to pick one situation in which it is particularly vivid, alive and active...let me know when you are in touch with it...*((wait for sharing))*...feeling its presence and energy...perhaps notice if its making its presence felt in a particular part of your body...that's right...just allow your awareness of it to gently grow...in a way that you are honoring its existence...appreciate its willingness to communicate...and allow yourself to open to this communication in such a way that it will be mutually beneficial...

[In a moment, I'm going to count to three...when I get to three, this part of you that embodies and controls the behaviors associated with this problem of_____ will manifest before you in some form, the most appropriate form that will enable it to communicate with you *most effectively now* for your mutual benefit...as I am counting I would like this part to decide what form it would like to take to communicate...it can be any form in the universe...a rock, a river, a cloud, a bonfire, a person or animal, anything in the universe...on the count of three it will be there.]

((Repeat [ ]))

Now I'm going to begin counting...just relax and go with your first impression of how it appears on the count of three...sometimes people have a sense of what it's going to be before I get to three...and that's fine...just understand that if it is different or the same as what you anticipate...that ...either way, on the count of three, even if it is the same, it will be new and fresh and alive in more interesting ways *to communicate for your mutual benefit now...*

Number one...relaxing and preparing to welcome this part into your awareness...

Number two...in such a way that you both feel safe and open to communicate to discover new learnings to benefit you both...

And...three...there it is....experience it there...go with your first impression...share with me what you experience...sharing with me causes you to be more fully involved with your experience, enhancing your capacity to communicate with this part.

> *((If necessary, assist in whatever ways are appropriate to establish the image: 1)small chunks, 2) create devices that will help, e.g. visualize a curtain with the part behind it (open the curtain or, if the part prefers, leave it closed, 3) generate a house- knock on the door or call the part out, 4) create an idyllic scene with a book, beautiful and ornate on an enchanting pedestal [describe them], have the client go to the book and open it to just the page that has a picture of the part, 5) if visual accessing seems futile, switch to body access, as in: "Where in your body do you feel it?"[usually tension or burning], "Ask it to speak...." This approach, as you know from Phase II, can be used to generate emotional release. That is not the objective here, but don't create a bias against it! 6) try anything that comes to you - remember this is theater!))*

That's right...allow it to reveal itself...notice you have a sense now of your connection...also, a sense of how you feel in its presence...and how it feels in your presence...share with me what you are experiencing...understand that it has the freedom to show you various qualities and aspects of itself, and can even change shape to do this, if it wants to...relax and, with a sense of gratitude for its willingness to communicate, make some gesture to it that communicates your respect and desire to establish a more beneficial relationship...*((share))*...

Ask, "What are you trying to accomplish in my life by acting and manifesting in the way you do?" ...and tell me its response...*((You can also choose to phrase this as, "What are you trying to accomplish that is positive," to get an answer phrased positively. If you get negatives, keep asking, "What does accomplishing this do for you?" until you get a good bottom line positive intent: peace, joy, happiness, wholeness, etc. Remember, thank the part for responding; incorporate the response in your next question: "Good, thank you...now, assume...(or, "contemplate having X, imagine, experience as best you can what it would be like to have X")...you have X fully and totally in a beneficial way in your life...what would that do for you that's even more significant?" Ideally, repeat process until you can go no farther, which should be some contact with an aspect of Inherent Purity.))*

Respond to the subp.'s answer...recognize what its motivation and desire has been in generating these behaviors...both of you reflect on this positive goal that you both value and honor...feel a bond of kinship and warmth growing as you both recognize you value the same goal...freely dialogue about this realization *as it is growing now*...and share with me about your exchange...*((Ideally, they have discovered that the most precious goal is a given and doesn't have to be strived for, but, if not, on the way to that, a growing friendliness between them will help the process.))*

((By this time, if they are in rapport, their discussion moves very fast, and they could cover this ground before you ask them to, but, if they haven't already, suggest:)) Reevaluate together, the beliefs and the choices of behaviors that this part was doing to accomplish this goal in the light of this new recognition of shared positive intent...and make any agreements necessary and appropriate to generate better choices of more effective behaviors that you can do cooperatively to really achieve this goal...

((Have them share with you and assist in the negotiation in any way needed))

((Alternate approach if you have reached Inherent Purity: Reverse the process of the steps uncovering the layers of motivation.)) Ask: "Experience fully experiencing being *peace (e.g.), and move into the situation of having X (the desire or motivation). Experience how it changes X." ((Share))*

((Repeat moving up through the steps of each higher X, each time taking with you the source aspect of Inherent Purity and the transformed X's, until you're asking about their very first response to the question, "What are you trying to accomplish?" i.e. the first presenting 'X')) Great, thank you...now imagine [contemplate, etc.] and experience as fully as possible fully being Inherent Purity and having the transformed X's and moving into

Y [the next X] and experience how that changes the dynamics of Y."
((Share))

Now that you have established this new bond and sharing of resources in the deeper realization of how you can truly benefit each other...I'd like you to check, before we come back to normal waking consciousness, if there is any residual concern that needs to be addressed...or if you sense that any other part has any objection that needs to be heard, honored, and reconciled...

((Depending on time available, share, or have them make a promise to resolve it on their own unconsciously, or to bring the issue to the next session. Handle whatever comes up - basically repeat the process getting to the fundamental positive intent that everyone can agree on, making new agreements for new behaviors and mutual support))

Good...in a moment you'll be coming back to normal waking consciousness on the count of 5...but before you do...[relax and reflect on all you have accomplished with your subp.(s) in this experience...as you do, allow your subp.(s) and your whole experience to become enveloped in a loving, healing, nurturing golden, white light...experience yourselves and your whole experience dissolving into this beautiful healing, loving light...enhancing and empowering the bonds you created here today...sense the power this light has to radiate these new learnings, new resources, and new love throughout your past into any and every situation in your past where they may be needed, now... for healing and the releasing of outmoded beliefs, attitudes, judgments or negativities of any kind...]

((Pause, repeat this last sentence within brackets [ ], take a moment to help it sink in, perhaps repeat a third time. With any encouraging non-verbal responses, or simply by imagining yourself talking directly to their unconscious, say, "good...that's right"))

...experience that now in some way, releasing...healing...recapturing your pure innocent life force...*not necessarily in detail or conscious of any specific event*...but relaxing into the presence of this loving light and energy...*it feels good*...carrying these resources now...into your past wherever they are needed...that's right...want it to happen... ask that it happen ...make an inward gesture giving your permission for it to happen now...that's right...*feeling just how good it feels growing in interesting ways now moment by moment*...the more you make this inner gesture with your whole heart...

Now feel that light radiating into your future in the same way...carrying these new resources in your being into your future...imagine yourself in future anticipated and future unanticipated situations perceiving, interpreting, and acting with the awareness and support of these new resources...see yourself...feel yourself...hear yourself moving in these future situations with these new ever growing resources...that's right...Now allow that light to surround your body...feel it permeating your skin as it dissolves into every cell of your body...permeating your entire being...imprinting these new beneficial powers on the awareness of every cell of your body...feel it dissolving into your cells...open to these living, healing resources as they integrate lovingly into your being...that's right...*((Repeat appropriate phrases as you sense they are indicated, and feel free to elaborate with your own inspirations))*

Now...coming back to normal waking consciousness at the count of 5...

One...coming back...feeling this wonderful new energy in your being...

Two...more and more...coming back...

Three... lighter and more awake...wiggle your toes and fingers (repeat).. coming back

Four...breathe in a deep breath of fresh air...breathe it in... balancing your energies...clearing your head...that's right...again...fully coming back... and

Five...open your eyes...open your eyes...that's right...fully back...fully coming back now

◆◆◆

3. Inner Guidance

Inner guidance can come in many forms. The ultimate inner guide is your own inner Self, the pure living, sensing, awake truth of your own being. This is *not an object of truth* but the awake realizing/experiencing of **living as the truth,** moment by moment, without any contrivance or need to make an effort to be O.K. This is the complete surrender to the mystery of your arising manifestation, to the **last** detail, in **every** respect, on **every** level of your being (physical, emotional, mental), accepting the perfection of your appearance and dynamic action without any movement to alter it. Totally relinquishing the attitude of *not being it* (i.e., shame/separation trances); understanding that it (you) learns and alters it (your)self by the simple application of your now innocent (but not naive) intelligence, rooted in a *constant intuition* of your unity with all manifest reality, **pragmatically,** *being by specific being, object by specific object, activity by specific activity, moment by moment.*

On the way to this state of awareness, we need and receive, inwardly as well as outwardly, assistance and guidance. As with every other aspect of relating to models, its best to have the most expanded, and therefore most flexible and open-minded concept of inner guidance. This would include and pace the client's ideas and experience of any such connections, as well as leading them into a greater appreciation of the resources that may be available.

A primary rule that seems to be a "law" that is stated biblically as: "Ask and ye shall receive," must be honored and expanded upon as: "Until you ask you may not receive," not because these sources are withholding, but because asking is an expression of your free will, another primary "law" of the game.

The variety of inner guidance available, as indicated by human experience, is vast, e.g., shamanic encounters with entities from the plant and animal kingdom. You can adapt trance scripts to focus on accessing any of these as required. For the purpose of this course, we are going to focus on the idea of there being a primary "True" Inner Guide, a being whose highest manifestation in form is human (light not being considered as a "form" here).

The True Inner Guide is your inner spiritual Master Guide, if you will, who knows you completely, and knows the terrain of the unconscious completely. He/She knows the best path for you to take, moment by moment, to becoming fully established in your awareness of yourself as fully being your Higher True Self. As such, the Inner Guide is the one you can always go to for support of all kinds, including how to access any other kind of guidance and whether such access is important or suitable. Therefore, this manual provides only a script for accessing the True Inner Guide in consideration of the time constraints and scope of this course. Keep in mind that you have the freedom to use the basic principles to modify and experiment to access whatever guiding "entity" the client may wish, but the capacity to establish a familiar working relationship with the True Inner Guide is an invaluable resource.

Just as with past life regression there is no need to "really" believe in the experience as a past life vs. a symbolic creation of the unconscious, there is no need to require belief in the Inner Guide as a separate entity. If the client wants to consider it an imaginary means of communicating with the unconscious, that's fine. The test, as always, is not "truth," but effectiveness. Does the experience carry transformative power and produce beneficial results, whether regarded as real or imaginary?

◆ ◆ ◆

4. Accessing the True Inner Guide

Discuss the concept of guidance and the True Inner Guide with the client to ascertain their knowledge, experience, and comfort level with the ideas. Also, listen for preferences of imagery (sub modality cues), either implied, (they are unself-consciously talking about their guide not noticing they are giving relevant descriptive information), or overtly: "I always call my guide like this..., or "My guide is always behind me to my left, all I have to do is <u>tune in</u> to her...," or "I want to do it this way...".

Do inductions, catalepsy testing, deepening (in this script, counting down a hill to a meadow, but some guides may be in towers or ancient libraries or temples, etc.).

Feel yourself standing, now, at the top of a hill in a beautiful natural setting...feel your feet on the ground...your head and shoulders *eeeasily balanced and <u>relaxed.</u>*..as you look around at the wonderful trees and greenery...*breathing* in the delightful scent of the fresh air...that's right...it feels good to find yourself here in this beautiful natural setting... feeling at ease in your body...and your mind open and alert in a delightful *eeeasy* way now...drinking in the scene...uplifted by the expanse of sky overhead as your feet enjoy their contact with the earth...as you listen to the sound of my voice guiding you into just the right state of relaxation and ease to effortlessly enjoy this journey to meet your True Inner Guide...that's right...breathing easily now...with each breath becoming more and more involved in the wonderful experience of standing in this beautiful natural setting at the top of this hill...as the sound of my voice makes it easy for you to follow my suggestions to the letter, for your own highest benefit, as you are about to walk down this hill to the meadow where you will meet your True Inner Guide...

That's right...opening...feeling the aura and protective blessing of your own inner purity, your own Higher Self awareness now...making it a heart-warming, touching experience, in a special way, you are discovering now as you prepare to approach your True Inner Guide...

In a moment, I am going to count from 7 down to 1...as I count you will walk down the hill to the meadow... each step...each beat of the count taking you to just the right depth and openness to meet your Guide...every step you take causes you to experience a profound inner alignment of your energies in an effortless delightful way...every breath relaxing you more...feeling better and better every step you take as I count you down the hill...

Number seven...going down...deeper...deeper...deeper

Number six...deeper...deeper...deeper...down...down...down

Number five...deeper...deeper...deeper...down...down...down

((When repeating like this, focus with interest on the client, imagine they are looking directly at you, and say each "deeper" or "down" like it is the first, only, and most important time you are saying it.))

Number four...even deeper...more relaxed...more in tune...your energies aligning eeeasily, effortlessly...that's right...

Number three...deeper...deeper...deeper...down...down...down

Number two...almost there...feeling the power of your own expansive pure being...being caressed by the energy of nature all around you as you go...deeper..and deeper...down...down

Number one...now at the bottom of the hill...feel yourself walking out into the meadow...easily erect and balanced...it's almost as if you could see in every direction at the same time...you are so at ease, alert, and receptive...

Notice a blanket in the meadow...notice its size, shape, color and design...as you walk to it...it's there for you...go to it, and, as you sit down on the blanket, you become even more attuned to this natural setting and to your own awakened inner energies...

In a moment...when I count to three...an animal will appear in the meadow...this animal will come to you to lead you to your true inner guide...

One...two...three...go with your first impression...seeing this animal approaching you...welcome it...look into its eyes...notice how you feel as you sense its awareness of you...sense the bond of friendship between you...share with me what you are experiencing...*((if the animal is there and they are in sync, proceed. Otherwise, do whatever may be necessary to help access the animal))*

Now signal the animal to take you to your True Inner Guide...get up and follow it...feel your body moving...watch the motion of the animal...notice the details of the terrain you are moving through, including any smells or noises...every bit of sensory information you notice enhances your feeling of aliveness and ease in your body...and of the fresh openness and alertness of your mind...that's right...

Now you sense the presence of your guide...watch as the animal leads you to the guide...extend your hand and feel the guide take your hand in its hand...feel its texture...its temperature...whether its rough or smooth...old or young...feel the energy of the guide's presence as you prepare to allow its presence fully into your awareness...share with me what your experiencing...*((respond and assist appropriately))*

Now allow your vision to move from the hand up the arm to the head and shoulders...see the guide's face...look in its eyes...experience how it regards you...experience how it is dressed...its sex...and whole appearance...share with me what you experience...*((again assist in any way necessary))* ...now very directly, with your whole heart and soul, knowing that in this inner realm you must be told the truth...ask, "Are you my True Inner Guide?" And tell me its response by word or gesture." Share his/her response.

((Whether yes, no, or uncertain, instruct the client to send a beam of pure white light from their heart center at the being and have them tell you what happens. Typically, if it is the guide, it will laugh, expand, send a blessing back, etc., but, if it's not the true guide, the light beam will dissipate it or send it away in some way-don't explain this to the client in advance, let them discover it))

((If it's not the true guide, tell them to walk around that place to the right and continue on to where the guide is waiting, and repeat the process. You may, in some cases, have to repeat 3 or 4 times. Always test with the light beam, and emphasize that they must be told the truth, and that they have the right to feel certain before proceeding.))

Now you can freely interact and dialogue with your Inner Guide. Please ask questions out loud and tell me the guide's responses...sharing with me in this way will enhance the power and vividness of your inner experience...*((As you listen, if it seems right to offer a question or some suggestion do so...also simple reminders to open more and more to experience the presence and beneficial power of the guide. For instance, make sure they ask in some way, "What do I need to do on a daily basis to become more and more attuned to your assistance and to deepen my appreciation of the significance of our relationship?"))*

We are going to return to normal waking consciousness in a moment...do you have a last question?...*((share))*

Now ...in the presence of your guide...reflect on this experience...and on the count of three offer your guide a gift...one...two...three...go with your first impression...experience giving the gift...experience his/her acceptance of the gift and watch as he/she takes the power and significance of the gift into his/her being...*((share))*...now experience your guide giving you a gift...a gift that embodies the power of your new bond with each other...experience taking the gift...and experience dissolving it into your being, integrating into your being completely the power and meaning of this gift...*((share))*

Now as we are about to come back...look at your guide with gratitude...experience as your guide and this whole experience dissolve into this golden white light that is surrounding you now...the light of your own true pure being...your guide and this whole experience dissolving into this light...charging this light with all the learnings and power of this new relationship...radiating this new resource into your past...causing your unconscious mind to reevaluate your relationship to your whole past in such a way that you become more and more free of any way in which your old relationship to your past experiences may have negatively limited you until now...and radiating into your future...sensing yourself moving into your future, now...step by step...breath by breath...moment by moment...day by day...more and more supported by this new and ever expanding and enriching relationship...that's right...

Now feel that light dissolving into your body...impregnating every cell of your body with the power and learnings of this new bond with your true inner guide...as I count from one to five...you easily come back to normal waking consciousness...feeling refreshed and wonderful in every way...

Number one...coming back...the light completely dissolving into your being...energizing and healing

Number two...breathe it in...breathe it in ...that's right

Number three...more and more awake...wiggle your fingers and toes...wiggle them...that's right

Number four...breathe in wakefulness...breathe it in...fully coming back

Number five...open your eyes...wide awake...clear headed...come fully back...that's right...

◆ ◆ ◆

5. Resolving Conflicts between Parts or Subpersonalities

*Appreciating that "parts" are devices of an essentially whole being managing its inner energetic state, it is important to remind the client's conscious and unconscious minds, and <u>the parts themselves</u> that they are one, and share the same positive intent. Being one being with this inner display of subpersonalities that have <u>apparently competing and conflicting agendas</u>, there must be an awakening to the (here we go again) theatrical nature of these inner conflicts. They are an act, **not real**, but <u>powerful</u> nevertheless. All the actors have forgotten they are just acting, and that there is complete freedom to rewrite their realities, choices, and outcomes, and to recognize there is actually only one actor, playing all the parts, who needs to wake up into self-love and genuine self-caring. To the extent that maintaining the inner parts is useful for communication, the actor of these parts needs to love itself **<u>as each part</u>** as well, honoring the play as an expression of creative self-delight.*

Identify with the client the "parts" that run a behavior or inner conflict they want to address. Make sure the client can relate to this model, i.e., thinking about themselves as having parts that run their behaviors. Remember, parts run their resource behaviors, too, so balance that insight in their awareness so they don't develop a subtle attitude against parts as bad. Since they have more than one subp. identified for this session, decide which to address first, or get their agreement to let their unconscious decide which is most important to communicate with first. (Note: many times, this is what happens anyway. Even if you get agreement from the client on the issue, once you do trance, something else pops up. Don't be so fixed in your agenda that you can't make the shift, and <u>take the client with you</u>. Think about how to interpret and relate to "resistance" from this perspective. <u>Comment or ask questions in class.</u>)

Do induction, relaxation, testing, and deepening. *[Utilize information, images, concerns, anticipate distractions based on discussions with client to build rapport (it lets their unconscious mind know you were listening- it humanizes the technique.)]*

Now that you are in this deeply relaxed state...allow your awareness to sense the energy of this problem...think about your experiences of it manifesting...it may be helpful to pick one situation in which it is particularly vivid, alive and active...let me know when you are in touch with it...*((wait for sharing))*...feeling the presence of the parts of yourself in conflict in this situation...perhaps notice if they are making their presence felt in a particular part of your body...that's right...just allow your awareness of them to gently grow...in a way that you are honoring their dynamics...appreciate their willingness to communicate...and allow yourself to open to this communication in such a way that it will be mutually beneficial...now call upon your True Inner Guide to be present to witness and assist in this process as needed...open to your Guide's presence...that's right...let me know when your Guide is present and you both are ready to proceed...*((wait))*

In a moment, I'm going to count to three...when I get to three, the first part that embodies and controls one side of the behaviors associated with this problem of_____ will manifest before you in some form, the most appropriate form that will enable it to communicate with you *most effectively now* for your mutual benefit...as I am counting I would like this part to decide what form it would like to take to communicate...it can be any form in the universe...a rock, a river, a cloud, a bonfire, a person or animal, anything in the universe...on the count of three it will be there. *((repeat this paragraph))*

Now I'm going to begin counting...just relax and go with your first impression on the count of three of how it appears...sometimes people have a sense of what it's going to be before I get to three...and that's fine...just understand that if it is different or the same as what you anticipate...that ...either way, on the count of three, even if it's anticipated, it will be new and fresh and alive in more interesting ways *to communicate for your mutual benefit now...*

Number one...relaxing and preparing to welcome this part into your awareness...

Number two...in such a way that you both feel safe and open to communicate to discover new learnings to benefit you both...

And...three...there it is....experience it there...go with you first impression...share with me what you experience...sharing with me causes you to be more fully involved with your experience, enhancing your capacity to communicate with this part.

((If necessary, assist in whatever ways are appropriate to establish the image: 1)small chunks; 2) create devices that will help, e.g. visualize a curtain with the part behind it (open the curtain or, if the part prefers, leave it closed; 3) generate a house- knock on the door or call the part out; 4) create an idyllic scene with a book, beautiful and ornate on an enchanting pedestal [describe them], have the client go to the book and open it to just the page that has a picture of the part; 5)try anything that comes to you- remember this is theater!))

That's right...allow it to reveal itself...notice you have a sense now of your connection...also, a sense of how you feel in its presence...and how it feels in your presence...share with me what you are experiencing...understand that it has the freedom to show you various qualities and aspects of itself, and can even change shape to do this, if it wants to...relax and, with a sense of gratitude for its willingness to communicate, make some gesture to it that communicates your respect and desire to establish a more beneficial relationship...*((share))...*

Ask, "What are you trying to accomplish in my life by acting and manifesting in the way you do?" ...and tell me its response...*((You can choose to phrase this as, "What are you trying to accomplish that is positive," to get an answer phrased positively, or leave it this way, and ,if you get negatives , keep asking, "What does accomplishing this do for you?" until you get a good bottom line positive intent (peace, joy, happiness, wholeness, etc.))*

Respond to the subp.'s answer...recognize what its positive intent has been in generating these behaviors...both of you reflect on this positive goal that you both value and honor...feel a bond of kinship and warmth growing as you both recognize you value the same goal...freely dialogue about this realization *as it is growing now*...and share with me about your exchange...

> *((Some questions that could be useful to stimulate the dialogue: "How do you feel about (the client)? "What do you want from him?" "What do you need from him?" "What is your function in (the client's life)?" Note: Stay away from "why" questions that lead into intellectualized discussions and explanations. For example, you don't particularly want to pursue the "why " of a part's dislike of the client. It's more important simply for the impact on the client of hearing and experiencing the part's statement. It makes the inner situation more "real," more vivid. So encourage the client to openly and fully experience the part as it expresses the answer to this (and all) questions and to notice how it makes them feel. Encourage a sense of gratitude even for negative sharings so that they both understand that they can freely express their truth without fear of blame or judgment. Then ask the questions that will reveal the shared genuine need that deserves to be honored by both and fulfilled by the integration of their energies and efforts.))*

((If they haven't already)) reevaluate together, the beliefs and the choices of behaviors that it was doing to accomplish this goal in the light of this new recognition of shared positive intent...and make any agreements necessary and appropriate to generate better choices of more effective behaviors that really achieve this goal...*((Have them share with you and assist in the negotiation in anyway needed))*

Now that you have established this new bond and sharing of resources in the deeper realization of how you can truly benefit each other...I'd like you to check if there is any residual concern that needs to be addressed...***((share, handle whatever comes up))***

Now invite this part to go with the Inner Guide for further empowerment of these new understandings as you call forth the competing subpersonality...***((Repeat the process of evoking, dialoguing with, and reaching resolution with the polar opposite or competing part. Go back in the script and lead in with, "I'm going to count to three and this other part will manifest in the most appropriate form to communicate with you now about these issues..." and continue from there to the same point of resolution you did with part 1.))***

Now send this part with the Inner Guide for further empowerment of these new learnings as the first part comes back before you...notice if it has changed in anyway from having integrated these learnings with the assistance of the Inner Guide...***((share))***...

Now bring back the second part and notice if it has changed from having been assisted by the Inner Guide. ***((Note: In the inner realm, time is very relative and non-linear, so the second part had just as much "time" with the Guide as the first. It's fair.)) ((share))***

Now invite the subpersonalities to dialogue with each other, telling each other what they need and want from each other in the light of their new awareness in order to fulfill their shared positive intent...listen very openly and with respect and gratitude as they do this...experiencing the support of the Inner Guide...the Inner Guide will assist them to work out any agreements necessary...***((share))***

Now ask the Guide to take you all to the super conscious level, the level of your Higher Self...up a column of golden white light to the level of awareness where these parts will experience themselves at their fullest level of actualization, free of limitations and confusion...now experience yourselves ascending this column of brilliant golden white light...feel it caressing and permeating your being...as you all go higher and higher...on the count of three you will be at the top of the column at the super conscious level...once at the top you and your Inner Guide will step out of the light and turn to watch as the parts step out one at a time...as they come out of the light they will have changed into a form that expresses their fullest actualization, free of limitation and confusion...

Number one...rising higher and higher...

Number two...higher and higher to the super conscious level...

Number three...now at the top of the column...step out of the light with your Inner Guide and turn and call forth the first subpersonality from the light...experience it there...feel its energy...*((share))*...ask, "What do you need or want from me in order to accomplish your goals?" Experience the answer with your whole being...its words and its energy being communicated vividly...respond establishing new bonds of warmth and cooperation...*((share))*

Now, on the count of three, experience yourself giving this part a gift that embodies this new healed relationship...one, two, three *((Do this fairly quickly, no long pause for the client to consciously decide what the gift should be.))*...experience yourself giving the gift...notice the gift...go with your first impression...experience the subpersonality accepting the gift and taking it into its being in whatever way appropriate...*((share))*...now experience the subpersonality give you a gift...one, two, three...go with your first impression...take the gift...experience it...it represents all the healing power of this new relationship...take it into your being in whatever way appropriate...*((share))*

Now have this part stand aside with the Inner Guide as you call forth the second subpersonality from the light...*((Repeat the process done with the first part.))*

Now all join in a circle holding hands *((or whatever, some parts might not have hands))* with the Inner Guide directing the flow and balancing of energies among you all...balancing and further enhancing the new bonds of warmth, power, and intelligence among you...let me know when the Inner Guide signals this is complete...

Now allow these parts, the Guide, and this whole experience to dissolve into a golden white light surrounding you...dissolving into the radiant light of you pure being...this light absorbs all the power and resources of this experience and these energies...and you feel it now as it permeates your body and dissolves into your body carrying these resources to the core of every cell of your being as it also radiates throughout your past...reevaluating your relationship to your past...releasing, healing, and empowering you in relationship to your past in whatever way is needed...as it also radiates into your future...imagine and sense yourself moving into your future with these new resources...see yourself, hear yourself talking...feel yourself moving...living more and more delightfully, expressing more and more fully the joyful purity of the enjoyment of your own life force...experiencing this, as your awareness comes back to this room on the count of five...

One...coming back...feeling the light...perhaps, kind of humming in every cell of your body...

Two...more and more...easily coming back...

Three...wakeful, light energy moving through your arms and legs...wiggle your fingers and toes...that's right...

Four:.breathe in fresh wakeful energy...breathe it in...that's right...clearing your head...aligning your energies fully towards delightful waking consciousness...

Five...eyes open...coming fully back...that's right...breathe it in...fully back...that's right...

Note: This process excluded the approach of moving through the layers from the subp. script (Phase III Chapter 2) because that "should" be so thorough that conflicts would be resolved, which would deny you the opportunity of exploring this approach.

◆ ◆ ◆

6. Important Factors in Managing Trance Communication

Especially in the beginning, as we combine more and more theatrical devices, you may begin to feel lost or confused about what you are doing, where you are going, and why!

Here are some guidelines:

A) *Keep your objective in mind.*

Resolution based on conviction in and reliance upon Inherent Pure Being and its <u>Function</u>:

1) **Separate pure intent from problematic behaviors.** Cultivate an exalted view of your client and their potential. Your capacity to do this, **genuinely,** will be directly proportional to your cultivation of an exalted view of yourself. <u>Don't *ever* put yourself down!</u> Understanding this simple statement thoroughly, on a moment by moment basis, in such a way that it sparks the awareness to burst "Put Down" thought forms, **<u>in all their subtlety</u>,** will allow an exalted sense of yourself to simply emerge naturally.

2) **Have the client hold behaviors in awareness at the same time they are holding awareness of pure intent.** This is an exercise of clarity, of True Intellect, of True Discrimination. Refrain from sympathizing with their dilemmas. Inappropriate sympathy, "idiot compassion" as coined by Trungpa Rinpoche (see reading list), will either offend them and break rapport, or suck you into a shared trance state of dilemma that reinforces that problem state, or both!

3) **Reevaluate behaviors based on awareness of pure intent.** Instead of following them in the dualistic teeter-totter that has maintained the problem, where the mind fluctuates between two poles in such a way that contradictions aren't highlighted and resolved, bring both poles into awareness as two aspects of one reality, two sides of the same coin.

4) **Restore recognition that an emotional holding, a contraction, a chronic defensive crouch, creates inner psychic shadows, false imaginings, which then are projected on to external situations and sought out for engagement to self-justify rationales for the crouch.** This creates a vicious cycle, circular thinking: <u>**all egoic thinking is circular**</u>. The sense of the need to hold emotionally is fused **unnecessarily** to actual valuable lessons from the traumatic (i.e., significant, and impactful lessons) situation.

<u>In other words, we learn to keep the lessons and let the emotional energy and bodily contraction relax</u>: *"You don't have to maintain this defensive state of alert to*

remember what you have learned to avoid, and you don't have to keep seeking out harm to verify that you have still remembered to avoid it (**see the circular logic?**), *anymore than you have to keep putting your hand on a hot stove burner to reassure yourself that you remember you shouldn't do that because it burns!"*

Most people clearly "get it" about the stove. Help them wonder what stops them from getting it about old dangerous and traumatic situations that are over with, that they have survived!

5) **Maintain rapport on the macro and micro level.** Keeping the insights, to let the emotions and the body relax, requires a sense of confidence, safety, and inspiration towards beneficial change.

a)Macro-level is up front resolution of any issues about hypnosis, the therapist, expectations and performance standards, fears and misconceptions in general. Encourage them to speak openly about these things, especially about what you may sense are the *secret* hesitations they think they shouldn't speak about, or which are unconscious. Recognize that the shadow side of their hope and trust that you can help them change, is a determination to defeat your assistance. The strength of this dynamic will vary from client to client, from moment to moment. Don't romanticize the therapy and get caught by this hidden persecutor because of your own naive idiot compassion. (Don't interpret this egoically and decide to flip to the pole of aloof cold-hearted cynicism, either!) Genuineness and clarity simply are required. Don't ever *try* to feel for your clients. Your clarity and genuine feelings are what will support them, even if it means you're not being "nice."

b)Micro-level is on-going, on the spot, adjustments to maintain rapport and to keep the client accessing resources. **This requires that you monitor your own "co-trance state:"**

[1] Your attitude, your breath, your bodily balance and tension, your thoughts and feelings,

[2] Are you getting caught in their drama?

[3] Are you trying too hard? Do you have a fixed agenda that sets you up to fail vs. remaining awake and focused on the process with an exploratory attitude?

[4] Is their "stuff" triggering your "stuff" causing you to get reactive and out of your resource state?

Remember, you don't have to be perfect; you don't have to have overcome the same problem; you can have "bad" thoughts and feelings. The crucial thing is to be able to acknowledge them and hold them in awareness with ruthless honesty without reacting to them or excusing them or trying to cover them up. Just let them be in their space, there is plenty of space for everything. Let them be, don't react, stay loose and focused on the client's process *with your own process in your awareness, freely moving in its own space.*

B) Remember your tools:

Theatrical submodality alterations, and emotional releasing and clearing:

1) **Scan for bodily sensations**, relate to them, have them speak or generate pictures.

2) **Use imagination and pretense.** If they "can't," have them pretend they can.

3) **Allow discursive information only as necessary to promote involvement in inner imagery and symbols**, e.g., the generation of symbols to represent vague feelings, or parts, lessons, gifts, etc. You want them to feel the power of images rather than chat about them.

4) **Utilize your understanding of dualistic mind's negative hallucinations of hidden polarity issues:**

   a) *"I don't know what I want him to do." "What don't you want him to do?"*

   b) *"I can't see..." "What don't you want to see?" "*

   c) *"I don't want to feel sad.." "Say you don't feel sad, say it doesn't hurt..."*

   d) *"I don't know..." "What would it be if you knew?"*

5) **Bring in resource entities**: inner guides, adult self, anyone who embodies the resource needed (including movie characters exhibiting the quality in a scene they know), Ideal parents (this is tricky if the client had abusive parents), etc.

6) **Employ dissociation and magical devices.** Rise above, float to the side, create a movie theater to safely view the trauma (e.g., the phobia cure), safety glass, force field, etc.

7) **Employ association.** Assist the client to feel the feelings, let the feelings speak, see the "other's" response (parent, persecutor, whoever is there) as the client communicates their truth in a way that wasn't available to them "then." Have the client act out their true desired responses monitoring responses from the "other." Have the client recognize how they are affected by the "other's" response.

   a) Clarify, in any way necessary, that all feelings are O.K. to feel. Many people may have strong prohibitions from their past, religious or cultural, that make it hard for them to release and experience strong negative or strong positive emotions (anger, hatred, joy, or delightful sexual arousal). This conflict has been an essential ingredient in the splitting off of parts. Give counter examples, or approach the belief as a subpersonality and work out the conflicts and contradictions. Especially be on the lookout for secondary gains and implications of arrogance and resentment hiding in the guise of purity:

   "It's fine if others swear, but I don't allow myself..."

   "I'm patient with other's mistakes, but I'm hard on myself if I make one..."

   It is not as hard to let go, as we all believe. It is hard to let go because the polar opposite of our desire to let go of the affliction is our desire to hold on, holding on to resentment- the desire to get even with a secret arrogance.

b) Remember this is theater. If necessary role play, or have them act out to get the energy flowing (e.g., hitting pillows, pushing against your hands).

c) Learn to associate with and *channel* feeling energy, not just in trance but in daily life. Do this for yourself as well as for your client. This is not merely a hypnotic procedure, but a method of developing inner strength to maintain focus of awareness, and the capacity to feel strong energy move through the body, and to consciously move it in beneficial directions. It involves developing the capacity:

[1] To "break state" from accepting habitual trance commentaries and directives about one's life, as they happen moment by moment, leading one repeatedly through useless endeavors that sap one's enthusiasm and generate unsatisfactory outcomes. After breaking state, which is {a} simply waking up to the pull of a habitual trance induction(usually V, A, associated with a K), and {b} staying dissociated from it (i.e., listening to its rap, but not buying into it, and scanning the body to release any tendency to contract, including the breath), one then,

[2] associates with the energy, the *feeling* of the feeling,

[3] breathes into it,

[4] maintains a *dual awareness* of the feeling energy and the thoughts the feeling energy generates and the memories it may trigger, without letting the thoughts and memories "knock one out" (put one into trance so one loses track of *feeling* the *flow and elucidation* of the feeling energy in present time through the body. I say elucidation because, if one isn't distracted into trance, but stays attentive to the energy, following it to its source, it reveals itself (i.e., the nature of its pattern or form such as anger, sadness, fear) fully and then returns to its formless liberated state of Inherent Purity which is experienced as peace, spaciousness and clarity.

This is an ancient meditative technique that allows one to follow any experience, any feeling, back to its source, i.e., back to one's liberated state, inherently free, awake, trance free. Becoming skilled at this makes one the master of his/her experience, aware more and more, moment by moment, of the sacred presence of one's own being (or God or whatever you like) beyond conception. When one can do this, one can channel the energies of supposedly "bad" feelings into beneficial endeavors, released from the trance realm of self-involvement. For example, when asked where she got all her energy to do hospital work, Florence Nightingale replied, *"Rage."* Or, *"Good indignation brings out all one's power,"* Emerson. [Examples of perseverance: Edison, Col.Sanders]

C) Develop mindfulness and awareness.

As with emotional clearing, this can be like riding a rapids. It is easy to talk about, but to actually do it requires the inner strength, stamina, and wakefulness. The way to develop this inner strength, more and more, is to take every opportunity to practice it, bit by bit. **Opportunities present themselves every moment.** Put simply, it's the constant practice of breaking state and acting independently of the "urge" of habitual thought/behavior. Daily life examples include:

1) Go slow when you want to go fast, and vice versa. When you feel like contracting in fear, expand. For example, if you are sliding into a poverty mentality, give something away. Return kindness for rudeness. Patience is a form of generosity. Cultivate it towards self and others. Give both space and time: take a deep breath and shift perspective - look at the sky, feel your feet on the ground. Affirm that there is plenty of time to do everything, and relax the contraction.

2) Do ordinary habitual tasks, like brushing your teeth, with wakeful attention as if for the first (beginner's mind), or last time (awareness of the imminence of death).

3) Do them faster or slower than usual, i.e. become attentive to habitual patterns and vary them so you **feel the friction**.

4) Don't base choices or behaviors on external, or internalized external, standards such as praise or blame, good or bad, or right or wrong (think more deeply about what causes harm), or other's expectations.

5) Take risks, do small acts of courage (and appreciate them), make arbitrary choices and plans and follow them through. Just do it!

6) Practice witnessing thoughts and feelings. Sit quietly erect and relaxed and simply label thoughts and feelings: *"thinking...thinking...feeling..."* **Label and witness, don't get involved.** Build up to 20 minutes or more a day with this simple exercise.

7) Cultivate mindfulness of all your actions throughout the day, and create your own exercises for breaking state, for waking up.

This is a discipline, and true discipline itself is an act of courage. The courage to step outside of the trance of narrow self-involvement and fear. To keep it real and fresh requires vigilance. <u>If it becomes a routine habit, you've fallen asleep. If it becomes a duty, an obligation, involved with hope and fear, guilt, or a gaining idea, you will become resentful.</u> **Right relationship to wakeful living is the goal of this course and approach to hypnotherapy, not trading in one trance for another.**

8) Become aware of how and when you are ruled by your **unexamined likes and dislikes**. What are they? Make a list.

9) As an exercise, create for yourself a script in which you represent your most important goal in life as a living symbol of some sort. Relate to it, feel its energy. Take some time to get fully established in relationship to it so it becomes alive and vivid. Then visualize it moving straight out into the distance to the top of a hill where you still experience its power and vividness, as you experience yourself at the beginning of a straight path out before you and up the hill to the symbol. Walking this path symbolizes you walking the path of your life to attain this goal. As you begin walking, on either side of the path are temptations and obstacles of all sorts, manifesting in varied ways: as people, objects of desire or fear, past situations, symbols of shame and fear, sadness or grief, seduction and distraction. These manifestations can do whatever they want to divert you from your path except one

thing - they cannot block your path or prevent you going step by step, wakefully, and intentionally walking the path. As you go step by step, knowing you are going to stay on the path, focused more and more on your goal, you can afford to take some time to experience these things to the right and the left, to hear and feel the pull of their cons, and then to "pop" them and move on. After taking the time you need to do this in a way that is beneficial to you to build your inner strength, you come to the bottom of the hill having left all those things behind. Take one last look back at them, reflecting on how good it feels to have overcome them, and then turn and proceed up the hill into the presence of this living symbol which has become even more vivid, meaningful, and powerful because of your efforts. Feel its energy permeating you as it fully merges into your being, dissolving into every cell of your body, carrying into every part of your being its resources and intelligence and power. Take some time to experience this, knowing and sensing it is radiating through your past and future in appropriate and beneficial ways, and then come back. (Adaptation of a guided mediation from What We May Be, by Piero Ferrucci.)

10) Rest in No-Self and allow Skillful means to flow genuinely. Be ready to be surprised! As you clarify and step out of your own egoic shame-based, fear-based trances, you'll be able to trust the Goodness of your True 'I-Don't-Know-Who-I-Am' Self. You'll be amazed at what comes out of your mouth and at how you behave, and at how it benefits the client. This effortless capacity is the fruit of sincere persistent efforts in cultivating the above described forms of discipline and self-inquiry. You can't sit and watch fertile ground, no matter how fertile, waiting for it to sprout a bountiful crop, until you have tilled it and planted good seed.

A client recently said to me: *"You operate on about 7 1/2% information and 92 1/2% laser intuition."*

This is a wonderful compliment. One can feel gratitude, give thanks, and then must let it go. Live in the rich poverty of No-Self.

◆ ◆ ◆

7. Problem Resolution
Using Subpersonality Dialogue and Regression to the Origin of the Subpersonality Formation

As in the prior scripts, identify the problem. Discuss the model of "parts" or "subpersonality" work. Discuss the regression model, going to the source of the problem, the critical mass experience where the part was formed, i.e., where the behavior became "<u>fixed</u>" and the mechanism of "<u>searching and projecting</u>" took over from open experiencing and learning.

This script is mostly a simple fusion of the subpersonality dialogue and regression scripts. Keep in mind, however, all your other resources: How could you introduce the Inner Guide? How would it be appropriate to go to the Higher Self? What else? Have you noticed how long the list has become? <u>Maybe you should make a list!</u>

Do induction, relaxation, testing, and deepening. *[Utilize information, images, concerns, anticipate distractions based on discussions with client to build rapport. This lets their unconscious mind know you were listening. It humanizes the technique.]*

Now that you are in this deeply relaxed state...allow your awareness to sense the energy of this problem...think about your experiences of it manifesting...it may be helpful to pick one situation in which it is particularly vivid, alive and active...let me know when you are in touch with it...*((wait for sharing))*...feeling its presence and energy...perhaps notice if it's making its presence felt in a particular part of your body...that's right...just allow your awareness of it to gently grow...in a way that you are honoring its existence...appreciate its willingness to communicate...and allow yourself to open to this communication in such a way that it will be mutually beneficial...

In a moment, I'm going to count to three...when I get to three, this part of you that embodies and controls the behaviors associated with this problem of_____
will manifest before you in some form, the most appropriate form that will enable it to communicate with you *most effectively now* for your mutual benefit...as I am counting I would like this part to decide what form it would like to take to communicate...it can be any form in the universe...a rock, a river, a cloud, a bonfire, a person, or animal - anything in the universe...on the count of three it will be there. *((repeat this paragraph))*

Now I'm going to begin counting...just relax and go with your first impression on the count of three of how it appears...sometimes people have a sense of what it's going to be before I get to three...and that's fine...just understand that if it is different or the same as what you anticipate...that ...on the count of three, even if it is what you anticipate, it will be new and fresh and alive in more interesting ways *to communicate for your mutual benefit...*

Number one...relaxing and preparing to welcome this part into your awareness...

Number two...in such a way that you both feel safe and open to communicate to discover new learnings to benefit you both...

And...three...there it is....experience it there...go with you first impression...share with me what you experience...sharing with me causes you to be more fully involved with your experience, enhancing your capacity to communicate with this part.

((If necessary, assist in whatever ways are appropriate to establish the image: 1) small chunks; 2) create devices that will help, e.g. visualize a curtain with the part behind it (open the curtain or, if the part prefers, leave it closed; 3) generate a house - knock on the door or call the part out; 4) create an idyllic scene with a book, beautiful and ornate on an enchanting pedestal [describe them], have the client go to the book and open it to just the page that has a picture of the part; 5) if visual accessing seems futile, switch to body access. "Where in your body do you feel it?"[usually tension or burning], "Ask it to speak..." This approach, from Phase II, can be used to generate emotional release. It's not the objective of this approach, but don't create a bias against it! 6) try anything that comes to you. Remember this is theater!))

That's right...allow it to reveal itself...notice you have a sense now of your connection...also, a sense of how you feel in its presence...and how it feels in your presence...share with me what you are experiencing...understand that it has the freedom to show you various qualities and aspects of itself, and can even change shape to do this, if it wants to...relax and, with a sense of gratitude for its willingness to communicate, make some gesture to it that communicates your respect and desire to establish a more beneficial relationship...*((share))...*

Ask, "What are you trying to accomplish in my life by acting and manifesting in the way you do?" ...and tell me its response...*((You can choose to phrase this as, "What are you trying to accomplish that is positive," to get an answer phrased positively, or leave it this way, and ,if you get negatives , keep asking, "What does accomplishing this do for you?" until you get a good bottom line positive intent (peace, joy, happiness, wholeness, etc.). Remember, thank the part for responding; incorporate the response in your next question: "Good, thank you...now, assume [contemplate having X, imagine, experience as best you can what it would be like to have X] you have X fully and totally in a beneficial way in your life...what would that do for you that's even more significant?" Repeat process until you can go no farther, which should be some contact with an aspect of Inherent Purity.))*

Respond to the subp.'s answer...recognize what its positive intent has been in generating these behaviors...both of you reflect on this positive goal that you both value and honor...feel a bond of kinship and warmth growing as you both recognize you value the same goal...freely dialogue about this realization *as it is growing now*...and share with me about your exchange...*((Hopefully this will include appreciating the discovery that the most precious goal is a given and doesn't have to be strived for.))*

In order to reevaluate together, the beliefs and the choices of behaviors that were creating the problem being resolved here...in the light of this new recognition of shared positive intent...and to facilitate any agreements to generate better choices and more effective behaviors for the future...invite the subpersonality to witness as we ask your unconscious mind to guide us back into your past to the situation in which these behaviors became fixed...the situation that is the origin of this old problem.

Now that you have a deeper appreciation of this subpersonality's positive intent in behaving the way it *used to behave* even though it created that old problem, we are going to go to that situation where it decided that these problematic behaviors seemed to be the best choice for trying to achieve this positive intent.

[While you're in this deeply relaxed state, *feeling good* about the new resources you have generated here...you can remember anything you have ever experienced. Everything you have ever experienced has been stored in your memory by your unconscious mind, and, now that you are in alignment with the helpful energies of your unconscious mind, you can easily notice as your unconscious mind accesses the important information about this problem from the past.] *((Repeat []))*

Invite the subpersonality to witness this journey into the past and to learn from it. Explain that it will be invited to participate at the appropriate time, and until then it can *feel safe* and *relax* and witness this journey. It will probably be profoundly moved by what it is about to witness: its birth, so to speak, its origination.

In a moment I am going to count from one to three...As I count from one to three...you will feel yourself *effortlessly drifting back* in time... guided by the power and knowing of your unconscious mind, your pure inner being...just relax into the light and energy that is permeating your being and surrounding your body as you *feel yourself carried back in time*...back to the origin of this problem...to experience it again in a new way with whatever resources you need...to *experience it and be freed completely from this problem.*

Number one...going back...drifting back...relaxing into the protective aura of your pure inner being...

Number two...farther back...protected and strengthened by this aura of light...on the count of three, you'll be there...fully aware of the root experience of this problem in such a way that you will easily be freed from this problem...

Number three...now there, fully aware...go with your first impression of what you are experiencing.

((Note: these instructions from the regression script could be superfluous because of the work done with the part, which is now standing ready as an ally: as necessary, assist client to orient into the experience. Do emotional clearing as appropriate, remember you have the flexibility to go forward and backward in time to gather resources and to process as required. Remember to chunk the experience into small pieces to help them build up their awareness of where they are and what is happening.))

((For very traumatic memories, it may be necessary and advisable to approach them first by floating up above their life stream and move back in time at a height that allows them to perceive the events without getting pulled into them. The vantage point for this will generally be from <u>*behind*</u> *the event, i.e. they have floated towards it from its future, over it in its present, and moved behind it to a position prior to its occurrence where they can see it as a future event in the context of all other future events stretching out in the life stream.))*

Share with me what you are experiencing...*((Assist them with input on whatever resources they need, e.g. inner guidance, their adult self to coming in as an ally, finding a way to make it safe for them to see new choices of action to take, and to let themselves see new perspectives on the situation that release blame, shame, guilt, resentment, bitterness, etc. and* <u>*then to relive, reenact the situation with these new resources. Note: the above are the directions from the regression script. In this case it should be natural and appropriate to have the part step in at this point with all its new*</u>*

resources. *From this point, you are going to have it move forward through time, i.e. take the position in the past at the critical choice point and "grow up" from there with the resources that were missing then.))*

Experience yourself as you were then *((or, if they are observing from above: "See the you down there"...etc.))*, as the transformed subpersonality with its new understandings and resources, dissolves itself into this younger you, filling this younger you with all its new power, clarity, and resources, causing this younger you to act and express in this situation in such a way that this whole experience is being transformed into an affirmation of your inner purity and freedom...you are completely protected and free to say and do whatever is necessary to affirm your inner power and truth...share with me what you are experiencing...

((Note: These instructions are included from the regression script, but should be unnecessary because the newly empowered part is stepping in to relive the situation with new resources rooted in Inherent Purity. Interact throughout the experience keeping them encouraged and focused and active in releasing the limitations and seeing with greater clarity...if they are above seeing themselves down there...see what effect you get if you have them run the old experience in black and white, and then the "new" reality, with resources and choices, in color. When that one down there really "gets it," have them jump into the scene and fully associate into the experience of this new power. If they need further "back up" try pointing out to them that they can maintain dual awareness, i.e., jump in, yet still be above as present time self, or come down as ally into the scene to support the past self relearning its right to hold on to its dignity as an inherently pure spiritual being.))

Good...now experience your unconscious mind taking these new resources, insights, and capacities that you have just created for yourself into the rest of your past...into every experience that needs to be reevaluated and released in the same way...give your wholehearted permission for your unconscious mind to *do this, now*...sensing this part of you growing up through all those past experiences, this time with all its new awareness and clarity and power...imagine it radiating the power of these new resources...seeking out and reevaluating all these experiences...transforming them *now* in the same way into resources for you as new learnings and new affirmations of your inner purity and inner strength and capacity to *take care of yourself appropriately, now*...relax into it... sense it in some way...*((Depending on your calibration of their state, you may ask for them to share to see if they need assistance, also, where and when it seems appropriate, feel free to repeat phrases and/or elaborate for effectiveness))* ...and you may notice that your conscious awareness is participating by *remembering something in a new way*...as you sense *in some way* your unconscious mind *directing the completion of this process throughout your past, now...*

Now experience these new resources and learnings being carried with you, as part of you, into your future...sense and experience yourself in familiar and imagined new situations in the future... experiencing yourself and expressing yourself supported by these newly activated energies of your own being...

Now call your subpersonality into your awareness and notice if it has changed in any way from witnessing, participating in, and learning from this experience, and from growing up with its new resources...*((share))*...with your whole heart and soul, invite the subpersonality to move into a more loving and alive relationship with you that will allow it to freely evolve to its highest integrated expression as an *inseparable* aspect of your pure being...on the count of three, experience yourself giving it a gift that embodies this new union...one, two, three...giving the gift...experience the gift, experience the subpersonality accepting the gift and taking the gift into its being...*((share))*...now experience the subpersonality giving you a gift...experience yourself accepting it...sense the living power it embodies and take it into yourself in whatever way is appropriate...*((share)) ((Note: it's possible that full integration may have occurred in which case there won't be a separate part available to share. Tell the client: "Just gift yourself."))*

Good...in a moment you'll be coming back to normal waking consciousness on the count of 5...but before you do...[relax and reflect on all you have accomplished with your subp.(s) in this experience...as you do, allow your subp.(s) and your whole experience to become enveloped in a loving, healing, nurturing golden, white light... experience yourselves and your whole experience dissolving into this beautiful healing, loving light...enhancing and empowering the bonds you created here today...sense the power this light has to radiate these new learnings, new resources, and new love throughout your past into any and every situation in your past where they may be needed, now... for healing and the releasing of outmoded beliefs, attitudes, judgments or negativities of any kind...] *((Pause, repeat this last section ([ ]), take a moment to help this sink in. Perhaps repeat a third time; with any encouraging non-verbal responses, or simply by imagining yourself talking directly to the unconscious mind, say, "Good...that's right))*

...Experience that now in some way...releasing...healing...recapturing your pure innocent life force... *not necessarily in detail or conscious of any specific event...* but relaxing into the presence of this loving light and energy...*it feels good*... carrying these resources now... into your past wherever they are needed...that's right...want it to happen... ask that it happen ...make an inward gesture giving your permission for it to happen now...that's right...*feeling just how good it feels growing in interesting ways now moment by moment*...the more you make this inner gesture with your whole heart...feeling the growth of new learnings... sensing them purifying your being.

Now feel that light radiating into your future in the same way... carrying these new resources in your being into your future... imagine yourself in future anticipated and future unanticipated situations perceiving. interpreting. and acting with the awareness and support of these new resources... see yourself...feel yourself... hear yourself moving in these future situations with these new ever growing resources...that's right...

Now allow that light to surround your body... feel it permeating your skin as it dissolves into every cell of your body...permeating your entire being...imprinting these new beneficial powers on the awareness of every cell of your body...feel it dissolving into your cells...open to these living. healing resources as they integrate lovingly into your being...that's right...*((Repeat appropriate phrases as you sense they are indicated, & feel free to elaborate with your own inspirations.))*

Now...coming back to normal waking consciousness at the count of 5...

One...coming back...feeling this wonderful new energy in your being...

Two...more and more...coming back...

Three... lighter and more awake...wiggle your toes and fingers (repeat).. coming back

Four...breathe in a deep breath of fresh air...breathe it in... balancing your energies...clearing your head...that's right...again...fully coming back...

Five...open your eyes...open your eyes...that's right...fully back...fully coming back now

◆ ◆ ◆

Table of Contents
Phase IV

◆ ◆ ◆

1. Shame & the Addictive Personality

In Phase II we examined the structure of the psyche from an eastern analytical point of view. This view is not to be believed without question. It isn't metaphorical like a mythical explanation of the mystery of the cosmos, e.g. that the sun is carried across the sky on the back of a turtle, or that God made the universe in 7 days.

It is empirical, experiential. It is to be tested, and can be verified by anyone willing to take the time to explore their own mind and perceptions. It, in fact, has been tested through the ages by people who, through their own self-inquiry and meditation, verified the observations and experiences of those who proposed these models.

This is a basic difference between the eastern approaches I have studied and the approach of much of Western religion. There is no issue of belief. God or not God is not the issue. The individual has remained in a position of empowerment, to discover the direct Truth for herself. The requirement is the conviction that you can have a direct experience of "what is true" regardless of what you call it, without any need for the intervention of an external authority. In a sense, it is a form of anarchy, but it is anarchy that renounces the deluding authority of internal trance states and affirms the inherent purity and capacity of beings to be awake and free from erroneous limiting ideas called false beliefs.

You see, having a transcendent experience is not that difficult, after all. The tricky part is what the egoic-minding, the trance-mind, the conditioned-mind, the full-of-ideas-mind, does with the _remembrance_ of the transcendent experience after it's over. The eastern disciplines have made a careful study of the working of this thinking mind, in order to transcend its delusionary aspects--but still to use it as the valuable tool it can be. There are extensive teachings about the pitfalls of the intermingling of _thinking-mind-trance-processes_ with the glimpses of awakened _no-trance mind_.

The mixing is happening all the time. It has glaring manifestations in the perversion of the _remembrance_ such as religious fanaticism, and other manifestations of addictive personality. What can be more absurd and pathetic than killing each other over different ideas of the same unconditionally loving God?. It has subtle manifestations that thoroughly pervade our ordinary daily lives.

The dilemmas of our daily lives are not the homogenous product of a constant continuum of confused trance states, but rather, of the dance of absolute(awake) mind and relative(conditioned/trance) mind, alternating.

Our seemingly solid ego identity is very porous - _what feels continuous actually is intermittent._ As you develop a mastery of this perception, your hypnotherapy work becomes more playful because you see egoic-minding switching on and off with your own eyes. You gain the confidence that, moment by moment, you have before you exactly what you need to deal with and that having a fixed agenda is not necessary. You guide the egoic display naturally where it needs to go to unravel itself as long as mindfulness (wakefulness) is maintained and interjected by you.

Such mastery of skills and wakefulness has several operative elements:

1) not being hypnotized by the client's act,

2) not being distracted by your own,

3) being inquisitive about and alert to:

   a)**unconscious assumed context**. Statements only have meaning in context, and our problems are perceptions placed in inappropriate contexts.

   b)**assumptions of cause and effect**. What is supporting the client's illusion of limitation? When you get stuck, that is merely a delightful reminder that you lost the thread of mindfulness. You merely pick it up again - *right where you are!* Simply, start listening carefully again and questioning their assumptions.

The transcendent, passionate experience is, in fact, the hook that keeps us coming back for more of the punishment that our confusion metes out to us. The addictive dynamic is an intense destructive strategy to return to the absolute without considering the cost on body, mind, and sanity at the relative physical level. For a while it can seem to work, until the psychological and/or physical toll gets to be so high one can't help but notice the law of diminishing returns taking over. In many cases, it's too late by then to do anything about it -one is addicted. Karmically, shortcuts to the transcendent that lack respect for the integrity of the inherently innocent human psycho-physical system are exceedingly costly and destructive.

How are the Eastern models useful?Historically, the translation of the Eastern analytical approach into Western language has been of limited usefulness. Misconceptions of translated terminology and concepts have been profound. These misconstrued formulations of Eastern wisdom have made it difficult to apply it to the actual details of our lives. How is one to relate to the skandhas?

There has arisen in the last 20 years a model and language that elucidates a similar understanding of the dynamics of egoic-minding, but in language that moves Western people powerfully. It is the model of "Toxic Shame" and family system dysfunction, one of whose main proponents is John Bradshaw (see recommended reading list). Though not intentionally, the Toxic Shame models ground the seemingly esoteric concepts of the Eastern analysis in concrete ordinary experiences. For example, in addressing the phenomena of addiction, Bradshaw's daily life descriptions and stories illustrate the origins of our pain and our confusion, hitting home in the heart and gut. The Toxic Shame model is a step of integrative translation that is effectively presenting aspects of the egoic model *in our cultural context* so we can begin to "get it." Bradshaw is very eclectic. He draws from Alice Miller, NLP, Milton Erickson, Western Theologians, and Virginia Satir, a pioneer in dynamic family therapy, among many others.

The "movement" to unravel the addictive process model hasn't approached the profound implications of the eastern experience of the intricacies of the psyche, but it is moving in that direction.

Toxic Shame and the Family System

Toxic shame is the feeling of **being** wrong, as opposed to **doing** wrong - flawed at the core, **irredeemably**. *There is no way out!*

Notice that this dilemma could not exist without the dualistic dynamic between the notion of flaw and the notion that there should be something other than the flaw. This split, this separation, from an Eastern point of view, is primordial. It has a mysterious, beginningless root. It is the affliction and challenge of incarnation on the earth plane. It is the manifestation of 1st Skandha, of anava mala. It **feels** like the core or ground of our being, and drives all of our behaviors as *the-one-who-we-think-we-are,* but our true ground is pure, at ease, light, and undefiled.

But metaphysical primordial roots are hard to work with for most of us. How does one relate to the 1st Skandha? Bradshaw's work, and contemporary recovery work in general, frames the dilemma in the context of this lifetime, and as an affliction that was inflicted upon us by our experiences of abuse, insult, and confusion when we were young, magical, and most vulnerable to indoctrination, good or bad.

For most of us it was our parents who gave us the message that we weren't good enough: in varying degrees, in varying intensities, and with varying levels of conscious intent. For the most unfortunate of us, it was done in a concentrated way over sustained periods of time on conscious and unconscious levels fixating the **chronically regressed states**, the **harmed Inner Children**, that run and limit our lives.. For those of us more fortunate, it may be residual hang-ups that don't really limit us that much, and that we outgrow.

The core feeling of separation, the root of shame and egoic thought, the root of the notion that one's good is separate and attainable independent of other beings' good, is the root belief of all problems, neurotic or psychotic. It manifests as clinging identification with the events of life, i.e., the past. It is the thought process of defining self and self's capacities and limitations based on past experience and indoctrination *disconnected from, and anesthetized to* a present moment-by-moment awake **bodily/feeling** awareness of being innocently, ecstatically alive as a temporary manifestation of pure dynamic life-force, just like everyone and everything else.

The thought process itself, with its speed, distraction and delusions, **is the anesthesia** to *present-wakefulness-as-eternal-life-force-in-a-temporary-form.* This confused thought is perpetuating and carrying, *outside of consciousness,* the terrible pain of the rejection of self: the contractions of our free-flowing energies upon themselves into knots of constriction. These contractions, and the rapid thought processes that cover them up, diminish our capacity to access the incredible intelligence that is available to us all as our own being.

The "awake" state is marked by the qualities of 1)**compassion** (not altruism -- altruism sees[because it thinks] self and other; compassion recognizes the identity of self and other beyond thought construct), 2)**wisdom**, and the 3)**creative power** to act spontaneously, whole-heartedly, and with good effect.

The best a person can hope for who is asleep to, disconnected from, the reality of pure inherent goodness, is to try very hard to be a good person: to be altruistic, to act kindly and do good works, to behave in those ways identified as good and nice, all the while being haunted by the shadow of the "Secret," the gnawing feeling that it's all a lie, that some day one will be found out, that one day the burden of the act will be too great to maintain. Recently, we have seen this act short circuit for many evangelists, caught with their pants down or their hand in the till.

The same problem is widespread among therapists who do good work, but feel drained. Those who know all the right techniques and get great client results, but find their own lives falling apart, find themselves becoming isolated. Healers with this problem generally have short life spans, dying with bodies destroyed by the diseases they cure in others.

We cannot beat the game by putting up a good front, but that is what we all try do when we are in the trance of egoic consciousness - that is its purpose! Its positive intent is to keep the terrible secret hidden and to keep us anesthetized to the core pain of the **conviction of being flawed** which is held in a painful on-going **bodily contraction** that is expressing the contraction that also exists on an energetic feeling level.

But the intent is deluded, the contraction is an unnecessary trance state. Therefore, we must not honor the intent and process of ego. At its core it is an insult, an act of violence against our own nature. It manifests only destructively. Whether directed at self or other, the nature of violence and destruction is the same. For example: *"I'm patient with others, but I'm really hard on myself."* The arrogant altruism of the perfectionist.

Be careful! We must not fight it, i.e. with resentment and anger, either. Since it is a phantom, the attacks pass through it to hit what is really there - the person, the life force. To act in violence against the egoic mind serves the egoic mind, is part of the trick of egoic mind! *Affirming and evoking the real is the required focus of action. Accessing __positive intents and vivid wholistic outcomes__ enables you to love the ego, to humor the ego, to confound the ego into dissolution -- gap! This is the path, not endless humorless recapitulation of ego's version of self and personal history.*

When the intensity of the conviction/contraction of shame is great, you get the addictive personality. The great insight in cutting-edge recovery work recognizes that:

- the addictive process itself, the toxic shame, is the core disease - not the substance abuse, not the compulsive behavior. And,

- the "addict" is not a problem in isolation, he is part of a system of shame. He is the "designated patient" in a family of shame, whose role is to carry the burden for everyone in some special way.

That 'special way' is predictable. It is the egoic projection of 'styles' of the constructed, desperate, flawed self.in the realm of the five poisons.(Ph.II, Reactive Model) It is the display of stereotypes: egoically twisted imitations of Genuine Qualities.(Also, see Ph.V, Archetypes.)

The addict may be living with the primary family players still functioning together in time and space on the earth plane. In other words, everyone is still alive and interacting. Or they may only be active in the addict's psychic space as inner **energy clones**, internalized versions of those *"real people of the past."*

Either way, **it is the inner clones that hold the real power.** The inner clones are the people of the past who hold the addict's shamed, *chronically regressed* self hostage to the past. The present time people only have power because they correspond perceptually to the inner clones. Free the client from the inner clones, and the present time people become "just folks," with transparent harmless labels like 'mom' and 'pop.'

This is what makes regression work and parts work so powerful. Many of a client's key "parts" will turn out to be mommy, or daddy, or whoever is a significant other. And it is the younger trance fantasy version of the client, the "inner child", that the significant others are affecting.

The good news is that it is all in the client's mind. Therefore, it is within his power to be at cause over it all and to change it all. Our job is to help him to recognize that at some psychic level, *he is already at cause and willfully, though mistakenly and unnecessarily, maintaining this house of cards (albeit a powerfully vivid, painful, and compelling house of cards.)*

Some Hallmarks of Shame:

1) *It is guarded by perfectionism and control*

As I said above, shame is inherently violent, so it is marked by rage and grandiosity. Its logic: *"If I can't be it (perfect), I'll do it perfectly."* i.e., I'll earn perfection, but the *feeling*, the true feeling, never arises from the doing because no amount of doing can release the core belief of being flawed. It is inherent to the sense of separate self, it can't be changed or touched by any action or good deed.

2) *It is sustained by dualistic thought process*

Good/bad, right/wrong, black/white, either/or, yes/no, best/ worst. Bradshaw makes a very funny notation of a third choice: you can be grandiose (the greatest) or a worm (the worst), or you can be a grandiose worm!

3) *The mind is always thinking*

Since shame is maintained by dualistic thought -*you have to be thinking all the time!*

4) *It is an immature psychology.*

It is the psychology of a harmed child: flawed, fearful, and abandoned. *The sad irony is that the abused child bonds to the abuse and idealizes the abuser the more he is abused.* He is chronically denied the right to do what a harmed child needs to do: cry his heart out! The trance is sustained by the child-like capacity of the mind, the imaginative, dynamic, creative source, twisted against itself. Bradshaw, by poignant example, points out the qualities of this mind:

a] it is magical - *"step on a crack, break your mother's back..." "You're killing your father, you know!"*

b] it is non-linear - ask a girl who has a sister if she has a sister, she'll say , *"yes"* ; ask her if her sister has a sister, she'll say *"no."*

c] it is ego-centric - it can't take a perspective outside itself. It can't step into the other's shoes. If something is wrong, then, it must be his/her own fault.

At this point, you should see all the powerful active ingredients necessary to creating powerful sustained trance states!

Fundamental to the magical, yet destructive, trances created under these conditions are **bogus cause and effect relationships** (simply naive assumptions on the part of a child or adult indoctrinations [that still trace back to naive assumptions and delusions], and **misunderstood, inaccurate, or improperly limited <u>contexts</u>** that signify erroneous meanings.) Develop your wakefulness to discover these, and to play with them in a way that dissolves their delusionary power. Bring them into the light of conscious intelligence where they cannot survive **<u>by asking the right questions about how things work.</u>**

5) *Leads to addictive personality traits*

Shame-based personalities harbor addictive traits such as illusion of control, perfectionism, self-centeredness, depression, crisis orientation, dishonesty, denial, dependency, defensiveness, negativism, obsessive pre-occupation, frozen feelings, and inability to trust.

6) *Addictive manifestations*

<u>Substance</u>	<u>Process</u>
Nicotine	Gambling
Food(incl. sugar, chocolate, etc.)	Sex
Drugs	Religion
Alcohol	Relationships
Caffeine	Work
Money	Possessions
Distractions	TV, shopping, games, risk-taking

The Way Out of Shame

Whatever the presenting problem, it is essential to understand that the core problem you are confronting is shame: a horrible pain of feeling wrong and there being no way out. Your job, directly and indirectly, is to help the client connect to the underlying purity that is there.

Keep clear that the problem is an act; that the pain is an on-going self-inflicted wound replicating an experienced wound of the past. *Therefore they are already hypnotized when they come to you; chronically regressed with some significant portion of their energy.* All the tools we have learned so far apply.

The power and complexity of the "act" in the addict is greatly magnified, however. It will probably take more conditioning to get them to drop their habitual trance states in favor of the ones you want them to work with. If there is a mate or family system of some kind present (even peers, not necessarily family of origin) in their life, you need to appraise their vested interest in the client **not** changing, and determine how you both can relate that. Get them to seek counseling as well; encourage the client to find support groups.

The addictive process operative here is called co-dependence. It defines the recent recognition that the addict is not a problem in a vacuum, but merely the representative of a *hidden family system problem*, the result of an unconscious agreement among the parties about who will carry the shame. The system has been the *hypnotist of choice* for the client's whole life, or a major portion thereof. Any work you do will be challenged by those in the system once the client returns to it. It is extremely difficult to change or heal if the system is unwilling to change or heal. It would generally require breaking from the system - an enormous task in itself, of proportions akin to death and rebirth.

Cultivating Wakefulness

Your capacity to assist with these powerful deluded dynamics will be in direct relationship to your awareness of them and wakefulness in dealing with them. Cultivating wakefulness is a process of education and practice.

It is fostered by concepts that increase consciousness.

We have been emphasizing the hypnotic delusionary power of thought/concepts/fixed ideas. But concepts are also the antidote to the extent that they are useful in waking one up from fixed mind states.

Don't be satisfied with one-liners of truth:

"God is Love."

"We are all inherently pure."

While these may be "true," they are not particularly empowering, certainly not across a very wide spectrum of situational demands. Do either of these statements get you through an aggressive obnoxious challenge on a packed subway? They don't give you **procedural applications or perspectives**.

To that extent, if you hold on to them, they are just run of the mill fixed ideas. You need more of the whole story to generate useful insights. Saying an "apple is red" may be "true" but it certainly doesn't tell the whole story about apples or give you any real feel for its qualities. If an ordinary person goes outside and looks at the night sky, does he see the same thing an astronomer standing next to him sees? With the physical senses, yes, but with the mind, definitely not.

<u>Education and contemplation</u> elaborate your consciousness and maturity of understanding. So, contemplate these perspectives and make lists of phrases that display the "truth" from different angles, that point out connections between seemingly disparate issues and reveal the path of associations that join the disparities in the dance of seeming contradiction and paradox. We're challenging your understanding of the notion of dualistic egoic thinking here!

Creating and contemplating a list of *functional expressions of the truth* gives you perspective in different contexts - different situations that create living demands upon you, making the possibilities for wakefulness increase. It makes your understanding more comprehensive, and the likelihood of being hypnotized less in a given context.

Everyone knows the truth, most don't have the necessary **concepts of application or concepts of functional qualities** that remind them that the truth counts. *"No, this is a special case where violent self(?)interest applies."* Functional knowledge of truth has an **aspect** that can be applied and aligned with in situations as they change, moment by moment throughout the day, day by day.

In other words, situations come up that throw us off, make us forget what we know, scare us, anger us, distract us, confuse us, **hypnotize us** *into believing and behaving as if we are less than, smaller than, what we truly are.*

This fact demands the perseverance of practice: developing the capacity to go along **moment by ordinary moment** through life staying aligned with the truth as it applies to changing circumstance. This involves the True Intellect, Insight-Thought, and the Compassionate Heart to reject, to cut through, the seductive, compelling illusions of the speedy hypnotizing egoic fear-based thought mind.

Example: I had a couple coming in for therapy. One partner who was very insecure and "clingy" was going through a list with me of dualistic traps. In the context of what she was saying, I pointed out that her hope was inseparable and the same as her fear. She got it. That good was the flip side of bad. She got it. That praise was the flip side of blame. What did she get?:

You can't try to have one side without getting the other.

The trick to freedom was not to get caught by sticking to either side. Notions of praise or goodness or rightness can't be attained to remedy life's dilemmas, because they automatically affirm their polar opposites and bring them along to the party. *The light and the dark are just manifestations of the core contraction that gives birth to the entire dualistic display in all its variations.*

In accordance with this insight, I commented that her protestations about wanting to let go, wanting to be free of this "clingyness," were merely the flip side of wanting to hold on - *the very "clingyness" itself!*

Suddenly, a light went on, and she exclaimed, *"Oh! I didn't know it applied to that! I thought this was different! I thought this was real, or special! But it's the same trap!"* She got it: trying to fight her attachment was just the opposite side of giving in to her attachment, and, whether she was giving in to it, or fighting against it, *she was still caught in the trap.*

She got it that one side is never the remedy of the other, never the way out of the trap, *both sides are the trap. But because she didn't have* **that application for that situation, that context on her internal list of functional concepts of truth,** *she got caught by it, hypnotized by it, made to forget what she knew so well - seduced by a special case!*

Example: A client, very cynical, very bright, very educated with Eastern spiritual concepts, lots of altered state experiences, drug induced or otherwise, lots of experience with therapy - *"I know all the games, all the trips, all the techniques."* In any discussion of reality or human interaction the response was always a somewhat huffy, *"I know that."* Yet this person was often suicidal, acted very distracted and scattered - an admitted strategy to protect himself and keep people at a distance, and was basically non-functional in the world. How was his vast knowledge and understanding helping him?

At one point, I was having him play with the submodalities of an experience with an abuser: making their nose get longer a la Pinocchio, their voice get squeaky, etc. Then I asked him to wonder what his father's experience was looking in the bathroom mirror, juxtaposed to his own experience and response to seeing himself in the mirror. He lit up, said, *"Oh! I just had an AHA! experience - I hardly ever have them anymore. I've never thought of my father in that way before. It never occurred to me that he may have walked away from the beatings he gave me with a burden!"* **He saw his father's burden in his own face in the mirror.**

The client, then visibly softening, went into a reverie of resorting and reevaluation of whole sets of attitudes and fixations about his past experiences that opened and empowered him.

He hadn't learned any new "truths", but he had discovered a new <u>perspective</u> from which to contemplate his experience.

It's one thing to know all the games; it's one thing to 'know-it-all.' It's another to know all the <u>perspectives</u> on all the games, and on 'all-that-you-know.'

And it's another to soften body/mind into all the contemplations and poignant insights and extrapolations that arise from entertaining these new perspectives.

To summarize:

We've discussed moving around, floating around in a situation, as a 'point of awareness' to gain a different "hit" on the meaning and power being projected in a memory.

We've also discussed the dynamic tension of traumatic memories, and how to dissolve this tension of dualistic fixation between victim and perpetrator by jumping into and becoming the one one *doesn't* habitually identify with. (E.g., rape victims constantly rerunning traumatic memory, not appreciating they are victimizing themselves. Having them identify with being the perpetrator in the memory deflates the whole situation. The horror ends. The unconscious recognition of being at cause over the memory creation is awakened. Space opens up, emotional attachment is released, and insight has a chance to occur. Likewise, powerful transformative work is being done in prisons with perpetrators having them take victim position to open their hearts to the pain they have caused in their victims, and to get them in touch with their repressed victimhood as children, which is invariably the case. Their victims in the outer world are discovered to be the projection of their split off, disowned, repressed victimized younger selves.)

Notice that three very familiar positions are being discussed: first, second, and third person locations in space. This is utilizing and expanding upon the old common sense wisdom of putting yourself in the other person's shoes. The expansion is third and fourth position which are not mentioned as often.

In the case of the example above, first person is the 'know it all,' himself. Second person is becoming his dad. Third person is a 'point of awareness', embodied as a person or not, outside the duality, witnessing or observing the dualistic players. Although he didn't mention it, I suspect if asked, he would discover he had taken a third person perspective in his softened revery.

Second person, e.g., moving into your child self, or walking in the shoes of your adversary, gives you the chance to break the self-centered fixation on your opinion of what is real. (Recall utilizing these shifts from Phase II emotional clearing guidelines?)

A very poignant utilization of second person is to hold a dual position or to oscillate between adult self and child self, with therapist suggesting that the adult self see the fearful question of survival(outcome) in the child's eyes, and recognize that he has the answer - truly, that *he is the answer to that fearful question*. Then let them both digest that. The resolution of this survival contraction releases the emotional gridlock on perceptual and cognitive intelligence, allowing the situation to be re-evaluated, allowing the child-part to grow up.

Third person, as witness/observer, is free of it all, free to see clearly, not indifferently. **This means that true third person has been in the shoes of first and second persons, and can freely and willingly shift to them.** There is no contractive avoidance about assuming those positions. If there were, it would indicate the bogus egoic mimicry of witness/observer that you may be familiar with from your own experience, or from observing others falling under the influence of egoic mind's version of Witness Consciousness, after learning of it in a meditation class. The egoic version is stiff, cold, & repressive.

It can be very important and powerful to specifically, and in careful detail, have the person build their experience in their new location, making sure they are seeing through the eyes only, hearing through the ears only, and speaking their own voice from the throat (if aloud)or in their head. Anything not theirs is to be pushed away to its proper owner. In third position, they should be standing at eye level and be the same size as the other(s) In other words, they are fully embodied and not fragmented. This is simply the full detailed description of what would happen if you stood in another's shoes. As a famous old Zen retort demonstrating realization goes: "My eyes are horizontal and my nose is vertical." Simple, natural, effortless functioning of the senses, free of hallucinatory contortions.

Fourth position is a special case. It is True first person as present-time awake, but not body-identified. The issue is over with, you've survived. Not only have you survived, but your identity is as Awareness, not as the personality or the body. You can choose attitudes, courses of action, evaluations of your perceptions without being inhibited by fear-based toxic shame - without being deluded by trance states of identity with any aspect of the realm of form. You are Awake(ness) in the Dream of being a finite some-body.

As True Witness one is *in it, but not of it* - allowing the spontaneous flow of energies: with clarity, experiencing the energies, but not swept into identification with them. (i.e., no fixation of 'i'.)

True Witness, **fourth position,** has no space time attachment, while third position is more embodied, like a person, watching the situation without bias, but in space time, in a body, i.e. identified with it. Think about it! Think about witnessing (as third person), then witness witnessing.

Please, utilize these flexibilities to develop long **lists of applications and lists of functional qualities and aspects of wakefulness** that will keep you awake to the traps being laid by the thinking mind, the shame-based, fear-based mind.

For example, what has more power:

"Love yourself." or *"Don't ever put yourself down."*

"Let go of the past." or *"You have the right to bounce back from each and every experience of your life. The right to bounce back and be completely renewed."*

Reading and studying Miller, Bradshaw, and all the others on your recommended reading list, will aid you tremendously in this challenging adventure of discovering and tapping into your own goodness and wakefulness, and assisting clients to do the same.

◆ ◆ ◆

2. Treatment of Addictive and Compulsive Phenomena

The tools and view for addictive treatment are basically the same, but you need to find ways to make it especially compelling. Many times the addictive or compulsive client will have a sophisticated understanding of their problem that only serves to keep it in place. It will often include a secret pride of knowing more than you, seeing through you, and an agenda to beat you at the game of fixing them. You have to be alert and creative.

It can also take additional efforts to condition such a client to hypnosis. Their mind speed is often so high that the experience of something other than their incessant mind chatter will astound them. You may discover, for all their street smart ways and elaborate denial systems, that they are very naive about other kinds of inner experience and communication. Or, they may have a full array of altered state experiences and expertise that obscures their vision about their human weaknesses because their egoic mind is clinging so desperately to their specialness as demonstrated by these capacities - again, a secret (or not so secret) arrogance.

Guidelines

1.) A preliminary emphasis on anchoring self hypnosis tools such as **"deeply relax"** can motivate their interest in proceeding further and in building rapport. A simple affirmation, a la Emil Coue, may also quickly demonstrate to them other dimensions and possibilities beyond their thinking/speeding chatter: *"Day by day, I'm getting better in every way."* Repeat 20 times with lip movement before bed and upon rising.

2.) Get your aversion ammunition from them. Why do they want to quit? Ask questions in precise detail to elicit and/or to educate them about the pitfalls, dangers, and consequences of their current path of action. You will use this information in trance to contrast with the healthy alternatives you generate. Remember, we have three choices of action: towards, away from, and neutral. You can further empower your attractive new healthy "moving towards" alternatives by contrasting with vivid "moving away from" scenarios about the consequences of current behavior.

3.) Let them educate you as needed regarding their disease. With substance abuse, for instance, they may have extensive knowledge about drug treatments, consequences of going cold turkey, (going cold turkey is not advisable in cases where seizures may result, such as extreme alcoholism), etc.

a) Find out if they are under medical care or taking medication and consult as necessary.

b) With smoking or weight loss, walk them through their day gathering information about when they smoke/eat. Look for patterns. With eating there is more likelihood of an originating trauma.

c) Remember to evaluate their target weight goal, and comprehensive physical activities. What are they going to do to stay healthy?

d) With smoking, *there might not be any trauma* with a simple link to smoking. In fact, Dave Elman felt that hypnosis wasn't really helpful for smoking, because there was no originating significant trauma, just natural pleasure seeking, no big deal, initiating ingestion of a physically addicting substance. He felt that will power was the answer.

Question: In the context of our presumption of inherent purity, might we not find causes for the debilitation of the will, in this life or another, that could be cleared to restore the will of the client so they can quit?

e) Discuss and evaluate whether to go for quitting or an initial phase of reduction of cigarettes smoked.

4.) Regarding alternative behaviors, help them construct specifics. Don't just suggest that they will generate them unconsciously and trust it will happen. You want to establish *specific behaviors* set in *comprehensive contexts in ordinary life*, and, when possible, set in a *greater context of mythic proportions* that frames *their outcome, their goal, which you help them specify,* with a larger more compelling meaning beyond personal pleasure and egoic self-improvement. If possible you want to give them a transpersonal reason for changing, something that starts them thinking that they may be more magnificent beings than they thought, with aspirations beyond fame, money, and sex. With alcoholic clients where generational alcoholism is present, I take them to a point outside of time where they chose to incarnate and take on this burden in order to break the generational chain of alcoholism for the sake of all their ancestors. When done with conviction and rapport, this is a powerful perspective that gives great meaning to their efforts beyond their own comfort. Such expanded perspective is transformative in a wide range of contexts. I would go so far as to say, you should always try to establish some form of legitimate expanded view regarding the meaning of a person's life.

A sample hypnotic session format for addictions:

1.) Do inductions and relaxation. Make sure you anticipate and diffuse any issues re: control and safety.

2.) Do subpersonality dialogue to elucidate the underlying positive intent of the addictive/compulsive part.

a) Clearly separate the positive intent from the problem behaviors in such a way that they "get it" as vividly as possible that their strategy was ironically self-defeating, while generating a compelling force, an irresistible urge, to continue it.

b) Elaborate and affirm the possibilities of manifesting the inner purity and get their agreement to open to such possibilities. Check for any objecting parts.

3.) Do regression to the origin of the problem, the "birth" of the subpersonality, to clear the trance and frozen feelings supporting the shame-based belief system.

4.) Do emotional clearing techniques, at point of regression or in present time (which, you understand, regresses them) to get them to feel their tenderness, their purity. **It cannot be emphasized too much that people need to recover their capacity to feel their feelings directly, without reservation or judgment, and to learn how to communicate them [and with them] beneficially. Do not read this to mean being "nice".** This can be a long, even a lifetime task. It doesn't have to be, but it can be, especially if egoic mind constantly diverts the process. <u>Perfectionism</u> is one key way that the process is delayed because so much allegiance is given to the hope and image of being more than ordinary and human, i.e. arrogance keeps pulling us out of our bodies and the feeling intelligence residing there.

5.) Invite the shadow to speak. Test, expect reservations and doubts, and the fear and hesitation to express them. *"This won't last." "How can I keep this feeling?" "I'm not going to remember this."* Recognize the set of feelings that may be permissible for a client, and help them explore their denial trances about those that aren't permissible, typically anger, rage, grief, and sadness. **Make sure that you understand that, as humans, we share the same capacity to feel or do anything any human has ever felt or done. <u>*Not*</u> understanding this is a key element of shame. Don't get caught by dualistic notions , e.g. *"I'm a good person." "My parents were good people."* Response: "So what, that doesn't mean you can't experience anger."**

6.) Antidote the shadow concerns by giving specific alternatives to the old behaviors. Get agreement. Anchor them. Anchor the urges to new behaviors. Don't think you have to eliminate the urge. Reframe it as a friendly reminder to practice using their power to make new choices to truly meet the underlying, newly honored needs that have a genuine right to be met. **Remember, underlying needs and secondary gain needs have to be addressed and tools for meeting them created, or the client will <u>not</u> let go of the problem because, right now, it is their only tool.**

7.) Walk them through 4-tuples of the new responses and test for agreement, reservations, or lack of clarity regarding purpose or outcome. *"Is there any reason why you would want to forget or forsake these new choices in the light of your new awareness of your honorable needs and ability to meet those needs? Is there any reason to be conned by the lies of those old behaviors?* **Make sure the resources can be accessed in any sensory channel, no matter where they "go." <u>Test for whole psyche access, in other words, any subpersonality can access the resources.</u>**

8.) I have found it very powerful to frame this lie in the image of a con-artist. *"Do you enjoy it when someone rips you off, tricks you? Have you ever been taken by a used car dealer, or boiler room salesman? Most people have some experience of being ripped off. Did you enjoy it? Do you see how this addiction is like a dishonest used car salesman, a con artist, tricking you out of your right to a high regard for yourself, tricking you out of behaving in ways that allow you to truly celebrate your precious life? Do you see how these inner urges and voices compelling you to act in these self-destructive ways are like a deceitful inner hypnotist, a con-man secretly laughing at you every time you follow its instructions?*

9.) Play with submodalities to ridicule the inner con, e.g. *"Change the voices to Donald Duck and listen to him try to push you around." "Since you know this stuff is a lie, imagine this con-man standing there trying to sell you a bill of goods as his nose gets longer and longer, his ears gets bigger and bigger, his voice starts changing into a bray.. that's right...and hair starts sprouting everywhere as his hands and feet turn into hooves, and shortly there is an astonished pathetic little donkey standing there in a ridiculous seam-splitting human outfit that can't possibly hang together anymore."* Walk them through such scenes until they have significant power for the client.

10.) Make it very clear to them that physical withdrawal can be a demanding test. Most people get caught and give up when the going gets tough because **they buy into the thought that if it feels bad, or hard, it *means* it's not working, or that they can't do it right.** Get this out in the open, anticipate it, and give them the recognition that they can just feel it and wait it out. It doesn't **mean** they have to buy into the old drama, and it doesn't **mean** they have to do those old addictive behaviors. **Just because they may *feel* like a failure doesn't mean they have to *act* like one.** Give them anchored responses to key them into relaxation and remembrance of their resources and their experience of their goodness to ride out such storms. Make it clear that they are just storms of emotional and physical agitation. They have a beginning, a middle, and an end, and they don't mean what the con-artist thoughts try to convince them that they mean. They don't have to react, or try to fix it. They can ride it out; they can practice relaxing into the energy of it, embrace it and stay with it until it takes them to a deeper level of themselves. This is a strength and capacity worth developing.

11.) Project learnings throughout the past, future pace, dissolve into light, bring them back.

12.) Utilize time perspectives:

   a) *"Sooner or later, you'll be able to do this...sooner or later everything comes to pass...think about it sooner or later, you decide, you'll be free."*

   b) Deathbed evaluation of present time circumstances and their outcomes. Deathbed evaluation of new choices. This is the ultimate outcome perspective. Utilizing outcome perspective, in general, is a powerful way to approach therapy: *"What do you want to have when you get up out of this chair today?" (if you could have whatever you desired?)* Insisting on constantly reorienting from an outcome perspective is a powerful way to create clarity and a shift to a more uplifted attitude. It naturally brings up relevant obstacles that need to be cleared.

   c) Pre-birth intentions. Viewing origination of trauma as future dissociated event, the whole life as future event from the point of time where you can evaluate and change intentions and attitudes. They will probably feel resistance, even anger. *"Go back before it, imagine determining 'X'...forget that it doesn't feel real...think about what it would do for you to have this new perspective."* Play with this even in pre-induction to soften the ground.

13.) Develop perspectives of all kinds. Brainstorm. It's O.K. to border on the ridiculous; its O.K. to cross the border if it helps break up the fixated problem dynamics! For example: undercut the euphemisms of the addictive trance:

   a) Getting "high," for a mother with young children, becomes reframed as "neglecting and abusing my children."

b) "Relaxation" from smoking, by clarifying the killing effects of the various toxins being ingested, gets reframed into a term I coined for cultivating one's own slow death: "encorpsment." "I'm relaxing myself," becomes, "I'm encorpsing myself."

Insert the new phrases into the situations where the old language was used. Act it out for them, walk them through it so the new language of <u>true effects and consequences</u> becomes an anchored replacement for the old comfortable euphemisms. Seek out these euphemisms in our thoughts and conversations. The egoic mind is constantly churning these out for all of us, not just for addicts. **What are some of yours?** This is a powerful awakening way to create aversion towards harmful behaviors.

The "awake" state is the only "state" without a reference point. If you are thinking, you're *always* inside a circle, a construct, a potential trap, a limited perspective, a point of view. All points of view have their shortcomings, their tendency to produce trance, to be dualistically fixated. Toxic shame is generated by very strong points of view. Addicts have very strong allegiance to their points of view, their beliefs. Changing their perspectives, their world view, is crucial to lasting change.

You are strongly urged to read Alice Miller's work and John Bradshaw's work, plus whatever else may attract you in the field of addiction and co-dependency to enhance your chances of being effective. **Their work is virtually a pre-requisite, in my opinion.**

◆ ◆ ◆

3. Anesthesia and Pain Relief

Do inductions to medium, or, better yet, to somnambulism. Use Elman numbers technique or progressive relaxation. Use a yardstick to measure depth. It has a moving pointer: 36 down to 25 is light trance, 24 to 13 is medium trance, 12 to 1 is deep. Explain that the unconscious will move the pointer down as you are giving suggestions to indicate proper depth. Get below 12 before you move out of relaxation and deepening. Utilize imagery conducive to producing numbness as well as suggestions that carry the prestige of physiological truth, i.e. facts about the mind's unconscious capacity to initiate, regulate and maintain incredibly complex and wondrous processes.

You may want to research obscure anecdotes that demonstrate the power of the mind over the body, e.g. old ladies lifting cars with one hand in a crisis, people curing themselves of cancer, etc., but make it a specific, vivid, interesting story. In most cases the specificity will be a more powerful inducement to them to do it, too. Of course, you build indirect suggestions into the story to that effect.

Now that you are in this deeply relaxed state...scan your whole sense of your being...physical...and emotional...and mental...to discover if there is any part of your being that needs clarification, or assistance of any kind in order to co-operate fully, *now*, in initiating and deepening and maintaining anesthesia, freedom from pain, in your body according to my suggestions.
((Pause/Share)) ((Clear any issues))

Good. As we begin, *now*, to demonstrate to you that your unconscious mind has the power to create beneficial anesthesia in any part of your body and will respond to your specific desire and direction to produce anesthesia anywhere in your body...for any beneficial purpose, including learning demonstrations...as we ask your unconscious mind to begin to initiate this process of anesthesia, *now*, in your right hand...remember that as we go along...if you sense any suggestion is needed by any part of your being to facilitate this process...remember that suggestion is immediately in full force and effect for your benefit, just as if I had said it...if anything at all is needed by way of suggestion for the benefit of any part of your being to participate fully and appropriately in this process of producing anesthesia...that suggestion is immediately in full force and effect for your benefit, just as if I had said it...

Now experience your right hand growing more and more numb.

((Note: some people may not have an experience of numbness to access. In such a case, create an understanding for them, e.g. affirming that the unconscious mind knows what it is and how to do it, and that it is a sleep-like state, etc.. This same thing can be a problem with the word 'relax.' Don't assume that it has an effective meaning for the client; you have to paint a picture.))

You may want to remember, sensations of numbness you have experienced in the past...kind of like an audio/visual set of instructions you are sending, *now*, to that control area of your unconscious mind...experience that happening, that request being delivered *now*, asking it to...*reproduce* and...*elaborate* and...*intensify* that kind of numbness in your right hand...and other kinds of sensations of numbness...that's right...all kinds of sensations of numbness coming together in your right hand...letting you know more and more quickly and easily, *now*, that your right hand is getting very, very numb...as you notice the kinds of sensations you have in your right hand letting you know that it is getting more and more numb now as if it were in a deep, *deep...deep* sleep...that's right...just your right hand...going into a deep...deep...deep sleep to demonstrate for your whole body how this wonderful power to be free of feeling and pain can be achieved and used for your benefit...*((Pause/Test:))* I'm going to touch your right hand now...if there is still some feeling in your right hand you will be able to tell me so, but, as you tell me, you will experience your right hand going numb to my touch, and each time I touch your right hand again, the numbness will double and triple until your right hand is totally numb and can't tell if I am touching it.

((When numbness is achieved:)) Now you are going to transfer that numbness from your right hand into your cheek. I want you to raise your right arm and hand slowly up to your right cheek...your hand may feel like a block of wood or an interesting kind of heaviness at the end of your arm that lets you know how to place it against your cheek, but I will help you if you need help...just let me know. *((Pause))* That's right...bringing that numb hand up to your cheek...*of course* *it's getting more and more numb the closer it gets to your cheek*...preparing to transfer all the numbness into your cheek quickly and easily as soon as it touches your cheek...*((touches cheek))* that's right...maybe you'll want to rub the numb hand up and down slightly to help the numbness drain into the cheek...experience your cheek becoming more and more numb as your hand transfers all the numbness...your hand waking up as your cheek goes to sleep into this beneficial state of numbness...you can let your arm and hand go back down to your side when all the numbness has drained out into your cheek...as you experience your arm and hand going down, your cheek becomes more and more numb...that's right..

((Option: therapist adds numbness with his own hand, suggesting in some way:)) I'm going to touch your cheek with my hand in a moment...my hand is full of numbness just like yours was...I'm going to transfer the numbness from my hand into your cheek by touching your cheek with my hand...you may not know when I'm doing this because your cheek is numb...or you may have some kind of other sense that it is happening...either way...when I touch your cheek, I will tell you I am touching your cheek, and just hearing me tell you that will cause you to notice your cheek going more and more numb and asleep. *((Touching))* That's right...more and more numb and asleep. Very good.

((Test. Pinch the cheek. Tell them you are going to pinch the numb cheek. Response))

Very good. Now I want you to think of some other part of your body that would benefit from or would simply like to experience this wonderful state of numbness. *((Share))*

Good. In a moment, I want you to raise your right hand back up to your cheek to transfer the numbness back into your right hand, because this time we are going to use your right hand to transfer the numbness, just like we did before...*of course, your right hand begins to get numb as soon as you begin raising it towards your cheek and this beginning numbness cause all the numbness in your cheek to quickly and easily drain back into your right hand.* So go ahead now, raise it up...getting more and more numb as it approaches your cheek...good *((Pause))*

Now place your hand _____ *((wherever. Note: if it is inaccessible to the hand you would give suggestions to move it mentally in some interesting way – think about how you would do that.))* Experience the numbness saturating _____ just like it did your cheek. *((Pause/Share))* Good, now we'll let this part enjoy the numbness for a moment...deriving all the rest and rejuvenation it brings with it...*((Pause))* O.K. Now it's time to put the numbness back in your cheek.

((Repeat the process in the same way you did transferring it into the hand and then into the cheek; bring the hand and arm down to the side))

Now that the numbness is back in your cheek, ask your unconscious mind to keep it there for the rest of this session.

((Option: Go to closing with post hypnotic suggestion or do the following:)) I'm going to be giving you some other suggestions to help you use this new learning for your own benefit from now on into your future...as I do, your

cheek will remain numb and *increase* its numbness as the sound of my voice delivers these other instructions. I want you to make sure all the numbness has left your right hand...and...as you do...your cheek will get more numb...that's right. *((Pause/Share))*

Good...now I'm going to explain how you can easily in the future use this numbness anytime you want to remove any *unnecessary* pain anywhere in your body...

((Direct their attention to appreciate the deeply relaxed state they have achieved. Explain that it is a learning that is now in their memory banks, and that you are going to give them a signal to use to direct their unconscious mind to activate this learning quickly and easily. Give them the Deeply Relax finger drop to come back to this state, relaxing just as completely with their hand getting just as numb as it did before. Repeat, then practice as you did with Deeply Relax, noting that, as they go in and out of trance practicing Deeply Relax with their hand going numb, their cheek will maintain its constant state of numbness when they are in and out of trance during this session only unless they wish otherwise.))

((Closing:)) Give suggestions to bring them back to normal waking consciousness, with their cheek staying numb for five minutes after their back to normal waking consciousness.

◆ ◆ ◆

4. Review:
Submodalities, Time Structures, and Tonglen

We live in our minds, not in the world.

The body and all our experience of the world, the outer, is still in the Mind, our Mind. The egoic 'mind' thinks differently. It's inside and separate from the outside. Contemplate the psyche models of Phase II to sharpen your awareness of your egoic mental processes of separating and projecting, but don't think of them as "yours." **To experience yourself as Awake Mind containing both inner and outer is to discover the beginning of True Magic and unbiased Love.**

Cultivate the notion of egoic minding as an impersonal infection that has virtually everyone in its grasp at some level of "feverish delirium" blocking the experience of life _as_ Awake Mind. This will help you separate your brothers and sisters, whom you can love and appreciate within the realm of True Magic, from their delirious behaviors, which you can constructively criticize.

I have no doubt you will discover the models' accuracy and practical application in aiding you to *"step out from"*, to *"wake up out of"* the trance logic of egoic mind.

Submodalities

'Submodality' is an NLP term that refers to the components we have available to construct and order our inner representations of our experience. (PII, pp.25-27) By this time, I hope you have begun to understand how:

1.) inner sensory components [seeing, feeling, etc.],

2.) association & dissociation,

3.) color & black and white,

4.) motion & stills [as in pictures],

5.) location in space, & time

6.) backgrounds & boundaries,

7.) textures & tonality,

8.) speed: rate of change (fast/slow, remember Buddha: Everything changes),

9.) language - syntax, grammar, inflection, etc., (PI, p.26ff., PII, p. 27ff.),

10.) and what else?(think about it!), carry the power of trance/delusion/confusion of our experience, in our inner/outer world.

I hope you have begun to develop an understanding of how to be curious (developing simple awareness and well-formulated questions; PII, p.27ff., PIII, adapting subpersonality dialoguing techniques) about submodality structures in your own states and experiences as well as your clients. And I hope you have begun to play with your own submodalities in order to change your experience in beneficial ways.

Do you see how all the techniques we are learning are simply examples of ways to affect submodality structure and therefore change the trance dynamics (and hopefully even spark wakefulness)?

When you understand this, you can be endlessly creative with technique in the most powerful way, spontaneously, because you will have grasped the nature of communication, experience and trance structure. Then you will never be afraid of encountering an 'unknown' challenge.

It can be a disturbing thought to regard mind as theater. Some students and clients may resist using techniques involving visualization, imagination, notions of Inner Guides, etc. because "something" in them, in their experience, knows there is genuineness, sacredness, real contact: intimacy. They react to these tools as deceptions, forgetting that when they are suffering, they are living in their own self-created deceptions, throwing away sacredness in the very way they fear these therapeutic devices may make them settle for self-deception. To the contrary, these theatrical deceptions are meant to dissolve and break the density of their pre-existing prison of egoic trance deceptions.

Reactive Model Dynamics - Submodality Mechanics

Referring to the reactive model (PII, p. 23), the egoic display is what the client brings to us as dilemma (also what we bring to ourselves as our own dilemmas). It is theater, and it is fear-based. Therefore any fear, including the fear of being deceived is not totally an ally. The primordial pulse of warning energy may be an ally, alerting us to boundary violation, but, by the time it reaches our "conscious" mind, it is fully clothed (5th skandha) in a role of defined notions of deception which reinforce the notion of being a victim to be deceived. We have to be alert; we have to look in two directions at once, inside & outside, to ward off deception.

Where is the sacred, genuine contact?

Referring to the reactive model, it is experienced when the egoic display is shut down, even for a moment. All that is left is self-existing sacredness, genuineness, intimacy of our True Being, always effortlessly there! The problem is that when egoic mind comes back on line, it has a memory impression of the sacred, but can only relate to it egoically, i.e., it regards it as:

1.) a separate object,

2.) something it did, therefore as something to create again or recapture,

3.) something to seize and solidify around a symbol (anchor) - person, place or thing, physical or mental

4.) something requiring great effort and strategizing,

5.) something that is missing in the meantime, and

6.) therefore, as a longing that generates despair, pain, motivation, etc. (5 skandhas, 3 malas, 6 realms, 5 poisons - not all bad because these things, in the end, cause us to make the effort to dissolve egoic mind).

When egoic display is "on" even your best friend, pure lover, is only a mental image. There is no real contact. But in the next moment the egoic display can go off; intimacy is felt. It is pointless to say between the people, because in this moment there is only one person. Egoic mind flashes back on with a memory impression of pure being, looks around for its source - Wham! *"It's you, my dearest, I can't live without you, I don't feel alive without you!"* Egoic mind fixates a source, assumes causal relationships, and puts all its passion into holding the object. Of course, since this is all egoic misperception, it is all an internal theatrical display doomed to failure and pain, because there is no real contact with the real objectless source "object" - True Being.

In a healthy love relationship, the blessing of many moments of grace, contact, respect, intimacy, i.e., egoic display "off", smooth out the effects of egoic display "on." Mature individuals have an intuition of Self (faith, humble self-esteem) that allows them to see the transparency of egoic display. The egoic "stuff" is workable because generosity and love infiltrate it through a very porous boundary from True Being - a felt sense of well-being and tolerance. The fear and delusion that egoic display is capable of generating between good friends/lovers, is so low that even when it comes "on", it is simply a reminder of TrueConnection/Love and therefore is regarded as very workable, no threat, and met with warm-hearted humor.

Addictive, abusive relationships of great passion, or substance addictions of great "passion" are, by contrast, very unfortunate. The boundary is not porous. The con of fear and delusion generated is very high. Thus, a "peak" experience of intimacy, peace, etc. creates a memory impression in the egoic display that is an extreme highlight in an arena of desolation. The egoic mind's sense of inherent desperation and emptiness is harshly irritated by this highlight, causing it to obsess in all manner of familiar violent and destructive ways in its attempt to return to the EXPERIENCE for relief. Since the boundary is "hard," (i.e., an unconscious, on-going, moment by moment, fear-based, willful rejection of light due to misperceiving it as a threat), love, patience, generosity, and intelligent inspirations to diffuse egoic trance in a healthy manner cannot infiltrate. The felt sense of well-being and tolerance is absent. Egoic mind's only alternative is some form of assault to attempt to tear a hole in the wall. This can be done. Egoic mind can intensify its negativity to such an extreme that it exhausts itself for a time - one pops through to experience some aspect of True Being. But it eventually takes an unacceptably destructive toll, physically and psychologically, returning more and more diminished "pay-offs" leading to more extreme attempts which, if not mitigated, end in annihilation.

This tragedy is internal theater acted out to the extreme. We haven't a clue that we are at cause, that we set the requirements for shutting grace/intimacy down moment by moment according to our attachments (5 poisons - building egoic world view - *"This is what is happening!"*) We do choose moment by moment to associate into egoic display, or to release it and rest in always-given TrueBeing - relax and breathe.

With our tools, we can construct new submodality displays.

All the players, friends and enemies alike, need to be loved and saved, because they are merely energy clones, our energy, of people of the past. Even if "they" are present, they are not who they WERE IN THE PAST, NOW, in our minds. The clones are the problem, not the outer people. Our internal clones, ourself dressed up as someone else, keep us anchored in limiting notions of self and limiting responses - not the external people. The truth of this is what allows therapy, or any change, to work. If it wasn't true, you couldn't change. Because it is true, you can change anything, including the past. Remember the past is a package of perceptions, misperceptions, arbitrary c/e assumptions, opinions, prejudices, etc. Therefore, you can change its **meaning** which was supporting a false notion of self, (praise, blame, and shame: *"you dumb jerk, you spilled the milk"*), without denying the **factual occurrence,** (the milk spilled), which, if denied, would be a form of brainwashing, (the milk didn't spill).

Time structures: *Timelines, Timepathways, Lifestreams, Time Continuums*

Time is entirely a trance state. If you feel you are living in time, and we all do, <u>most of the time</u>, you are living in a trance in your mind. To experience being in timelessness, the trances of the skandhas have to stop. Then you see clearly without reactive mind interference. Movement in timelessness, that is what is marked to create the notion of time. To lose the feeling of timelessness with movement, which is very spacious, we identify emotionally with the "passage" of time because it is anchored to notions of getting things done that matter in proving our worthiness - so **time is a shame issue.**

Movement in timelessness is real. It is truly being present, not being in the present which is a time notion hooked to past and future. If you are awake, you can deal with movement, i.e. change, the truth of suffering, the truth that everything changes, dies. You keep awareness of space and workability.

Dealing with movement looks like dealing with time.

The difference is that the person dealing with movement is relaxed, experiencing bodily presence and spaciousness, a felt sense of timelessness, and almost anyone feels the Presence of someone in this state. It may be threatening to egoic minding, and therefore quickly blocked or avoided.

Dealing with time is to be in a trance of self-identity.

Something is at stake. How could something be at stake if you had all the time in the world? There is bodily contraction, stress, pressure, all trance phenomena: code words for fear. No feeling of timelessness, no sense of spaciousness, no humor. The most extreme forms of compression are trauma and phobia, and these are radically and quickly affected by playing with time and space, and perspective: submodality variables.

Time and Space variables? Consider:

Fear is the distance in time between egoic consciousness and Awake consciousness. [True Being or Source consciousness]

Mass is an illusion.

We know scientifically if we remove the space from our body, we would be smaller than a grain of sand. Size, mass, is an illusion of electromagnetic fields.

Past emotional trauma is an electrical storm in the space of the timeless presence of our Being.

The trance quality produces and maintains the effect of time-displacement and separation. Therapeutically, theatrically, each of us plays with time and space to affect the meaning of experience in relation to the one creating. We then forget, as creator, and then get stuck experiencing the limited, prejudiced meaning of our creation.

A primary *motivation* at the root of <u>meaning</u> generation and maintenance is to save the injured one, to sort out what happened and why, to make it better.

A primary *belief* at the root of <u>meaning</u> generation and maintenance is that <u>*re-experiencing the trauma is necessary to acquiring the learnings*</u> from a constant rehash of the events.

Since the <u>*motivation is misguided*</u> because the past and that person of the past are over with, and since the <u>*belief is erroneous*</u> because you don't need to keep injecting your system with shock in order to contemplate and gain understandings, in fact <u>the shock treatments inhibit learning and insure on-going bewilderment</u>, the whole process is futile.

All our learnings in this course are designed to facilitate the shifting of **meaning** of all trance states ("present," past, & past projected into the future: all chronically regressed states). Actually, it is to eliminate their shame generating, shock generating meaning so wakefulness and real learning and growth can occur. In wakefulness there is no egoic ascribing of meaning to phenomena; phenomena simply speak to us of their uniqueness, their momentariness, and hence their poignancy and sacredness. We learn about the movement of life, but not about a particular shamed individual, isolated and unredeemable.

Since all problems are of the past, all problems are of **Time.** Did you notice?

Past, Future, and Present are trance states in our egoic minding display.

All techniques therefore are techniques in the realm of regression.

ALL TIME STRUCTURE TECHNIQUES ARE SIMPLY REGRESSION or PROGRESSION METAPHORS. APPLIED PROPERLY, THEY ARE POWERFULLY EFFECTIVE TOOLS TO ACCESS RESOURCES, ALTER SUBMODALITY DYNAMICS, AND GENERALIZE LEARNINGS.

Regarding the generalization of learnings, *it is very important to ask the conscious mind to notice it has been and is learning by the end of a session, and anywhere in the midst of a session where it might be appropriate.* This is built into the scripts. If the conscious mind isn't told to notice, it might not, and therefore, it might persist in thoughts that it can't and isn't learning. These techniques release the power of innate intelligence to learn rapidly, even instantaneously. You will come up against the conscious doubt and resistance that you are expecting too much of clients too fast. You need to help them have the experience of learning happening, and then to point it out to them. For example, the phobia cure works in 6 - 40 minutes, whereas standard psychological dogma says it takes 7 -10 years of therapy.

Generalization of learnings is built into the end of every script of this course, but *using the theatrical device of timelines is an enchanting way of getting the conscious mind to participate and to notice that it is learning.* **Like any other technique, it is enhanced by repetition and vividness, (emotional impact).** Running a client through their timeline more than once with their new resources causes it to happen each time more easily and more powerfully. Why? The same with any learning, the more you do it, the more parts of you participate, and repetition causes the learnings to be more powerful. Why? Same as above, more of the parts are "getting it". Review: in submodality sensory language: always anchor a desired *kinesthetic*, i.e. feeling, component to the *vision* of your outcome state. You see it, you feel good about it; that creates movement towards the outcome state. Do you understand that this is another way of talking about generating emotional impact? Notice it gives you specific guidelines about **how** to generate emotional impact.

We unconsciously store events in time in some order. How can you tell what happened yesterday vs. 3 days ago? Think about it. Positing timelines is one way to elicit a person's storage style, or to suggest one. It is important to note that one can be flexible, and that even if they weren't doing it in some way until you suggested it, they still get the benefit of learning to play with their mind in this way:

1.) Ask client: if their past had a direction, what direction would it be? Please point.

2.) Same re:future.

People may typically point behind for past, and in front for future. They may also point up or down , at angles, or have the past displayed in front of them so they can't see the future, like a peacock turned to look at its tail. (Get him to turn around.) Experience may be stored on cards, like a deck of cards, and be in a neat order, or thrown all over the place in a fragmented array.

It is interesting to ask a large number of clients to point to their past and future to experience the varied responses.

Time Structure Illustrations

Everything is situated **somewhere, sometime** in inner psychic space. Everything has a space and time location that seems to be a key factor in the power any given thing has to affect us.

A most important point is that *we can do this ordering process any way we want to* at different times as it suits our needs since it does affect one's state. **Now we know about it, now it is something we are considering consciously. Now that we have a new submodality toy to play with--instead of being unconsciously a victim of time--experiment.**

How you have time displayed directly affects your ability to approximate Presence Itself, and your ability to function effectively. The approximation is called "being in the present."

For example, it has been found that people who are good planners are dissociated from their timeline and have it laid out in front of them just below eye level from left to right. This makes sense. They can see the whole thing in order to lay out their plans. But to be stuck with this structure unconsciously makes it difficult to be spontaneous and enjoy life.

People who are spontaneous and active generally are on their timeline in the present with the past behind and the future in front. They may know how to have a great time, but their lives are chaotic because they can't plan.

In this example, it is a great learning to give these people the awareness that they have the flexibility to switch structures as the situation demands. Time to go to a party? Get on your timeline, put the past behind you, and the future in front of you. Time to plan a project? Get off the timeline and lay it out in front of you where you can look at it objectively and make your planning decisions.

Want to do a regression? Float up above the timeline and float back to where you want to go. If it's trauma, float up as high as you need to, to feel safe enough to see the events **down there** happening to **who you used to be**. If necessary, float back behind the events, i.e. into the past before they ever happened, turn around and see them up there in the future, noticing you can also see all the future after the event up to real present time. Therefore you know the **one who you used to be** *is going to survive, is surviving as you, now. What does that suggest about the fear/trauma shock injections?*

What resources would you like her to have with her to move through these events and to move on into her future?

Playing with this returns to the person a significant aspect of **being at cause**. One course graduate shared that she had played with this with a friend by phone, simply having her float around to different locations relative to a disturbing experience. At one point the person exclaimed, **"Oh, I just got that I have control over this!"** Enough said.

Another client that I had float back in time before she was "anyone" and send healing energy forward throughout the timeline exclaimed, *"This is really healing, this is really happening for real."* I also had her float forward in time past being anyone she would ever be, and send the healing back. She thought we were "just" pretending. *We were pretending,* but **when you pretend with pretense in a certain way, when you imagine in accordance with the truth of Inherent Purity, you get reality - the release of real healing reorganizing intelligence.**

When you go back before you were anyone, and forward after you were everyone you're going to be, where do you go?

You go **here, now**!

Who is **here, now** once you get **here, now** by detaching from anyone you have been or will be, i.e.,. you've dropped all the trance identities?

I-don't-know-who-I-am Awareness/Intelligence is **here, now** once you've done that. True Being awareness is **here/now**, and that is the source of all healing loving energy, and that is how she suddenly found herself experiencing real healing by pretending. This is a wonderful way of getting someone to experience what in the East is called Witness Consciousness, which is an aspect of True Being: Awake, not identified with any small self trance state - the timeless space of Love.

*"An intersection of the timeless with time, is an occupation for the saint.
But no occupation either, but a lifetime given and taken in love."* --T.S. Eliot

This is the secret, in my opinion, of timeline. The "travel" implies disidentification with selves rooted in time, so the only One left is Timeless Self with True Healing Qualities. You can use the metaphor as directed in the scripts and the examples above to "go" to significant times safely and effectively to do work, and you can go beyond time to **Now** to get a true taste of Being.

There is also a specific structure, the Phobia/Trauma Cure, that I believe was stumbled upon through playful experimentation that provides fast healing for phobias and all classes of trauma. As we go through the steps of these processes, it should be clear that the magic of these procedures is the elegant way in which they directly and indirectly communicate to the conscious and unconscious minds: **"Dissociate!"**

Trauma and phobia are addictions to highly charged negative experience. They illustrate the tendency of contracted egoic consciousness to be fixated by intensity regardless of its quality, positive or negative. Remember the unconscious judges level of reality by the vividness of the stimulation.

Egoic contracted consciousness also seeks intensity, positive and negative, with a romantic fervor idealizing the quest as an exalted condition and awareness above that of the herd of the rest of sleeping humanity. In those individuals thus driven, this not so subtle prideful attitude overlooks the fact that all egoic states share a certain deadness because of the split from a true experience of Being. It doesn't really matter if they are sleepwalking and resigned, or "intensely" driven to seek pleasure, thrills, anger, danger, or whatever. Both categories are reactive strategies for dealing with the core unconscious toxic shame/pain split from True Being.

Phobias can be viewed as states of strongly anchored bonds to a specific stimulus. This specific stimulus: elevators, heights, snakes, etc., is held in (un)consciousness as itself without being projected or generalized. In other words, it is only triggered by the presence, real or imagined, of the specific stimulus.

Trauma is more complex in that it is generalized and projected more widely in various contexts, and therefore is more likely to be "on" most of the time, thus exhibiting (i.e. it is acted out) as compulsion or addiction. It is still a strongly anchored state, but it is anchored to a generalized class of experience, even though the initial trauma may have been specific. For example, someone traumatized in a war may be triggered into fight or flight mode by being bumped by anyone at anytime in any setting. (Although I guess you could look at it as being a phobia of being bumped.) It is less discriminating in its requirement as to the character of the trigger. Because it is more generalized and all pervasive, it also takes on the character of a ritual.

An anchored state is an associated state. So, from a process point of view, the objective in treating a trauma or phobia is to get the client to dissociate from the charged stimulus, thus breaking the anchor. Again, this is always the objective in therapy work, to reorient the client in such a way that they associate with what it is appropriate to associate with, True Being, and to dissociate from what it is inappropriate to associate with, egoic, shamed states of self-image (identity trances). Remember, you don't so much have to work at connecting with True Being. Rather, as you disconnect from the identity trances, True Being emerges.

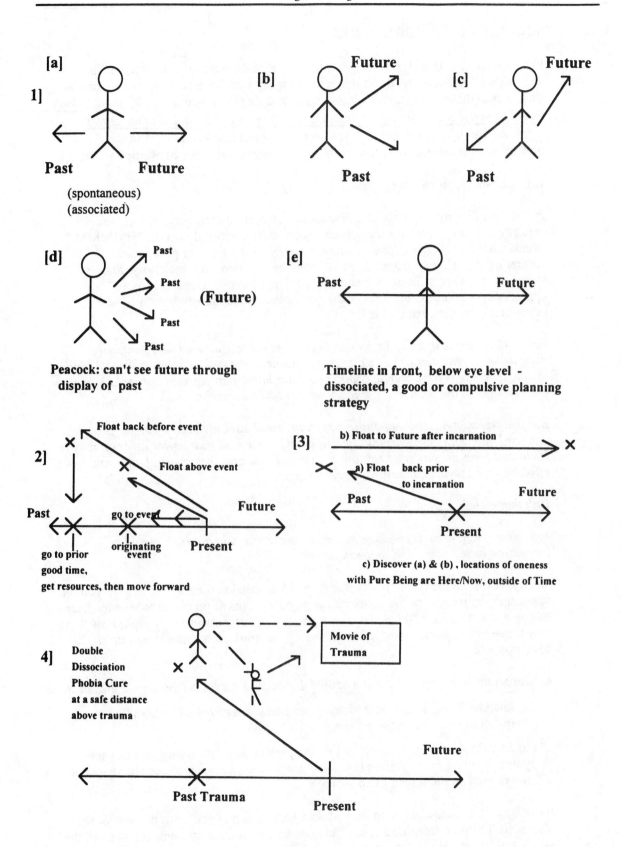

[a]

1]

Past   Future

(spontaneous)
(associated)

[b]

Future

Past

[c]

Future

Past

[d]

Past

Past

(Future)

Past

Past

Peacock: can't see future through
display of past

[e]

Past   Future

Timeline in front, below eye level -
dissociated, a good or compulsive planning
strategy

2]

Float back before event

Float above event

Past
go to event

go to prior
good time,
get resources, then move forward

originating
event

Present

Future

[3]

b) Float to Future after incarnation

a) Float   back prior
to incarnation

Past   Future

Present

c) Discover (a) & (b) , locations of oneness
with Pure Being are Here/Now, outside of Time

4]

**Double
Dissociation
Phobia Cure
at a safe distance
above trauma**

Movie of
Trauma

Future

Past Trauma

Present

The Miraculous Fast Phobia Cure

I believe Richard Bandler, co-originator of NLP first devised this technique. That such a simple process can do so much for so many who have suffered for so long is truly extraordinary. As you learn these steps to doing the process "by the book." *don't forget to notice the underlying principles that have been assembled to make this work*. **As you learn *to recognize*, and *to think* about applications of these underlying principles, you, too, may create a powerful piece of change work.**

1. Establish Rapport - always the first step, right?!?

2. Reframe the problem state as a demonstration of their creativity, power, and capacity to learn. Watch for the contemplative shift that should occur. "HMMMM." (Remember discussions of this in subpersonality work? Finding pure intent, separating the behavior from the intent, noticing all the power, creativity, and learnings that were utilized to create the problem behavior. Generate a new appreciation of these in the light of the pure intent to inspire generation of new beneficial behaviors, remember?)

E.g., *"Most people learn to be phobic in just one experience that was genuinely dangerous, or was perceived as dangerous. Generating such a quick, powerful, and lasting learning is a wonderful capacity of your mind, that you can appreciate, now, even though, in this instance, the learning has had its drawbacks.*

But you can appreciate that your unconscious mind has only been trying to protect you, and that, with new learnings, it will be able to use all that power and capacity to learn and generate powerful responses to reevaluate and create even better and more effective and appropriate protective responses.

Isn't that right?

Yes, all we want to do is enhance its ability to care for you appropriately by increasing its learnings and understandings."

3. Trigger the phobic reaction - **partially**. The purpose in doing this is to give you the opportunity to recognize and calibrate the physical signs of phobic response for later testing and evaluation: *"What makes you phobic? What if it were here right now?"* As they move into it, break state: tell them to stop imagining that, stand them up if necessary, etc.

4. Instruct them in the creation of a <u>double</u> dissociated state. Use the movie theater model:

a) imagine sitting in a theater looking at a blank screen (or a black and white snapshot of yourself on the screen.)

b) now float out of your body up into the projection booth where you can see yourself sitting in the theater seat *down there*, and you can also see the snapshot of yourself on the screen *out over there*.

It can be helpful to anchor them in the booth so they don't "pop" into the seat or the screen. Tell them to imagine a clear Plexiglas barrier in front of them. It lets in all the sights and sounds. Have them put their hands on it and feel it while they watch what happens next.

5. Instruct them to pick a time when they had the phobia - the first, the worst, or a recent time.

   a) Tell them to run a black and white movie of the event on the movie screen.

   b) Tell them to watch the whole event starting **before** the beginning of the phobic response through to **after** the end of it when they felt better. Have it be a B/W movie with sound and running at normal speed.

   c) Tell them to watch that <u>younger</u> self <u>over there</u> going through the experience. Watch it as a detached observer, even as a stranger. As needed, emphasize they are safe in the booth, feeling the glass with their hands and also noticing the other self in the theater seat watching - it's just a movie.

   d) Instruct them to run the movie to the end of the situation and stop the film on the last frame, like a snapshot, and to tell you when they have done that.

6. Instruct them to leave the booth and to float into the "you" in the still picture on the screen. When you're fully there, run the movie backwards, in color, in about 2 seconds (make a sound indicating this -- *"Just run it back real fast...shooouuup!"*), all the way back to the beginning. O.K. Do it.

7. When they indicate they have done it, test. Ask again a question that would have elicited the phobic response. *"Here comes a snake slithering by your chair."* Calibrate their response. If there still is a phobic response, check with them about how they ran the process. Take them back through it, making sure they do it correctly (Steps 4-6). Repeat as necessary.

8. Ecology check. Discuss with them the need to learn about those situations, to reevaluate them, now that the fear response is gone, to determine appropriate responses under those conditions. Encourage them to carefully take their time as appropriate.

Technically, utilizing the phobia cure for trauma is simply a matter of combining it with regression [using timeline or any other regression theatrics]. Take client back to the incident but floating safely above it, and run phobia theater floating over the incident at this safe distance, running a movie of the incident.

Triple Dissociation Phobia/Trauma Cure

The phobia cure is brilliantly simple and powerful in its rapid effects. To some, it seems so "pat" that one could just tell a person to follow the instructions and that would be that. Indeed, for some phobias it goes very quickly, 2-3 minutes, and you're done! With trauma clients in particular this will not be the case. They will make demands on your skill and artistry to help them actually follow the instructions, from visualizing the scene and deciding upon its content, to making it possible for them to stay dissociated through the entire viewing. It is important to emphasize that rapport skills are needed to use it successfully.

I have had clients tell me that they have done this process on their own and with therapists without good results. The results we subsequently got were very beneficial. It is not my job to ferret out the mistakes of others, so I don't know what happened in those other attempts. I strongly suspect the ineffectiveness had to do with rapport issues with their therapist, and with the need for convincing theatrical creative elements that they couldn't provide on their own from following the process in a book, and that the therapist also didn't provide. I want to stress again the importance of understanding underlying principles versus just memorizing technique. Such understanding allows you to improvise appropriately when you have a client that blocks the expected efficacy of a technique.

This happened with the phobia cure in a training I was doing. One subject said her trauma was so severe she couldn't do the movie, even from the projection booth. All the students were stumped about what to do. Understanding that the underlying principle is dissociation, I immediately came up with a <u>new technique</u>! The Triple Dissociation Phobia/Trauma Cure.

1)I had the client sit in a new chair to the side of the chair she had been in, "in the booth."

2)I told her she could not see the movie screen (e.g., a wall to block her view) and didn't need to know what the other "her" was about to <u>successfully</u> view.

3)I told her she was clearly not the "her" she was watching in the booth who was about to view the movie and <u>successfully</u> follow all the other steps.

4)I told her the "her" in the booth, and in the seat below, were going to do the process and watch that movie that needed to be watched, but that she would not know its contents, but, perhaps, if she had a sense of it, that was O.K..

5)She was to give her unconscious permission for the contents of the trauma, which she sensed but did not know, to be made accessible to the other "hers" so they could do the process.

6)She was to carefully watch the "her" in the booth to notice changes in her state as she repeatedly did the process successfully. She was to decide if she wanted those changes for herself.

7) I then took the "her" in the booth through the process, asking the client to tell me when "she" had finished each step. At the end, I asked her to comment on how "she" looked and to sense "her" state, and determine if it was desirable. I repeated the process with "her" twice more with her watching, sensing, and letting me know when "she" finished each step.

8) After running the process several times, when it looked and seemed to her like the "her" in the booth was very resourceful and free, I invited her to step into that "her" and absorb and claim all the new resources and freedom. She did it and it worked. Conclusion: At a certain point, the other her was not intimidated by the content of the movie, and she was able to step in and run through the steps of the phobia/trauma cure herself. This is the test of effectiveness.

Remember, the structure of experience is theatrical. Stay creative and experiment with the staging. And remember Einstein's criteria for solutions: **They should be as simple as possible, _but no simpler._**

Subpersonality Manual Integration (CF. NLP Visual Squash)

1) Sit with palms up on knees or chair arms.

2) Focus on a conflict. (part vs. part) Visualize a subpersonality on one palm. Dialogue to get to positive intent.

3) Ask it to observe as you call forth the conflicting subpersonality.

4) Visualize second subpersonality on your other palm. Dialogue to get positive intent. {Positive intents should reveal common intent which will be the basis for their reason to integrate. Continue to dialogue until you get such a formulation.}

5) Ask them to notice they share the same intent. Ask the parts to come together, pooling their power, learnings and resources **as the client's unconscious mind begins moving their hands together,** *only as fast as this integration can occur appropriately, keeping everything that is truly of value, releasing everything that is unnecessary.*

6) When their hands to come together: "*Experience this new integrated part of yourself, more powerfully resourceful for you than the sum of the separate parts, and bring it into your body with your hands, wherever appropriate.*"

7) Test. Share.

This process is a quick easy way to disperse inner turmoil. It streamlines very quickly with repetition to the point where you can simply visualize your hands holding the parts & going through the steps, even while driving. It can streamline so that just noticing and identifying the conflicting parts triggers a synthesis and resolution.

Tonglen

Exchanging Self for Others - The process of egoic mind's final dissolution - the Holy Secret

At this point, I hope that you have some sense of conviction in True Being which underlies the transpersonal approach to the techniques of this course. The power and possibility of rapid change demonstrated by the techniques hints at the power of our innate intelligence to produce rapid radical change in the direction of liberation from suffering.

The phobia cure, in particular highlights how powerful, easy, and enjoyable change can be when one knows what to deal with, knows **what** *ideas* to communicate (remember Erickson? "Hypnosis is the communication of **ideas**.").

In particular, it demonstrates how much power and intelligence gets bound up by inappropriate association/identification and inappropriate dissociation/misidentification of self.

This is the core fact that is highlighted. How powerfully contracted, bound, and solidified our energy and intelligence can get around an *idea* **of self** which is nothing more than a bundle of associations with and dissociations from **objects**: *physical, emotional, and/or mental objects.*

The whole process is a product of thought in *initiation and substance*, (i.e., thought creates it, and thought creates it out of thought. There is nothing there but thought.)

The following process, Tonglen, is taken from the Buddhist tradition. Its principles are known in all traditions. It is a demonstration of process that dissolves the misidentification with false notions of self (notions being nothing but thoughts) completely, if sincerely practiced and cultivated.

There are many variations in presentation, but the essential form and structure are the same. Personally, I have learned and practiced it in several formats with my various teachers. What I present here follows very closely the directions found in Sogyal Rinpoche's book, The Tibetan Book of Living and Dying. **I urge you to read this book, it's on your recommended reading list.**

A word to those who feel wary thoughts stirring about this being "religion." In my opinion, this is not religion. It is communication free of confusion. For example, Christianity, and most major and minor "religions" I know of, subscribe to the 2 primary Commandments:

1) Love God with your whole heart and mind, and

2) Love your neighbor as you love yourself.

To love with all your heart and mind means to recognise and to experience self-existing oneness with God. That's what you recognise and experience when you love anything with your whole heart and mind. The same is perhaps more obvious with loving thy neighbor as thyself. Again it means to experience the self-exisitng oneness. 'Self-existing' meaning it's already there; you don't have to make it or fake it - relax into it. This is the Sun of Pure Being/True Self.

One thing that makes religion dysfunctional and unattractive to many is that these commandments have been misunderstood. They have been taken as **"shoulds."** This is what you **should feel**, and this is what you **should be like**, in other words, they are taken as **moral statements**, reflections on an idea of self that needs to struggle free of being "bad" and succeed at being "good," and at having the proper set of thoughts and feelings.

This struggle is watched over by an idea-of-God. Because it is egoically centered: idea-of-self struggling and separated, from idea-of-God, the notion of "shoulds" quickly cause the process to degenerate into a game of **"SUCK UP"** (a technical term).

Idea-of-self futilely trying to live up to these "shoulds" as morally absolute statements in order to SUCK UP to idea-of-God for redemption. The shadow side is, of course, shame, resentment, and frustration. No wonder people are wary of religion!

These commandments are not moral statements. They are not about being good. They are about what works in a very matter-of-fact way. They are titles to operating instructions showing you how to use thought to unravel the egoic mess created by thought. But when they became morals, emotionally charged instead of matters of fact, they stopped being headings in the instruction manual and they became absolutes and the instructions got thrown away. Without the actual instructions you are stuck with faking it. Posturing, grunting, and groaning, and grimacing to keep on a happy face - and there is a lot at stake.

Since Buddhism is a non-theistic "religion," it is harder to set up the "SUCK UP" game. There is no idea-of-god there to suck up to. Don't be fooled, however, egoic mind does find a way! It is easier to keep clear that the game is not about being a good boy or girl. It's about getting clear of confusion, no shame, no blame.

Tonglen, exchanging self for others, is the instruction guide to realizing the commandments effortlessly: no posturing, no good boy/good girl pose necessary. All that is necessary is to do the steps no matter what you think or feel about yourself or anything else. Just do it and experience what happens.

1) Take a comfortable position and posture. Breathe easily and relax. Extend your awareness into the space around you and clear it of disturbance, lighten it up easily in your imagination. Want it to happen.

2) Give your allegiance to the idea of Pure being - with your **Intellect**. *No faking of feeling or belief necessary.* Remind yourself of Scientific Fact to hook into it. We know now that everything is just a manifestation of one indestructible energy and that there is no such thing as a "thing": quantum physics. From this idea of one energy follows the entire logic of the process as a challenge to egoic logic which believes in solid "things." The primary solid thing being ME! ME! ME!

3) Let yourself relax and expand into this notion of Oneness by dissociating from all egoic thoughts and feelings as they arise. Remember, dissociation doesn't means egoic "stuff' goes away. It doesn't means trying to make it go away or pretending it isn't there. It means you just hold on to the thought, "I am not this" or simply "not this" in response to every thought feeling, experience that arises moment by moment. Let it be there, just don't be it.

4) From the perspective of being the True Being, welcome the presence of your egoic self completely in all its facets. Since you are pure indestructible being and this egoic self is a mere tiny momentary display in the expansive infinity of your True Being, you can easily afford to open to it with caring energy.

5) As you breathe in, imagine breathing in all its suffering, anger, confusion, greed, pride, etc. Breathing it in willingly. You breathe it in, and it is immediately transmuted into light and pure loving healing energy which you breathe into the egoic self when you exhale. Just do this for a while as you breathe. Breathing in all the impurities, exhaling pure healing energy, thinking thoughts of the very best wishes for your "self" to be truly perfectly happy forever. If fear or reluctance arises, don't identify with it. Recognize it is an aspect of egoic self "over there" coming into awareness and breathe it in as an impurity. As you do this, the feeling that may arise is one of expansiveness and relaxation and perhaps much more. The key is to remember **not** to identify with anything that comes up, but to remember it is an egoic impurity. You breathe it in, and breathe out pure healing energy when you exhale.

6) Now imagine a loved one present and, without reservation, breathe in all their obstacles, wanting the highest for them. Breathe out pure healing loving energy filling them completely. Make it real, feel it happening. (Imagine and pretend.)

7) As you get the hang of it, bring more loved ones into your awareness, then friends and acquaintances, then strangers. Start locally with your neighbors, your town and/or city. Keep expanding. Include your state & country, then the whole world. Include all beings as you realize all beings want the same happiness and freedom from suffering. Open more and more breathing in the impurities of all, remembering resistance, fear, & thoughts that it's too big for you are not your thoughts but manifestations of egoic impurities and suffering. Relax, open more and breathe them in. Breathe out pure healing loving energy more and more vividly on each exhale. Expand your awareness to include all beings in the whole universe, known and unknown. Sense your willingness, as True Being, as Source of all, to lovingly include all beings, known and unknown.

8) Now focus on enemies if you haven't already. Breathe in their "stuff," exhaling pure healing energy and the highest best wishes. Make it real. Open more and more, breathing gently through any resistance, fear, or hesitation.

9) To test how your doing, think of a situation in which there is a strong negative charge of some kind. Breathe in the negativity from your "self." Breathe out pure healing energy of the quality of whatever is needed, e.g. forgiveness, patience, forthrightness, accepting your part in the creation of the pain. Breathe in everyone's egoic pain and confusion in the situation, breathing out pure healing energy without reservation. Do this patiently until you feel you've made it real.

10) Continue with this for 20 minutes or more if you can. Do it at least once a day. Twice a day would be best, first thing in the a.m. and before bed. How powerful it becomes is up to you, just like "hypnosis" - want it to happen, make it real, no one can do it for you. Let the remembrance of the fact of oneness, scientifically known, inspire you through your Intellect to put energy into it even if you egoically don't feel like it. You know that feeling is part of the con of egoic mind.

I have not included Buddhist images here because I didn't want to create any notion that you had to subscribe to Buddhism, or its iconography. There are specific powerful images in the complete Buddhist version, as found in Sogyal Rinpoche's book. If you read them, it will be clear to you that Buddhist teachings understand the power of submodalities and how to create vividness to make something real.

More importantly, however, Tonglen is an expression of the ultimate Transpersonal Vision and Commitment to Action - the unceasing *action of renunciation* of violence and exclusive self-interest *forever*. One does not merely settle for ascribing to the consoling conceptual ideal of oneness and brotherhood. Day by day, moment by moment, one directs one's *life force* and *interest*, dedicating, silently from the heart, all the fruits of one's thoughts, words, and deeds to the unceasing *action of cultivation* of Unbiased Wisdom/Love, the awakened heartfelt intuitive *knowing* of being one being, brothers and sisters in one being, not leaving anyone out.

One commits to *this practice, this effort,* forever. In my opinion, this is what is meant by surrendering to the Will of God (He already has the Infinite Vision and Commitment). This also embodies elements of what Carl Jung called the third and fourth(the highest) developmental stages of modern man's spiritual maturation: the notion of selfless service (3rd), and of complete awakening into being Life Itself as Witness manifesting in a limited form, but not being entranced by it(4th). Thus, in each case, one lives *in time* with a commitmenrt to life that is *outside of time*, that trancends time. This is expressed in Native American religious views honoring all life, all traditions, and praying for, not simply mankind into the future, but praying for the species that will arise out of man. If one can live in time, in day to day challenges, with such an expanded sense of concern for and vision of context, one's mind is very deep, very quiet, very sharp, very strong, and very tender.

We are learning tools and insights to relieve personal suffering and confusion. That is hypnotherapy. Some may think that accessing Superconscious allies and resources for personal growth elevates hypnotherapy to transpersonal hypnotherapy, and, in a sense, it does. But when we go beyond such personal goals to accessing and cultivating this eternal selfless vision and capacity, we have true Transpersonal Hypnotherapy/NLP. Our own very personal and intimate focus and commitment determine what level we are practicing at, regardless of what we call it. This vision is not something one requires of one's clients. If it is our sincere orientation for ourself, we can get out of the way, and let the authenticity do what it may.

5. Clinical Scripts

These scripts are presented as reference material for your information. They are not the <u>right</u> way or the <u>only</u> to approach their respective issues -- they are just one way someone could do it. Hopefully you will recognize basic hypnotic principles and interesting turns of phrase that will enhance your composition of suggestions under varied circumstances.

Our emphasis is to point out and understand the underlying principles, plus to develop the skill to see, hear, feel, and think appropriately about presenting situations in such a way that you will be able to generate a <u>living heart-felt</u> beneficial interaction with you client, whether it looks and sounds like an old technique or a spontaneous inspiration.

To review again, a basic template to follow to resolve the presenting symptom would be:

1)During pre-induction talk, gather details about the symptom and its effects. Establish rapport and prepare them to induce trance.

2)It can't hurt to begin any process by invoking inner guidance and protection from the Higher Self or Inner Guides to facillitate all processes.

3)If it is an issue of pain, it can be very useful to have them visualize the pain, giving it a 2 or 3 dimensional (experiment) shape and color. Associate the intensity of the pain with the intensity of the color, and give them a device (e.g. a reostat) to slowly increase and decrease the intensity of the color, which will directly change the intensity of the pain as well. For headaches this may be all you need to do! But where deeper work is required this is a good preliminary step to introduce the <u>element of control</u> and the <u>magical effect that visualizing pain as an *object* can have on the *experience* of pain.</u>

4)Once they have demonstrated to themselves that they can have control over the pain (and this can be used for emotional as well as physical pain), you have, again, three options:

a) You can move the pain out of their body placing it into the proper receptical and/or the proper location anywhere in the universe where its energy will be reprocessed for the benefit of the entire universe. This can be done in one direct step, or if necessary in gradual steps moving out of the body in stages along the best route that the client determines. For example, with a migraine, it might be through a channel down the shoulder through the arm and out the fingertips into a special kiln, jar, or, as for one client a cosmic toilet! (Laugh, but her intense pain was gone in moments!)

b)determine its positve intent - subpersonaility work, **and/or**

c)regress to its origin and uproot the need for it by resolving the unresolved issues there.

5)Anchor the resources obtained in (4), generalize throughout the past, and future pace. Then walk them through specific near future anticipated challenging situations calibrating their responses as a test. Make the tests strong - strong enough to make the real situation a breeze.

Confidence Builders

One new graduate of the course took an office in a dental building. A patient was referred to him with severe TMJ - severe grinding of the teeth during sleep, a very widespread ailment many times requiring expensive teeth guards to be worn. **The graduate didn't know what TMJ was - had never heard of it!** He had the client explain the symptoms and, even though he felt totally at a loss, he followed the above steps. After one session, the patient's problem was gone! Of the many benefits to the graduate (besides real faith and confidence in the tools) was to witness the touching revelation in regression trance that the root of the fear,anger, and tension in her jaw went back to an experience as an innocent 6 year-old being handed a religious card in Sunday School quoting some requirement to be good that she misinterpreted, but carried unconsciously ever since - carried and constantly failed at achieving. There was significant emotion and clearing as this naively conceived burden was released. This personal experience of the absurd poinancy many of our burdens, established in the innocence of childhood, deeply touched this graduate. It gave him a glimpse of how rewarding and beneficial this work can be - even when done in apparent ignorance!

He came to mentorship class asking for guidance on how to work with TMJ. I told him to trust the evidence of his work and to recognize he was the guide!

Another new graduate used the dental script that follows with her spouse, and he had extensive oral surgery without anesthesia!

Another student immediately achieved facillity to personally go to ultra depth states within seconds using the Deeply Relax finger drop method. This stuff works! And it works even if you're new at it! **Your own faith and consent are crucial however.** Doubt and hesitation create mixed results and even "failure."

Weight Control Script

After initial induction and relaxation suggestions:

You are now feeling so peaceful, calm, and relaxed, and this feels so much better than food ever made you feel **(check with the client first to verify that they are experiencing a state of well being)** because this good feeling comes from within you, and cannot be created by anything external to yourself. **(Feel free to elaborate this concept in any appropriate way.)**

Communicate the following string of suggestions with careful attention to pacing the client's ability to absorb them. Make sure you give them time to savor each suggestion and be encouraging to any responses that indicate this is the case:

As a result, your body feels more and more relaxed every day. The cells of your body are relaxing and releasing all excess liquid and fatty tissues. As a result, your body is easily and naturally assuming its normal weight, size, and shape, a slimmer trimmer you. You feel more energy, your body functions more efficiently, your taste buds are more sensitive. As a result, you extract more flavor and benefit from each morsel of food. You are eating less and enjoying it more. After a small quantity of food **(option: after eating the amount of food that meets your true essential needs...)**, you feel full and satisfied. You push your plate away after savoring a small quantity of food. You are eating delicious, nutritious, leaner foods enjoying fish and poultry, vegables and fruits, and avoiding fatty foods like beek and pork, processed starches and sweets. Sweets are now sickenly sweet, like syrup on white sugar. Natural fruit sugar from fresh fruit is so much more satisfying to you now. Fresh fruit tastes so good to you now. Processed starchy foods are tasteless like cardboard in your mouth. You are now eating lean, delicious, nutritious meals, eating only at mealtime, drinking refreshing glasses of water between meals, enjoying the increased vigor and energy of the slimmer trimmer you.

(Adapt for vegetarian diets; substitute their ideal diet; make all suggestions attractive.)

You enjoy doing one of your favorite physical activities every day. Envision yourself_____(insert designated activity, e.g. going for a walk.)
Experience how your body feels, your energy moving, active and dynamic.
Experience how relaxed and refreshed you feel afterward.
Every day, in every way, you are feeling better and better, leaner and stronger, lighter and freer than ever before.
Soon I will count from one to five and you will bring the awareness you now experience into your waking consciousness. Each and every day you are slimmer and trimmer than before, rapidly achieving your ideal body shape and lightness. Now I will begin the count. When I get to 5, you will open your eyes feeling peaceful, calm, relaxed, refreshed. 1...2...3...4...5.
(This script is obviously simple positive suggestion. You will want to augment it with therapy work to uproot any inner agendas that are designed to sabotage movement towards slimming and healing.)
Options: Make a tape for the client, inductions and suggestions included, to be played each night while falling asleep.
Agree on the eating plan to be followed and monitor adherence. Have the client

keep a log of what they eat and what they are feeling before and after they eat. Have sessions weekly for at least a month as long as there is need for weight loss and they can afford the sessions. Then bi-weekly or less frequently as needed.

Smoking Reduction Session

After inductions, appropriate deepening, and creation of receptivity:

During the coming week, you will experience your alternative behavior at least half of the time (i.e. alternative to smoking), and the other part of the time, smoke one half or less of your previous number of cigarettes.

When you wake up in the morning, you will empty a cigarette pack to one half of your former level. (If a pack a day was smoked previously, then empty the pack to 10 cigarettes.)

Make up your mind right then and there, calmly but determinedly, that those XX cigarettes will be more than enough for you. Your subconscious mind will apportion those cigarettes over the day in such a way that you will be quite comfortable with that many or fewer cigarettes during the day. You will find that XX cigarettes a day are more than enough for you. And don't be surprised when you go to bed at night if you have one or more cigarettes left over.

Also, you will now be aware of your smoking. That is, from the time you reach for a cigarette, light it and start to smoke, you will be fully aware of what you're doing every moment of the time. Thus, since the main element of a habit is its unconscious or unaware aspect, you are eliminating the smoking habit by its roots. Since you are aware of what you are doing, you are no longer in the habit. In fact, your awareness of your smoking may actually annoy you, so that you put the cigarette out while you are only half way through it. You may find that it tastes unpleasant and you simply will wish to put it out halfway.

Every day, you are smoking less and breathing better, more deeply. You enjoy breathing fresh, clean air into your lungs.

Now at those points in time when you have smoked, you can demonstrate to yourself that you are in charge, that you can take it or leave it. At each of those times, you can choose either to smoke, or a more healthy activity, like drinking a glass of water, or having a fresh mint or breath freshener in your mouth. Now, mentally view your day, pulling the plug on the cigarette habit at each point where there was a habit before, creating a free, highly conscious choice at each point:

- at the first smoke in the morning;

- other key times: at breakfast, driving to work, on the phone, at or after mealtimes, leisure times, stressful times, etc. (Refer to pre-induction interview for smoking schedule. Obtain agreement to substitute decaffinated coffee for regular coffee.)

You enjoy the benefits of becoming a non-smoker. Your breathing is improving, your health is improving, you experience more energy and vibrancy. Every day, in every way, you are feeling better and better, freer and freer. This feels good.

Count them back.

Smoking Cessation

After inductions, deepening, and creation of appropriate receptivity:

You have decided to become a non-smoker, an act of self, loving your body, loving yourself. You look forward to the benefits that being a non-smoker brings into your life: better health and breathing, fresher breath, more money available for healthier choices, enabling you to do good things for yourself and others.

(Utilize information from pre-induction discussions to elaborate on the motivation and benefits of stopping.)

As you breathe deeply now, experience the feeling of fresh air coming into your lungs. As you exhale, experience yourself expelling all tars, nicotines, poisons and toxins from your lungs that were depositied there by the destructive cigarette smoking that you did before. Experience how you feel. The very thought of cigarette smoking is increasingly distasteful to you now. Cigarettes are a form of self-destructive pollution. Cigarettes disgust you now. **(Repeat any of these statements with emphasis as you see fit.)**

Seeing these truths about cigarettes in your mind's eye, and feeling the truth of the harm they have caused your body, makes it easy and inspiring to change your daily routines:

In the morning, upon rising, you have a glass of water by the bed and drink that glass of water, feeling full and refreshed as a result. At breakfast, you change your routines somewhat, substituting decaffinated coffee for caffeine coffee during your first days of being a non-smoker. On going to work, you may put a mint in your mouth or chew chewing gum, and this satisfies you orally. During the day, whenever stresses come up or a thought to smoke enters in, you take a long slow deep breath and relax very deeply, blowing away any stress or thought of smoking, experiencing how much better it feels than that distasteful cigarette ever made you feel. You now drink water in an enjoyable realxing way whenever any thought of smoking arises, and it washes the desire away. Cigarettes taste terrible and you avoid them now.

(Add any additional aversive images, particularly specific to their life with cigarettes that they may have expressed.)

You are now a non-smoker. You are now among that special group of people who are non-smokers, and you've made the intelligent realization that your body and well-being were being undermined by cigarette smoking. You enjoy being healthy, active, happy, and free of the addiction. You feel a sense of pride in your accomplishment. You notice that the smoker has cigarette burns and ashes on the clothes, and stained teeth and bad breath. On the other hand, you enjoy your increased vitality, dynamism, and attractiveness to others. You enjoy the fun and fellowship of being with others who are like this also, yet being around others who smoke does not affect you in any way. You are a non-smoker and enjoy life more as a result.

Now I am going to repeat the statement, "I am a non-smoker," ten times. Repeat it silently with me as I say it. Experience your own sense of conviction and determination as you mentally sat it with me 10 times, beginning now:

"I am a non-smoker." **(Repeat 10 times with varying inflections and emphasis.)**

That's right, you are a non-smoker. As a result, you're enjoying improving health. Your health is getting better each and every day, now that you are a non-smoker. This is your personal victory. You feel pride and satisfaction at being a non-smoker. Having to quit has increased your self-esteem. You feel good that you are in charge, not a victim of something external to you. You are being good to your body, good to yourself, and this feels good! You enjoy breathing fresh air into your lungs. You're a fresh air breather. Your sense of taste and smell is more sensitive now. You are eating less and enjoying it more. It feels good to be in charge of yourself. You are pleased and proud of yourself. Others are pleased and proud of you, too. You are now enjoying life more and more each day in every way. Every day, in every way, you feel better and better. (**Build in future-paced scenes with 4-tuples of the new ever healthier person.)**

Count them out.

Nail Biting

This brief piece of scripting assumes initial induction and emotional clearing of the root cause of the nail biting. Actually, such a piece could very well be unecessary once the cause is cleared. Standing alone it is obviously simple direct suggestion.

Whenever you have the slightest desire to bite your nails - in fact, just as soon as you start raising your hand towards your mouth - you will instantly become fully aware of what is going on. You will therefore stop your hand about midway to your mouth and you will pause and think about whether you actually do want to start biting your nails. You will be fully aware of your hand and you will stop to decide what you intend to do and what you really want to do. If you feel you really do want to bite your nails, go right ahead and do it. But chances are you will have no desire to do so. The chances are you will prefer to lower your hand again. That is, the mere awareness of your hand will tend to dissipate the compulsion to bite your nails. You are not being prohibited from biting your nails - you simply are being given an awareness of the compulsion. As a result, the compulsion disappears. The energy behind the compulsion becomes completely dissipated - and you find you enjoy having more attractive nails. **(Include more elaborate positive reinforcement based on pre-induction information about ideal outcomes.)**

Dental Applications of Hypnosis

Script for the day prior to dental appointment.

Inductions, etc.

You are going to the dentist tomorrow to have some teeth cared for. You have some cavities which must be taken care of so you will feel better and in order that you may rest contentedly with the knowledge that your teeth are all healthy. The dentist's chair was designed in such a way that you cannot help but feel very relaxed while you are there. You are going to have a very pleasant experience in the dentist's office. It is going to be pleasant because you are going to have your own hypnotic anesthesia. Because you do not have any novacaine, you know that you will feel just as fresh when you leave the dentist's office as you did when you entered.

My hands are very numb. They are numb and insensitive. I am going to place my numb hands on your face and jaw. I will count from 10 to 0. As I count, the numbness will move from my hands into your jaw. I am touching you now! **(Place hands on their face and jaw.)**

Now I am counting: 10...9...feel the numbness moving from my hands into your face. You may feel it most keenly in your lips. A very slight tingling in the lips...8...7...feel the numbness. Feel the tingling, especially in the lips. Some people don't really experience tingling, but feel a strange sort of feeling which they can't describe. Some do experience a profound numbness. It doesn't matter what you feel so long as there is something, like the sensation in your llips to which you can relate...6...5...numb and insensitive...4...3...2...1...0! **(Lift hands away.)**

This very pleasant tingling and numbness will remain with you until exactly 15 minutes after you awaken from your hypnosis. Exactly 15 minutes after you open your eyes, all sensation will return to normal.

When you awaken in the morning, the numbness will return. The moment your feet touch the floor, you will feel a very slight tingling in your lips. As you move about the house, preparing breakfast, the tingling will become more and more obvious. You will be pleased by the tingling. It will be a reminder to you that your hypnotic anesthesia is working. When you leave the house on your way to the dentist, the tingling will grow more and more intense. The closer you get to the dentist's office, the more numb and insensitive your face becomes. As you approach the door of his office, you will be aware that your mouth is very numb. It is a very secure feeling. When you walk into the dentist's office, you know that you will be incapable of experiencing any discomfort because your anesthesia is so profound. If you must wait in his office for a while before he can attend to you, you will just sit there and enjoy the numbness and tingling.

The dentist's chair was designed with the patient's comfort in mind. The moment you sit in the dentist's chair, you feel yourself becoming relaxed and comfortable. You derive a feeling of absolute security from the tingling in your mouth. The sound of the drill is surprisingly relaxing. As the dentist works with your teeth, you may be aware of slight pressures from time to time, but these pressures bring about their own numbness. The more pressure you feel, the more numb and insensitive your mouth becomes.

Your numbness is most effective in the gums and teeth. You will experience no discomfort whatever from the dentist's working on your teeth. The longer you hold your mouth open, the more relaxed you feel. It is very relaxing to sit with your mouth open. You breathe naturally and easily and there is no sign of gagging or choking. Your mouth and throat are very relaxed and comfortable. Your mouth remains just moist enough to keep you very comfortable. The instruments placed in your mouth by the doctor are solely for the purpose of repairing your teeth. You know they do not represent food and are not to be digested, so you do not salivate in response to the dentist's work. Your mouth will remain comfortably moist. As the doctor works on your mouth, you feel relaxed and comfortable. The longer you sit in the dentist's chair, the faster the time flies. An hour seems to go by in only 15 minutes. When he is finished, you will be amazed by how little time was required for him to do his work. You will be even more amazed when you realize how quickly time flew by.

When you leave the dentist's office, all numbness will recede to those specific areas on which the dentist operated. All numbness will move to the teeth and gums directly affected by the dental procedure. The rest of your mouth will return to normal. The numbness will remain in the gums and teeth on which the doctor worked for a perod of 24 hours...24 hours from the time you leave the dentist's office all sensation will return to normal. Your mouth and body are rapidly restored to normal healthy functioning.

For 15 minutes after you open your eyes right now, all sesation in your mouth will return to normal. Tomorrow morning **(the morning of the appointment)**, the tingling will begin to return to your lips the moment your feet touch the floor... the numbness and tingling will intensify as you prepare to go to the dentist, just as I have already suggested to you. By the time you arrive at the dentist's office your mouth will be completely numb and insensitive. The longer you sit in the dentist's chair, the more comfortable and relaxed you feel. Time flies by very quickly and you are pleasantly surprised by how little time was required for the doctor to finish his work. As you leave the dentist's office, the numbness will recede to those particular gums and teeth on which the dentist worked. The numbness will remain in these areas for 24 hours from the time you leave the dentist's office.

Count them out.

The post-hypnotic suggestion will serve as a test of the acceptance of the session's suggestions. If it remains for 15 minutes as suggested, this indicates favorable acceptance. You may want to discuss the client's concept of numbness and tingling. All clients won't be the same. Some will experience slight tingling, others complete numbness. With those who have minimal numb response, it is important to explain that hypnotic numbness is not the same as the incapacitating effect of novacaine.

Pain Relief

Inductions to medium depth or somnambulism:

Remember what it felt like when a part of your body fell asleep. Now experience that feeling spreading in your (left or right) hand, as if your body has been sitting on it. That hand is growing increasingly numb and insensitive.

(Option: As you continue to drift on down deeper and deeper to sleep, I'd like you to picture and imagine youeself walking down a mountain path. It's midnight and the middle of winter. You are bundled up in a coat, gloves, cap, and boots. Picture and imagine yourself outside in the cold winter air, and, as you do, just take a deep breath of fresh mountain air. That's it, it feels so good to breathe. Your entire rib cage collapses in total utter relaxation. The moon is full and silvery and it's 20 degrees below zero, a bitter cold, and you can see your breath in white puffs, and as you walk down that beautiful path you see tall, deep green pine trees laden with snow. The snow is knee deep and everything has a bluis tinge to it. Even the snow looks blue. 10 minutes pass...20 minutes pass...30 minutes pass...now you can stop.

You take off the glove on your (r/l) hand and you thrust your warm hand into the snow, making a fist, compressing the snow into an ice ball in the palm of your right hand. And as you do, you can feel a numb, wooden, leatherlike sensation beginning in your right palm, spreading throughout your hand. And as you sit there in your chair, I'd like you now to picture and imagine and feel this numb, wooden, leatherlike sensation. You won't hear my voice for the next few minutes as you do this.)

(Alternate suitable images and scenarios to preference, e.g. hand in bucket of ice, hand asleep as if you had been sitting or laying on it, etc.)

Very good. You relax even deeper as I now take your (r/l) hand and place it upon your right cheek. Begin rubbing that right cheek very gently, and as you do, just let all that numbness drain from your hand into your cheek. Your cheek becomes numb, leathery and wooden...just as if novacaine had been administered. Take a few moments now to do this...I'll lower your hand now.

My hands are very numb and insensitive. I am going to place my numb hand on your face. I will count from 10 (or 20) to 0. As I count, the numbness will move from my hand into your jaw. I am touching you now! Now I am counting: 10...9...feel the numbness moving from my hand into your face...you may feel it most keenly in the lips...8...7...feel the numbness. It doesn't matter what you feel, so long as there is something, like the tingling in your lips to which you can relate...6...5...numb and insensitive...4...3...2...1...0!

Now I'll pinch both sides of your face **(pinch cheeks)**. Notice which side is more numb than the other. Now, again, place your hand on your cheek. Now let all that numbness in your cheek drain back into your hand. Take a few minutes to do this now.

Notice how your hand is becoming once again leathery and woodenlike, just like a block of wood. And your cheek is becoming flushed and warm. The blood is rushing to the surface of the skin on your cheek, and when all that numbness has drained from your cheek back into your hand, once again you can place your hand at your side. Take a few moments to do this.

Now take a few minutes and allow your hand to return to its normal feeling.

As you now return to this time and place, in that chair, you are drifting deeper, even deeper into trance. And in the future, when you wish to rid yourself of any discomfort, anywhere in your body, all you have to do is close your eyes, take a deep breath, and as you do, picture and imagine yourself just as calm and deeply relaxed as you are now. Just let your mind drift back to this time and this place, so relaxed. You can reinforce and strengthen this relaxation by saying to yourself 5 times the word "Relax."

And after you've done that, at that time, picture and imagine the hand of your choice becoming very numb, woodenlike, and leathery, just as it did a few moments ago. You then place that hand on the part of your body that is causing you discomfort, and allow this numb and heavy wooden feeling to transfer from your hand into that part of your body. Within a few minutes, you find that part of your body very warm, restful, and relaxed, free from all discomfort, and that feeling remains with you for a very long time afterwards. And each and every time you use this technique, you find it easier than the time before, and it leaves you even more comfortable and at ease. Your subconscious mind helps you in every way to experience profound comfort now and in the future.

Count them out.

Tension Headaches

Headaches are most always caused by an inner conflict - tension between warring parts. *However, always keep in mind the possibility of a physical cause. Carefully question the client about relevant medical history.* This script is an example of suggestion without addressing root cause directly. I generally use parts therapy and regression to get to the root of the pain. Not only does it bring relief, but the client gains insight and the ability to reorganize his inner process as well. Clearing root cause is appropriate for migraines as well, and generally mandatory for lasting results. If you successfully clear root cause and clear emotional holding and don't get results, a physical disease could be indicated and they should consult a medical doctor. <u>You should always advise medical consultation.</u>

If the headache returns after clearing, check for secondary gains and ecology issues from other 'parts.'

Induction.

(Stand behind your subject. Place your hands firmly on the subject's neck and shoulders, feeling for tense muscles which are usually obvious to the

touch. As you suggest a diminishing of the tension and pressure, gradually ease the pressure of your hands. The obvious illusion serves to impress the subject, prompting him to anticipate total relief.)

Co-ordinate this scripting with your actions:

Headaches are caused by tension. Most of the tension is centered in the muscles of the neck and shoulders, where I am placing my hands now. These tense muscles exert pressures against the walls of the arteries and veins, therby inhibiting the natural flow of blood to and from the head. Your headache is your body's way of begging you to relax. It wants you to stop worrying. It wants you to let up on the pressures which are preventing your body from functioning naturally. As you relax these muscles, the release of pressure will allow your circulation to normalize and the headaches will disappear.

Be aware of the pain in your head. Imagine a shape that represents the pain. Allow the shape to have a color and size. **(Ask for sharing)** As I count from 1 to 10...allow the pain to intensify and the shape to grow ever larger and the color to intensify, reaching the maximum intensity and size at 10.

1...2...3...intensifying more and more...4...5...6...more and more...7...8...9...now at maximum intensity...10.

Now that you have demonstrated that you can make the pain intensify, this shows that you have the control over it to decrease it as well by simply reversing the process.

As I count from 10 to 0, the pressure and tension will leave, and the headache will fade away. It will feel as though all the tension and discomfort are leaving through my hands as each number becomes smaller. **(Note: you could have the numbers get <u>physically</u> smaller as they go down.)** All tensions and discomfort fades away, as each number becomes smaller. At the count of 0, there will be no tension and no discomfort. At the count of 0, your head will feel clear and comfortable because you will continue to feel relaxed and comfortable, even after you come out of this experience.

Counting now: 10...9...8...feel the tension fading away as each number becomes smaller **(begin to lessen the pressure in your hands)**...7...6...the headaches is leaving now **(lessen pressure)**...5...4...it may feel as though my hands are drawing all tension and all of the headache from your body...3...2...fading...fading...1...0! **(Remove hands)**

Your head is clear and comfortable. Relax. Don't worry about things you cannot control. You have been through many crises, large and small. Looking back, you can realize that worrying and fretting never resolved one of them. In fact, you probably found the correct solution to problems after you became calm and did something constructive to ease your situation. Things always have and always will take care of themselves. All is well and you are feeling better and better. Your head is feeling clear, feeling good, feeling better and better, every day in every way.

Bring them back.

◆ ◆ ◆

Table of Contents
Phase V

1. Superconscious Considerations:
Archetypes, Myths, Poetics of the Psyche

Now we begin to explore the most magical level of working with the psyche. The superconscious level, the "home" of the archetypes, is the repository of timeless intuitive truths and transformative energy. At this level, it is **the truths themselves that are the transformative energy**. In other words, they are alive as the ground of our being, *in our bodies, as our bodies*, not merely conceptual. They are beyond the thinking mind, they inform the thinking mind, but they are what they are, in the process of revealing what they are **as** truth, about which conceptualization is only an approximation.

As such, they communicate and inform as **energetic feeling movement, thought movement, and as the reconfiguration of subtle and gross structures** in our bodies: our physical, emotional, and mental bodies. Discursive conceptualization is merely the shadow, the residue, of energetic reconfiguration. Discursive thought is a tool for sharing about the experiences of energetic transformation, but such conceptual sharing alone does not communicate the attainment of reconfiguration itself.

Therefore, in trance work, it becomes even more essential to assist the client attempting to access archetypal energies to have a vivid fully involved experience of the living symbolic imagery and a felt sense of energetic movement, supported by necessary discursive information, but not distracted by it.

This is the level of Divine Ignorance where living as *"I- don't-know-who/what-I-am"* equates with *"I AM THAT"* in its fullest expression. I am not suggesting that people are going to become fully liberated on the spot in your sessions, but who knows? At this point, concepts about 'living beyond concepts' are still devices to spark glimpses of wakeful confusion and contemplation in relationship to our comfortable association with egoic/dualistic trance thought/mind. Contemplation held in such a state of confusion can create gaps in egoic trance for the Light to shine through.

Regarding Striving to Attain

The egoic mind sees the words *"I AM"* and immediately wants to own this state. It imagines what this experience must be, but in terms of its idea/trance about "i," the egoic version of self.

The level of Divine Ignorance is where "i" has dissolved and the transpersonal "I" is shining through steadily, moment-by-moment. There is a constant intuitive recognition of identity/unity with all beings/phenomena/existence that allows, rather than obstructs, the full expression of individual personality because false, *trance-imagined*, self-'identity has dissolved.

This is the paradox that has confounded egoic mind from the start. Egoic mind conceives of loss of individual/separate identity as a vegetative state, as loss of awareness and personality. The egoic mind is founded on ignorance, 1st skandha, and all the other skandhas are more elaborate levels of 1st skandha's ignorant reactive (i.e. false, mistaken) mind. The skandhas are the construct of identity and self which the egoic mind believes in as the true self that needs to be preserved. In fact, this is our false, shamed, restricted self, our act.

Thus, when it is proposed that all reactive modes be given up, the ego, <u>as always,</u> responds by **trying to create a representation, IN ITS FRAME OF REFERENCE, of what this would be like.** It dissolves the skandhas on the spot as far as it can go - all the way back to the 1st. It can go no farther without dying. *And it can't/won't willingly do that!* Egoic mind cannot completely and finally dissolve itself, but it can dissolve into the root 1st skandha and hold itself there briefly.

Since it can't "pop through" 1st skandha into the light of pure transindividual being, what it is left with is the sense of its own true nature - ignorance and fear, a major sense of terrifying "DUHHH!"(The black disc of the diagram, in PII.)

> *Exercise: Forget you are reading about the inner workings of egoic minding. Now, imagine what it would be like to have all your beliefs erased, being conscious but with no beliefs. Or imagine having your chattering mind, your thinking, stop. What would either of these be like? The typical answers are: "I'd fall asleep." "Oblivion, I'd be oblivious." "I'd be a vegetable." "It's scary; it makes me fell sick to my stomach." Each response indicates the person has contacted first skandha ignorance, the "DUHHH!" The difference answers indicate the emotional responses one can have to first skandha experience: go unconscious; go blank, into the ignorance; and fear or revulsion.*

Since it was trying to create an approximation of non-reactive, transindividual beingness, it identifies what it is sensing *("Here it is, I found it!")* AS non-reactive transindividual beingness instead of recognizing that it has stumbled on to the root ignorance of its own true on-going nature.

Experiencing root ignorance is unpleasant, to say the least. The egoic mind reacts to the misperceived experience of transindividual being with disgust, disgust with its own unrecognized emptiness. It also fails to recognize that it is too late to avoid becoming what it is disgusted with, *because it is intuiting its own core nature which it has mislabeled as transindividual being.*

Thus, it reacts; it bounces off the experience, i.e., it regenerates skandhas 2-5 on the spot, and the futile dance starts over again. I call it a dance, but the more appropriate image here would be that of a dog running away from its tail.

At the Superconscious level of trance work we are going to invite in living transformative energies, aspects of our transindividual being, that are beyond the confused level of dualistic egoic separation.

It would be valid to consider it a form of prayer, of supplication, of invocation.

As such, it is important to cultivate an attitude of trust, and openness without expectation: "Thy Will be done." To the degreee that a client's image of a Higher Power is infused with qualities of abusive parental figures, preliminary clearing work will be required before such trust and openness can be expected to be accessed.

The Superconscious is the level of mythic truth, and archetypal energies. It is beyond psychology which is focused on the small conceived self. Psychology is concerned with the storyline and varying conceptions of 'happiness' of the constructed 'i' self in its constructed world. In the mythic realm, the archetypal realm, **one _constantly_ stands in awe of the universe**, and one's concerns are to live and act in universal harmony with all _apparently_ separate entities, **with an 'awake' _intuition_ of oneness.**

Archetypes are the universal organizing principles and energies of the universe. Think of white light, sunlight, as the Source, the unmanifest, passing through a prism. The rainbow display of pure but distinct colors and energies that results is the first level of manifestation, the archetypal level. The colors are pure, primary, and the source of all levels of manifestation to follow. While they are distinct and primary, they are, nevertheless, fully aware of their unity and inseparable oneness with each other as display of Source. They are beyond being concerned with egoic notions of survival, for themselves or for humans. They embody effortless display as Truth free of struggle. Coming into alignment with their impersonal dynamic dance, we discover, paradoxically, our True Individuality.

I want to make it very clear here that there are many models of archetypes, as many as the myths that tell their stories.

For our purposes we are considering archetypes _exclusively_ as Superconscious, pure, energies that are not tainted by the twists of egoic/dualistic mind.

Many categorizations of archetypes include the shadow aspect, the dark, negative, or destructive (i.e. fearful/violent) as part of the archetype. These qualities tend to blur the line between archetypal and psychological domains. I choose to relegate those aspects to the subconscious realm. In my opinion, they belong there because they are egoic qualities.

Therefore, my point of view is that, if you encounter "someone" when invoking archetypes in trance work that is less than pure, awake, humorous and dynamic, _similar to Inner Guide qualities_, you are accessing at the subpersonality level and you need to relate to it as such. This could happen quite often with client's who are guilt-ridden or doubtful of such capacities. Preparatory work may be called for - don't interpret that as a failure. If in using this approach you get something clearly less than brilliantly transformative energies, recognise that you are being shown what needs to be cleared up first. Regard what is invoked as subpersonality expression and use your tools:

    1) Get the pure intent of the part or situation,
    2) separate pure intent from false beliefs and behaviors to evaluate the contradictions between them,
    3) raise the part with its new appreciation of pure intent to the Superconscious level, free of shame, using any or all of the techniques we have studied. Then you have the possibility of encountering the archetype for which the subpersonality was an egoic veil.
    4) pursue deep self-inquiry("What does that do for you that's even more important?") which can take them to an experience of Pure Being which is the archetypal level.

Since the archetypes are universal principles, **they are transcultural** and show up repeatedly in various guises in all human societies as their myths, their stories, their theater. In fact, **the theater of the egoic self is merely a devalued version of these greater mystery plays** which we have been learning to play with, in order to release our client's potential,. Indeed, there are therapeutic approaches, (e.g. Jungian, shamanic), that directly work to help the client uncover **the deeper archetypal roles they are attempting to portray in their lives**. We are working to do this also.

Our culture has fragmented the ancient myths: demystified them with egoic/dualistic rationality trances, with psychology, and, as a consequence, robbed us of the awareness of the organizing principles and the sacred meaning of the activities of our lives in the context of the unified field of being.

It is as if the theater of our subpersonalities is the struggle of these disoriented inner parts to recreate the reality of the greater morality (i.e. meaning) plays of the archetypal level. *It is very empowering for a client to realize that a "neurotic" aspect of behavior has been a protector of soul-truth and survivor of the destruction of meaning,* struggling to portray the lost archetypal script, to dance the forgotten sacred dance.

◆◆*Do you see, in terms of meta-process, what is happening here? Phenomena only have meaning in a context, therefore identifying the archetypal role, the universal aspect of the energies in play, elevates the person's life to a grand new context, dissociating them from the petty personal (egoic, separate, isolated) level into the timeless realm of universal dance. The shame and judgment in the restrictive context of "i" is then more easily dissolved.*

◆◆*Not only does the client get to the positive intent underlying those "bad behaviors" but they discover the glorious transcendent nature of that pure intent. Reframing, dissociation, expanded perspective, association with pure intent, etc.: the same process dynamics we have been working with are still the tools at hand. The insights gained from using them keep raising the client's perception of meaning to a higher, clearer, more expanded level.*

Recognizing their role in a family system can release a tremendous amount of shame because it reframes the client's behaviors giving them an expanded perspective of the meaning of their role in the context of supporting the family dance.**(transindividual awareness, 1st level up)**

Identifying and elevating the family roles to timeless universal themes releases even more of the sense of shame-identification with what is going on.**(2nd level up)** It's not about "me" anymore: "me" can afford to relax the contraction of shame, and acknowledge being less than a grain of sand in this mysterious universal play of energies.

A sense of connectedness arises, a recognition of the shared human dilemma that raises one above the absorption of the personal drama into the experience of **the birth of compassion.(3rd level up)**

Shame is not one's dirty little personal secret anymore. Egoic shame and process are seen as an indiscriminate infection, afflicting virtually all our pure brothers and sisters. Praise and blame are released, as is the struggle to be O.K. One cannot take seriously the pursuit of isolated personal happiness any longer. Humility arises and is, paradoxically, tremendously liberating and empowering. Egoic mind's feared death is discovered to be a greater birth:

"When the drop dissolves into the ocean, it becomes the ocean."

With expanded vision, we see the greater interconnected process of life, freed of the fear-based, self-absorbed, judgmental, fragmented egoic reference point, which arrogantly subsumes all events in the context of its all-important personal storyline. We move into the objective level of "Witness" awareness that does not identify fearfully, egoically, or dualistically with the events in our lives. Unlike egoic "objectivity" which deadens and represses life energy in its struggle to survive, "Witness" objectivity is not identified with the body, with the false idea of self. It is easily aware of the mortality of the body and all things, including self. IT is ever mindful that all beings and things dissolve into the one true being, and therefore do partake of immortality beyond the endless change of forms. Thus, contrary to egoic expectation, "Witness" objectivity releases the robust display of personality and individuality free of hubris (pride), fear, and shame.

One does not have to go into "trance" to get this. The ordinary but persistent focus of intellectual awareness of where we are, and of our shared dilemma/opportunity will work. Contemplate our shared mortality until the significance of our temporariness causes you to have a **felt sense of softening**, *in a persistent fashion, of the <u>heart-mind</u>.* Such contemplation challenges the assumptions of every thought that walks through one's mind, and brings a <u>felt sense</u> of slowing down and quieting down of the turbulence of the mind as petty concerns dissolve in this expanded awareness of significance, this opening to Superconscious, archetypal relationship. These are the qualities I choose to identify as archetypal for the purposes of this course:

> **<u>Awakened energies free of egoic contraction.</u> Dark energies are included to the degree that they are "just dark" (e.g., the force of a hurricane) vs. "dark" because of resentment which relegates them to the subpersonality level (egoic/dualistic level).**

In eastern iconography, for example, archetypal pure energies such as compassion (selfless love) and wisdom have wrathful as well as peaceful manifestations. The wrathful manifestations are terrifying, bloody, crushing bodies, spewing fire, etc., but all the objects of their wrath are understood to be egoic manifestations. Therefore, these pure energies will appear to a person as wrathful or peaceful depending upon where the person's allegiance lies - with their true heart or with the false self. As noted and implied, archetypes and their myths define many levels of meaning for us:

1) Personal identity

2) Transpersonal identity on various levels

    a) family

    b) community

    c) global

    d) universal

3) Moral values and ethics

4) Stages of life and challenges for individual unfoldment and maturation into True Authentic Self.

5) Context for and order of community in the midst of the mystery and chaos of existence and with the mystery of natural cycles

We are going to examine several archetypal models to begin to give you an understanding of how such information can be useful and enlightening. The subject is of vast potential for study and is certainly worthy of a lifetime of interest.

First we are going to take from the Greco-Roman tradition the archetypal representations and myths of the zodiac. This is an eternal, timeless, "static" model that encompasses all the "life areas" of an individual, and can provide a useful overview to approach the structure and meaning of life's situations. A reminder: the Gods of the zodiac in the myths are quite susceptible to the egoic passions and poisons. This can be very valuable and enjoyable information to learn, adult fairy tales, but when we invoke energies at the Superconscious levels, we are **not** invoking these gods. We are invoking a higher level of manifestation free of the vanities of egoic mind. This higher level manifests in human form as its **highest** expression **in form,** but it could manifest as animal or plant, etc. *At the appropriate place in the scripts, you can simply ask for its highest expression in human form to appear.*

Second, we will present a "through time" archetypal model that represents themes of development in a person's life, male or female. These themes will not be totally pure archetypes as you will see. Some themes we could call forth at the subpersonality level, and some at the archetypal level.

Third will be a presentation of archetypes of male psyche development.

And *fourth,* a model of archetypal aspects of the female psyche will be presented.

◆ ◆ ◆

2. Pantheon of the Gods:
Archetypes of the Zodiac

1. **Saturn** (Cronos), Inner Father, father of Jupiter (his successor), Father of all, organizes all, establishes security, ambition, status, rules of society. Government, Politicians, Historians, <u>Capricorn.</u>

2. **Jupiter** (Zeus), Wisdom, Inner Guidance, activates the laws and principles of the universe, generates understanding and signifies meaning. Large corporations, Advanced training, Foreign trade and interests, <u>Sagittarius.</u>

3. **Pluto,** Lord of the Underworld, death, sex impulse, merging impulse (i.e., partnerships- emotional issues) -- physically, emotionally, spiritually, financially, hidden and mysterious. CIA, Medical research, recycling, <u>Scorpio.</u>

4. **Venus** (Aphrodite), Goddess of love, "yin" energy, life and business partnerships (formation and dissolution), harmonizing, attracting. Beauty, Horticulturists, Diplomacy, <u>Libra.</u>

5. **Chiron** (Vesta), the Virgin, practical application of creative efforts, desire to perfect, to improve, to rectify, to purify, to make useful. Doctors, Medical technology, Bureaucracy, <u>Virgo.</u>

6. **Apollo** (Sun), Inner Child, creativity, spontaneity, exuberance, enthusiasm, entertainment, play and fun, romance, adventure. Arts, Gambling, Dealers in precious commodities, <u>Leo.</u>

7. **Gaeia** (Diana, Rhea), Inner Mother, home life, family, nest, inner nurturing and security, empathy, ancestral roots. Nurses, Hotels and Motels, Restaurants, <u>Cancer.</u>

8. **Mercury**, Messenger of the Gods, inquisitiveness and communication (speech), wanting to learn and share, physical, informational, and social networks. Teachers, Data services, publishing, <u>Gemini.</u>

9. **Vulcan,** Blacksmith of the Gods, the capacity to transform raw materials into finished products, to capacity to earn and to own, constant dynamic creative projects. Stocks and bonds, Movable possessions (i.e. not real estate), <u>Taurus.</u>

10. **Mars,** God of War, "yang" energy, assertive, active, Inner Masculine, body structure and physical appearance, self-discovery and primary coping strategies. Soldiers, Investigators, Athletes, <u>Aries.</u>

11. **Neptune,** God of the ocean, urge to transcend[+] or escape[-], right-brain non-linear modes of experience, dissolution of self[+ or-], relaxation, renewal. Meditation, Waste management, Film industry (images and abstracts), <u>Pisces.</u>

12. **Uranus,** God of the heavens, visionary, greater causes, unusual and non-conformist ideas, change and upheaval, rejection of the commonplace, desire for freedom and independence. Anarchists, Local and central governments officials, Aquarius.

These signs of the zodiac, as they are arranged around the circle of the heavens, display the dance, or war, as the case may be, of polarities of essentially unified energies. They are complimentary and balancing to each other when awake. They are adversaries and convinced of their separateness when in shame-based trances.

This is the list of the polarities by number:

Saturn--1	7--Gaeia
Jupiter--2	8--Mercury
Pluto--3	9--Vulcan
Venus--4	10--Mars
Chiron--5	11--Neptune
Apollo--6	12--Uranus

3. Archetypal Forms, Focus, Manifestations, and Vocations

ARCHETYPE/SIGN/PLANET	FOCUS	MANIFESTATIONS/BODY PARTS RULED	VOCATIONS
1. Aries ✧ Inner Masculine ✧ Mars	Search for Separate Identity, personality, mask, role, name. Aggressive and destructive elements	rugged life, athletics, competitiveness, tools, high-risk hobbies, assertiveness, leadership, outdoors-person, ◆head, eyes, vision	Defenses, security, mechanical trades, surgeons
2. Taurus ✧ Inner Producer ✧ Vulcan	Search for value and meaning, Self-worth, skills, possessions, resources	Loyalty, strength, fertility, sensuous, perseverance, results-oriented, ◆throat, ears	Personal finances, stock brokers, foundations
3. Gemini ✧ Inner Inquirer ✧ Mercury	Search for variety, communication, immediate environment	mental quickness, curious, versatile, adaptable, relations with siblings, neighbors, ◆breathing, lungs	Trade and commerce, Agents, printing, travel
4. Cancer ✧ Inner Maternal ✧ Earth/Moon (Gaiea)	Search for Mother Goddess, roots-ethnic, cultural, family environment	Nurturing, comforting, empathetic, bonding, relations with mother, ◆stomach, skin, breasts, digestion	Caring professions, marine trades, catering
5. Leo ✧ Inner Child ✧ Sun (Apollo)	Search for Whole/Beingness, Creativity, play, children, entertainment	Celebratory, enthusiastic, self-expressive, relations with children, childlike behavior, ◆heart	Authority, public relations, entertainers, sports
6. Virgo ✧ Inner Perfectionist ✧ Vesta (Virgin) ✧ Chiron	Search for meaning Service, Analysis, discrimination, service-oriented	problem solving, daily routine, schedules, maintenance, relations, coworkers-workers, ◆ general health, intestines	Unions, civil servants, armed forces.
7. Libra ✧ Inner Feminine ✧ Venus	Search for Soul-Mate, Cooperation, unity, love, affection, peace, harmony, litigation	Social intercourse, identify partners, negotiations, enemies, ◆liver, kidneys, lower back.	Luxury trades, artists, designers
8. Scorpio ✧ Inner Merger ✧ Pluto	Search for transformation, birth and death, use of power, destruction, sex	Intimacy, shared resource, OPM, intense emotions, passionate, public finance, trust funds, grants, loans, ◆ genitals, excretion	Underground workers, secret agencies, shrinks, archeology
9. Sagittarius ✧ Inner Guide ✧ Jupiter	Search for Wisdom, higher education, ethics, panoramic environment, travel long distance	Philosophical, optimistic, expand horizons-seek freedom, relations with teachers, religious organizations, ◆ hips and thighs	Ph.D.'s, lawyers, bankers, librarians, clergy
10. Capricorn ✧ Inner Paternal ✧ Saturn	Search for Dharma, position and reputation, worldly, life-path, career	organized, responsible, sets boundaries, discipline, relations with authority, ◆ bones, teeth, knees	Construction, Realtors, scientists, police, agriculture

11. Aquarius ✧ Group Instinct ✧ Uranus	Search for Holy Grail, groups, goals, future vision, causes, the greater good	Eccentric, inventive, utopian, breaking old patterns, relations with friends, ◆ankles, nervous system	Psychologist, inventors, pilots, sociologists, government officials
12. Pisces ✧ Inner Mystic ✧ Neptune	Search for Peace, Higher Power surrender, trust, faith, intuition	Compassionate, psychic, imaginative, healing, spiritual, seclusion. ◆ health of feet and immune system	Dancers, fine artists, hospitals, prisons, welfare, tobacco and oil trades

Note: These catagories are not to be regarded as absolute guidelines. An accurate determination of qualities in astrology relies on a complex interplay of planetary positions; a person's manifested tendencies cannot be "pigeon-holed" by a simple one-dimensional interpretation. Nevertheless, familiarity with this chart can make you aware of important patterns and characteristics in a way that will enhance your work.

◆ ◆ ◆

4. Applications of Archetypal Information

Hopefully questions are arising at this point. Questions such as:

"What am I supposed to do with this information?"

"How am I supposed to use it?"

"Does this mean I have to learn astrology and educate my clients about the meaning of archetypes?"

You do not have to learn about astrology or educate clients about the archetypes. Such intellectual information isn't necessarily useful or not useful. In general, it will be beside the point, but with some it may help establish rapport, and generate resources.

The information being given you in this phase is information about the language and imagery of the unconscious mind, **not** the conscious mind. Clients will be experiencing their inner world in terms of this kind of language much of the time, and it may be helpful to you to know how to pick up on the "hints." It can be helpful to recognize when an image has implications of a transpersonal nature indicating the deep motivating forces at work in the client's drama of being.

This does not change the perspective of the work, however.

I am not suggesting an added burden of having to be able to interpret their inner experience. Understanding the implications of some of the imagery may provide you with some footholds, some ground to support your explorations, but the view and approach remain the same, i.e.:

1) *To work with the submodalities (the theater) of the experience in such a way that you release limiting entanglements with the content of the experience (shame-based beliefs and frozen emotional energies).*

2) *To enhance and create beneficial resources in relation to the content and anchor them.*

3) *To generalize these new resources throughout the past and into the future.*

4) *To do all of the above by guiding the experience of vivid transformational inner experiences that don't get diluted by analytical, discursive speculations. Make it real.*

5) *Always remember you are relying on the inherent purity of their being, the built in tendency of the unconscious to self-correct in a beneficial, life-affirming way once the erroneous beliefs are cleared.*

6) *Constantly, by contemplation and self-inquiry, deepen your capacity to explore without getting "fixed"[tranced out] by agendas of hope and fear, praise and blame, right and wrong, etc.*

Thus, you do not necessarily need to mention the word archetype to access the archetypal realm. You could just suggest that you are going to access *the fullest expression, the fully evolved, awake, empowered manifestation of the pure intent at the core of this problem behavior.* Of course, you can establish the imagery of going "up" to the superconscious level if you choose. Going deep inside into the sacred inner sanctum of their "heart of hearts" would be equally as acceptable. As would other images - remember, **your criteria for choosing is: "What works for the client?"**

In that regard, having this information can help you discover what may work for the client. The previous "timeless" chart of the houses of the zodiac encompasses the whole of human life issues. The following questions, addressed to the client in your **first** interview, can give you a wealth of information about how to proceed with them. They will think they are answering questions because you want the content. *Take the content*, but be attentive to the other 90% of what they are communicating: their nonverbal indications of sensory channels of access, anchors, strategies, beliefs, and imagery (*which you can feed back to them in trance. Remember, they generally won't be aware of the power and implications of their imagery; they are used to it; they take it for granted; they don't really <u>hear</u> it anymore*).

Such an initial interview will give you tremendous data to work with: **content data, and, more importantly, process data.** Remember, trust your unconscious mind to be listening and comprehending in a much more comprehensive way than your conscious mind. Relax **bodily and with your breath** into a state of focused alertness. *<u>Don't grasp with your eyes and ears; let your senses effortlessly deliver their information to you.</u>*

As you develop the skill to persist in an unselfconscious state of attention to your whole experience of the client, as you allow space for your inner experience to flow uninhibited by (fear/shame-based) self-judgment, you will reap greater and greater rewards of creative inspiration from your unconscious mind.

You are entering the magical expansive realm where we are more than our ordinary idea of ourselves. The realm which can enrich the ideas we have of ourselves, and, hopefully, move us beyond the ideas into full delightful awakened participation in the cosmic dance of life, intuitively perceiving the movement of the Greatest and Most Profound in the smallest and most mundane.

Based on his experience exploring these realms with his clients, Carl Jung wrote:

> *"A Negro of the Southern States of America dreams in motifs of Grecian mythology and a Swiss grocer's apprentice repeats, in his psychosis, the vision of an Egyptian Gnostic."*
>
> --<u>Archetypes of the Collective Unconscious</u> [Princeton: Bollinger Press, 1959], p.50

Based on our models of possibilities, the implication of past life remembrance in this quote is obvious. It is important to understand that the archetypal <u>themes and patterns</u> are still of a higher order of significance because they still *<u>inform</u>* these past lives with meaning - a past life being no more important than this life because of its "location" in time.

The following questions will enable you to assess the client's relationship to each life area in the zodiac model, **by what they say and how they say it, by what they don't say and how they don't say it!**

They are numbered to correspond to the zodiac houses on page V-8. **This interview process should be allotted at least a full hour session.**

Overview question [not numbered]: Ask them to describe themselves, their life, and where they are at. Notice **how** they do it, e.g. do they **see** themselves, do they **sense** how things are **going**, do they **feel** good/bad about this or that or themselves, etc.

1. Re: Assertion, sense of self: How do you evaluate your sense of confidence in "who you are" and your ability to affirm that in the assertive expression of your needs and desires?

2. Re: Sense of self-worth: Do you feel worthy to have a totally abundant life? How does this correlate with the state of your finances? Do you feel over or under paid?

3. Re: Communication and mental life: How would you assess the quality of your mental life and your interpersonal communications? Are you curious about life? How frequently are you inquisitive about something new or unexpected in your life?

4. Re: Home and family of origin issues: Describe your relationship with your mother. How does your upbringing mold the way you relate in your current home environment?

5. Re: Wholeness and creativity and play: How do you relate to [your] children [or in general.] Do you take out time to play; do you have hobbies? What do you do for fun?

6. Re: Service and daily routine: Evaluate your management skills and interest in ordinary daily routines. Do you enjoy problem solving at home or at work? Do you like to be of service to others?

7. Re: Soul-Mate and social intercourse: Do you have a life partner? Describe: yes/no, want/don't want, etc. Describe your capacity to communicate harmoniously in any form of partnership. How are your negotiating skills? Have you ever been in a lawsuit? If so, how did it go; how do you relate to it now?

8. Re: Sex life, joint resources, use of power: Are you happy with your sexuality? Are you expressing it in a satisfying way? If you are in a business partnership, how is it going - is it successful financially? Are you happy with your understanding of how to exercise power in situations?

9. Re: Wisdom, higher knowledge, travel: Are you fulfilled in your spiritual, & philosophical interests? Are questions of deeper meaning and ethics important to you? Do you travel at all; do you enjoy it? What about it do [don't] you enjoy?

10. Re: Career, father: Are you happy in your work? Do you consider that you have found your vocation? Is that important to you? Describe your relationship to your father.

11. Re: Friendship, causes, groups: Do you have close friends? Are you involved in any causes or group activities? Describe how they enrich your life?

12. Re: Transcendence, escape, faith: Do you engage in any activities to take you out of yourself? Regularly, or in times of stress? Evaluate whether you choose beneficial or destructive means, i.e., do they transcend or escape?

As a last question, ask about general health and then specify about any particulars and locate their house. This is not a specific zodiac association, although it could be. general health is associated with 6th house.

Completing this series of questions can be quite a profound experience because it causes the client to do self-inquiry and to think deeply about their life in a comprehensive way. You can proceed from this into prioritizing with the client which areas are most important to work on. As we discussed previously, these houses are either polarized or complementing each other in their arrangement in the zodiac (see PV, p. 8). This provides you with a ready made treatment plan and gives you a means of providing the client with a sense of structure and direction for the therapy.

Remember, regardless of how impressive the imagery may be, don't get lost in the meaning of content. Consider their answers with these questions in mind:

- *How does this information help?*
- *How does it hinder?*
- *Does it confuse and limit?*
- *Does it awaken and generate resources?*
- *What can you do by way of changing and/or enhancing the relationship in and to their drama to empower the client as the Actor in a [playful] play vs. being the captive in a prison?*

Imagery may come up that is very impactful and can remain as an echo in their life to contemplate. When I took this course and did the practice session of accessing an archetype, I had a very magical, sweet image of a Centaur (half man-half horse) in a dark sky with the crescent moon. I had no words for it and didn't particularly try, or want to try, to communicate with it beyond just communing with it. I was even less versed in astrology than I am now, and my therapist had no insights either. The image stayed with me in a pleasantly haunting way. **Four years later**, a client was commenting on my chart and the relationship between Chiron and my moon. I had never heard of Chiron and asked what it was. In the course of her description she mentioned it was represented by the Centaur, and it was conjunct my moon! The image from four years before flashed into my mind. I still haven't investigated the conceptual meaning of this astrologically, but just that much insight enhanced my sense that I had tapped into a deep aspect of my being and can continue to commune with it. This is one kind of enriching response to this work that clients may have.

◆ ◆ ◆

5. Induction for Accessing Archetypes

Begin by discussing the relevant issues/life areas to be addressed selecting one to enhance in relation to its archetypal "well-spring."

DO INDUCTIONS EMPHASIZING THE CAPACITY TO RELATE TO THE SYMBOLIC PLAY OF IMAGES TO BE INVOKED *(versus a discursive, intellectual dialogue, or interpretive approach - this approach emphasizes the visual/kinesthetic impact.)*

Now experience yourself standing in a meadow *((or another appropriate setting – if necessary to facilitate accessing the archetype, go up column of light to the superconscious level))*. Experience the meadow; see the plants and trees, feel the wind gently against your face, listen to the sounds of small animals, perhaps hear the singing of birds, experience your body erect and at ease upon the earth. Take some time to vividly experience this situation in such a way that you know and feel yourself opening to the communication with _____
((the archetype governing the life area at issue. Not necessary to name the archetype, you could say, e.g., "the pure intelligence governing the area of life of the problem, that wants to come through to heal and release this problem"))

((Therapist repeats and elaborates appropriately to enhance the vividness of the setting and the receptiveness of the client))

As you become more in tune with your surroundings, now, in preparation to meet this pure (archetypal) intelligence which is simply an aspect of your own true pure intelligence, you call forth and experience the presence of your Inner Guide, now. *((Pause))* Let me know when your Inner Guide is present and you are ready to proceed.

On the count of 3, with the assistance of your Inner Guide, you will experience before you in the meadow the inner archetype (pure intelligence) whose energy supports this area of your life. Number one... number two... number three...now there...go with your first impression of what is there. *((Pause))* You can share with me verbally what you are experiencing and, as you do, you will notice that sharing in this way enhances your inner experience in every way. *((Share)) ((To test the genuineness of the archetype, send a beam of light from the heart, as done testing the Inner Guide.))*

Experience the archetype communicating with you by the manner in which it reveals itself. Relax and allow your intuitive sense, and your bodily instinctive sense to absorb this communication completely for your highest benefit, always feeling the support of your Inner Guide...making this process more delightful and effortless moment by moment, now, in every way. *((Pause))* Experience the feeling emanating from the archetype. *((Pause))*

Now ask with your whole heart and soul, knowing that you will receive answers for your highest benefit: "What changes do I need to make in order to fully receive the gift of your energies and teachings (guidance) in my life?" *((Receive reply and share))*

Now ask: "What is it within me that has been blocking your pure manifestation in my life?" *((Receive reply and share))*

On the count of three, you will experience this blockage being transformed into a symbol by your unconscious mind...a symbol that embodies its full meaning and significance... one.. two... three... experience the symbol and tell me what you experience... *((Share))*...now present this symbol to the archetype and experience the archetypal energies transforming this symbol in such a way that you are freed from its limitations and the problem completely solved. *((Share))* *((Test: ask archetype if it is done. If yes, ask client if they feel it has happened — instruct them to sense if any part of them did/didn't participate. Test in this way after each segment))*

and/or

Now, on the count of three, the subpersonality that embodied this problem will appear...one...two...three...experience the subpersonality...*((Share))*...now experience as the archetypal energies envelope the subpersonality, blessing and educating it, releasing all limitations, transforming and integrating all that is of value in the subpersonality into your being. *((Pause and share))*

and/or

Now, on the count of three, visualize a characterization of yourself in some situation, a scene personifying this state of old limitations...one...two...three... there you are...*((Share))*...now experience the archetype moving into the situation and doing whatever is necessary and appropriate to completely release you from these old limitations, and integrating all learnings and resources. *((Share))*

Guide the client to give only what verbal information is necessary to allow you to assist them to make the experiences alive and vivid. Avoid analyzing the symbols. Rather encourage them to feel the power and significance of the interactions taking place. Tell them to know that many learnings are being generated in their being and they will understand consciously whatever is appropriate to understand consciously and to relax and let their greater being absorb ALL the learnings for their highest benefit. *((OPTION: repeat process with polar opposite archetype.))*

((As needed or appropriate, do regression here to the origin of the problem, or anything else that seems right.))

Now invite the archetype to go back in time with you to the significant emotional experience in the past that gave rise to this problem of _____ IN SUCH A WAY THAT YOU WILL BE FREED FROM ANY REMAINING LIMITATIONS. REMEMBER, YOU CAN KEEP ANY LEARNINGS OR RESOURCES THAT TRULY UPLIFT YOU AS YOU LET THE LIMITATIONS GO. As I count from one to three you will go back in time with the archetype to the source of the problem. One...going back, farther back...back in time, two...floating back farther, effortlessly, comfortably. When I get to three you'll be there, fully aware in such a way that you will be freed of this problem...now...three! Go with your first impression of where you are and what is occurring.

((Continue as necessary with all appropriate procedures to process the experience.))

Now come back to the meadow with the archetype *((Pause))*... experience on the count of three the archetype giving you a gift that embodies all the power and significance of your new relationship...1...2..3...take the gift...*((Share))*...feel the energy of it with your whole being...examine it in a way that allows it to reveal itself fully....and ...then...take it into your being in whatever way is appropriate, absorbing completely its blessings, power, and teachings. *((Pause and share))*

Now experience yourself giving a gift to the archetype on the count of three...1...2...3...give the gift... experience the archetype taking the gift...honoring its significance...and taking it into its being in whatever way appropriate. Open to how this effects you. *((Pause and share))*

In a moment you're going to come back to normal waking consciousness, but before you do...[allow this whole experience to dissolve into golden white light] *((repeat))*...[a light that captures all the power, blessings and guidance of this experience and radiates them throughout your past, causing every experience in your past to be reevaluated in the light of these new learnings and healing powers.] *((repeat))* [Want this Light of True Wisdom, Loving Kindness and Beneficial Power to fully awaken deep in your being to completely cleanse the younger *((their name))* of your past of all (his/her) shame, guilt, fear, and confusion. Experience the younger (you) growing free of all victimization and need to blame and resent.] *((pause and repeat))*...experience the Wisdom, Love and Power radiating into your future as well... *((pause and repeat))*...experience yourself moving through future anticipated and new situations guided and empowered by these new learnings and resources, guided by your own awakened pure intelligence to perceive your life as a precious and sacred gift. Waking into this sacred appreciation of life causes you to experience your thoughts, feelings and understandings expand beyond the narrow boundaries of small-minded fearful ideas about yourself and others. More and more, day by day, you learn how to act truly for the highest good of yourself and all beings.

((Dissolve the light into the body, pervading their whole being, activating and sustaining this process from now on forever in every way for their own highest good... EMBELLISH AND ELABORATE, BE POETIC AND COMPELLING. Bring them back.))

◆ ◆ ◆

6. Archetypal Formations and Evolution

Whereas the zodiac gives the overview of archetypal organizing energies in each area of our lives, this section is presented to give a sense of some predominate roles that evolve in reaction to the dualistic dilemma of separation/shame/loss of innocence through time.

We begin at birth with the assumed state of innocence and its inevitable loss and subsequent adoption of reactive styles or roles to cope with the pain of the loss of innocence -- the loss of true living-as-self.

Again, as you learn about these roles and no doubt become moved and fascinated by the chords they strike within you, strive to develop the capacity to appreciate the underlying movement of dualistic splitting and its subsequent "topsy-turvy" twists of perception, thought, and action. In my opinion, there is a danger of getting distracted by the content and interplay of the archetypal (& subpersonality) roles in such a way that, while you become familiar with them and they help you to order, interpret and even become more aware of your motivations as they express in these roles, you still can miss the more central point of cutting through altogether the reactive egoic process.

Just as with emotional abreaction where people have become disillusioned with emoting because it doesn't change anything, people can start viewing and appreciating and interpreting the inner symbology of their limitations, but not experience that symbology evolving in a transformative way. In each case, the undetected problem is one of fixating in a closed loop relationship to the emotional dramas or the symbology that prevents clearing or transformation. It's a kind of familiar nesting that the egoic mind loves to do. It usurps the energy and insights, makes a storyline about itself using them and fixates this as another part of self-imagery.

*Cutting through this "egoic root" doesn't mean elimination of the roles necessarily at all. It means they become free-play -- skillful means to dance with life in the awake state, with one not identified **as** the role but able to **act out** the role as a useful tool. As Jesus said, "Be in the world, but not of the world."*

The Six Archetypes

The six archetypes here presented are: **the Innocent, Orphan, Martyr, Wanderer, Warrior, and Magician.** They represent one interpretation, but not the only interpretation, of archetypal roles that govern our behavior as we navigate through this world.

Archetypes as universal organizing principles are amoral. They are not good or bad; they simply "are," embodying and expressing manifest reality as itself. When the "twist" comes in, the sense of "i am this" vs. "i am doing this to accomplish something in accord with universal principles," the archetypes take on caric**aturiz**ation to greater or lesser degree. Just as this word, caricaturization, has a catch in it, so the free flowing energy of being experiences a catch in its flow upon the birth of the awareness of "i," the primordial separate self.

When these impersonal energetic patterns become identities instead of roles, they lose their flexibility to arise, persist, and dissolve according to the appropriate dictates of on-going situations. Clinging, fixating arises as the sense of "i." Agendas become set as overlay trance states that misperceive and misinterpret the on-going display of reality. Intuition of goodness, sacredness, spaciousness, power, freedom to choose and act truly, peacefulness, and more are diminished as the forgetfulness of "i" consciousness solidifies.

This is what makes all the roles mentioned _between_ the Innocent and the Magician problematic. They are the roles we inhabit as trance states of identity, whereas the Innocent is the pre-identity state and the Magician is the post-**fixed** identity state (but a true "I don't know who I am" trans-identity state). As such, according to our more strict definition of awakened archetypes, these roles are not archetypal, but stereotypical patterns suffused with egoic confusion. I will continue to use the term archetypal in this discussion to stay in correlation with the source author mentioned below. Maintain your awareness of the distinction, however.

The Magician is the master of the roles, and is archetypal. Magician energy is the energy that wakes up anyone relating _in a role as the role_ to their freedom from such bondage. All these "archetypes", being reactive strategies to the same dilemma, are simply different aspects of the same thing -- the primary egoic separation. Each one embodies the others; while we may act out in one predominate way, we inhabit them all, and therefore, to fully move into the mastery of the Magician, we must master each of them. This does not mean it has to be focused in a linear way, one-by-one, at all. There is no set plan. It could look rather orderly or very chaotic. The essential factor will be tapping into the Magician energy, or, perhaps more appropriately, it will be the Magician energy tapping into us. He knows the Wisdom of Action, i.e., he does things when they need to be done, as they need to be done; not too soon, not too late, not too little, not too much. The Magician can act skillfully in any role, without forgetfulness, and move on without clinging in any way to anything when it is time to do so.

Following is a schematic of these archetypes. Although they are presented in linear form, do not fall into assumptions about their process of appearance and function being linear. It would be helpful to consider them as the underlying molds of the subpersonalities. As subpersonalities, they pop up instantaneously and haphazardly as situations trigger them, while simultaneously generating atmospheric, persistent meta-themes through various life stages. You could begin to consider a hierarchy of subpersonalities, some momentary, some generalized over long periods of time, like radioactive isotopes with varying half-lives.

The Six Through-Time Archetypes

	Innocent	Orphan	Martyr	Wanderer	Warrior	Magician
Goal	none	safety	goodness	autonomy	strength	wholeness
Task	fall	hope	give up	identity	courage	joy
Fear	loss of paradise	abandonment	selfishness	conformity	weakness	superficiality
Posture	trusts	mourns	gives, loves	names own truth	asserts own truth	life=gift

Reference:Carol S. Pearson's, <u>The Hero Within</u>, (San Francisco: Harper row, 1944).

The Innocent

The innocent lives in a state of grace; the orphan has to confront the fact of the fall from grace, as do the martyr, wanderer, and warrior. These last three are styles of, *strategies for*, living in the world after the fall (or in our terms, after that first trance intuition of separateness).

The Orphan

The attitude of orphan compared to these three is somewhat passive shock -- just the insult and confusion and pain of loss, followed by mourning.

The Martyr

The martyr copes with the pain by trying to antidote it with a shift of focus, denying self to give to others. He develops the feeling capacity to commit to love, to let go for the sake of others. The twist here is that altruism looks good and can lead to subtle (and not so subtle) pride -- a sure indication that living life beyond the need for validation has not been achieved.

The Wanderer

The wanderer's response is somewhat one of sour grapes. If he is out of the garden, it isn't that good anyway, and off he goes to find his sense of self apart from others -- he makes a virtue out of separateness.

The Warrior

Although the warrior embodies the qualities of assertion and power over others, at his core, he is still expressing a confused passive acquiescence to the fall. He affirms the illusory reality of the fall by his actions to master the art of self defense. Morihei Ueshiba, the founder of Aikido, movingly describes his awakening to the ultimate archetypal sense of warriorship. He describes what occurred when, as an accomplished master of many martial arts, he defeated a master swordsman, **_unarmed_**:

> *"Suddenly the earth trembled. Golden vapor welled up from the ground and engulfed me. I felt transformed into a golden image, and my body seemed as light as a feather. All at once I understood the nature of creation: **the Way of a Warrior is to manifest Divine Love, a spirit that embraces and nurtures all things.**"*
>
> (My bold -- Excerpted from <u>The Art of Peace</u>. by John Stevens.
> c.1992, Boston: Shambala Publications.)

This is the warrior realizing the magician within -- the transpersonal "I" that is and embraces all things as itself. No doubt, all his years of cultivated focus and bodily alignment, coupled with the sustained intense focus of dueling unarmed with a master swordsman caused his mind to pierce the veils.

Until his awakening he had pursued an egoic stereotypical warrior ethic. <u>Notice the paradoxical discovery of the True nature of Warriorship vs. the worldly egoic view</u>. Notice also that extreme dedication to any of these coping roles has the potential, by virtue of the effect of sustained renewed focus (beginner's mind), to transcend itself, to pop out of trance into the realm of "ordinary magic," the archetypal realm.

The Magician

The Magician lives in sacred space and time, and all things partake of that sacredness. He therefore recognizes the abundance of the universe, and, being at one with the universe, has the capacity to powerfully move the energy of the universe, not by selfish will, but by being in accord with the law of synchronicity that implies "not my will but thine." Since he trusts the infallible supportive intelligence of the universe to provide perfectly for what is truly needed when it is needed, this is not the scary sacrifice the egoic mentality imagines. It looks like the Magician is exercising his will, but his will is in accord with the Tao or Will of God to which everything is possible. He fully values himself in an all-inclusive way, where his esteem for his form is in the context of his recognition of and esteem for his true boundless formless Self -- the Self of all. Thus, in a mature way, he comes full circle back to innocent, but not naive/ignorant, trust. He trusts himSelf.

Gender biases in Through-Time Archetypes

In our culture there have been some sexual biases towards certain roles, and we all experience the on-going unsettling shifting of their relevance.

Women typically would be attracted to martyr/magician archetypal energies embodying as they do feminine qualities of interdependence, interconnectedness, networks, webs, and affiliations. A typical female pattern would be to go from orphan to martyr and stay there.

All roles have their time and place. For example, a martyr mother may not survive the parting of her grown children unless she can shift to the guiding influence of another more phase appropriate archetype such as wanderer, in this case, to redefine the meaning of her life.

Some modern women have found themselves getting strung out by adding roles to adapt to their expanded vision of their possibilities, rather than transforming roles completely. An example would be the career mother: martyr at home; warrior at work.

Men typically would gravitate towards wanderer/warrior masculine energies of separateness, isolation, competition, and hierarchy.

A typical male pattern would be to go from orphan to warrior and stay there. Like the dilemma of the martyr mother, the warrior man will inevitably feel the trauma of going out of phase. We call it mid-life crisis, when he is challenged to move into the guiding influence of a more phase appropriate archetype. Like the woman, if he survives the challenge to become "unfixed," he regains the opportunity to be enlivened by phase appropriate archetypal energies that naturally carry him towards the magician state. But the tendency to cling, bind, and nest under new more expanded, but nevertheless fixed, dualistic trance standards can limit or stagnate the flow. Constant wakefulness to renounce the fixating tendencies of the trance/mind is essential. Fortunately, wakefulness can become a beneficial habit in itself.

The flow of the life force is defined by the patterning of the archetypal forms. When we bind them, we are damming up the free flow of our life energies, and we experience the harm that such restriction causes. When we flow with them, they empower us and enable us to flourish.

◆ ◆ ◆

7. Male Archetypes

Before presenting this material, I want to again emphasize that, for my purposes and from my point of view, the most important thing to understand is <u>not</u> simply the content of these archetypal categories as intellectual knowledge, but:

*1) How the underlying dualistic, egoic process, which we mistakenly identify as self, devalues and obstructs the manifestation of the inherently pure, sane, and awake expression of archetypal energies as aspects of our own **True** self, and*

2) How to relate to the obstructing dualistic dynamic in a way that sparks the inherent wakefulness of archetypal qualities to manifest spontaneously, dissolving the obstructions, bringing the client out of the egoic trance.

This is a most terrifying notion -- that we could be totally spontaneous without any guardedness (i.e., exposed - the TRUE ME) and discover that we always are thinking/feeling/acting appropriately and that things work out.

It has been my experience that people who have approached this type of material as a tool to understand themselves and to grow, get stuck in identifications with the tool in ways that are subtle forms of denial. *As stated previously, the egoic mind stands ever ready to embrace, <u>even and especially</u>, the knowledge, ideas, and processes designed to destroy it. By embracing them, it perverts them, and bends them to its purpose of creating fixity, and false identity - commonly known as **Pride**, of ownership and of knowledge. This is true in any field of thought, in any endeavor, not just here.*

We can detect it in such statements as,

> *"**My** warrior really came out last night when he did that...I **knew** better but..."*

or,

> *"I felt such anger, then had a flash of a vision of **my** black panther. We accessed the panther; it's caged, and even though the door is open, it can't get out."*

There is an over identification with the archetypal imagery that causes an inappropriate dissociation from the <u>temporary patterning of one's own energy (i.e., just having a *feeling*)</u> - in these examples, anger. In each example, the person had stopped progressing in their capacity to relate to their anger, but having a sophisticated image and means of "holding" and identifying it, <u>and creating a melodrama</u>, gave them the illusion of progress and hid from them work that still needed to be done.

The attempt to gain a perspective to understand and to work with these energies of feeling, then becomes a way of boxing them and fantasizing about them instead of embracing them and feeling them as our own living being. It stops us from finding out that, by becoming one with them, they have an integrity of process that is independent of the fantasies and their implied danger. Left alone without mental contrivance, they arise, persist, and dissolve back into the ground of our being without having to subscribe to or affirm the meaning that the fantasy thought-trance drama tries to give them. {This is what we learn in real emotional clearing work: to separate the feeling energy from the storyline and let it release, keeping the learnings from the storyline as simple data, not ammunition for shame attacks.}

Feelings are just Feelings

Feelings are just feelings, think about it, contemplate this:

1) They don't *mean* anything (re: what the fear-based thoughts try to convince they mean: "Bad person" or, "Bad consequences" if you *let yourself know* you are feeling this -- and I mean *let yourself know* because most people get caught by the egoic trance suggestion: "*if* I let myself feel this" not realizing *it's too late!* -- *we wouldn't be having this struggle with ourselves, trying to decide if and what to feel or do if we weren't already feeling it and trying to pretend we weren't!*);

2) They don't have to pull us out of present time or put us in trance; we don't have to (and can't really) run away from them, they are our own energy, so we can afford to learn <u>how</u> to embrace them, which is what this course is attempting to teach.

3) The point is not to push thoughts and/or feelings away, but to participate in them with full body/mind awareness. How? - breathe, relax, stay alert to the fact of thinking and feeling, without becoming hypnotized by thinking and feeling, using sensations of contracting and releasing in the body to keep anchored in the body/present-process -- easier said than done, but a worthy endeavor to practice, to play our part in saving the world. This allows a *feeling appreciation* of their energy and a *discriminating awareness* of their relative nature (i.e. they are not fixed solid truths as phenomena, and they are not about any fixed "I" personality -- but a play of energy in an intuitively felt, *free* field of awareness which is our True Self, No-Self, I-don't-know-who-I-am-self. Yes, even you can feel it, it's there/here all the time, it just takes practice.

On the following page is a diagram that I have constructed to illustrate the underlying dynamics and qualities in relationship between the archetypes and their mutation in the phenomenon of egoic dualistic splitting:

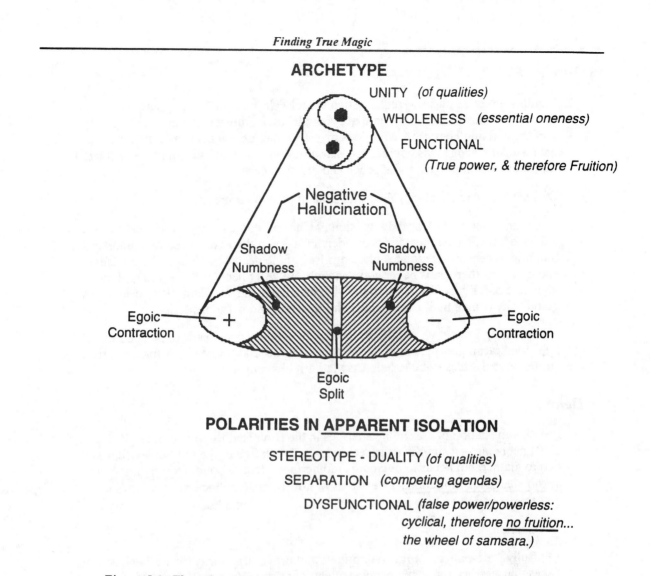

ARCHETYPE

UNITY *(of qualities)*

WHOLENESS *(essential oneness)*

FUNCTIONAL
(True power, & therefore Fruition)

Negative
Hallucination

Shadow
Numbness

Shadow
Numbness

Egoic
Contraction

+

−

Egoic
Contraction

Egoic
Split

POLARITIES IN <u>APPARENT</u> ISOLATION

STEREOTYPE - DUALITY *(of qualities)*

SEPARATION *(competing agendas)*

DYSFUNCTIONAL *(false power/powerless:*
cyclical, therefore <u>no fruition</u>...
the wheel of samsara.)

Figure 5.1: *The relationship between the archetypes and their mutation in the phenomenon of egoic dualistic splitting:*

Notice how this phenomenon plays itself out in the descriptions of the Boy and Male Psyche (by the way, there will be significant relevance here for the female psyche as well.)

As we go through this, it will be quite evident that, in our culture and in the history of the world, Boy psychology is very prevalent in adult behavior. The problem being that we have lost touch with the power and process of myths and mythic rights of passage and initiation that create and induce a shift of being and outlook in the initiates, moving them from boyhood to manhood.

The Boy Archetypes

The Boy archetypes are: Divine Child, Hero, Precocious Child, and Oedipal Child. They transform respectively into: King, Warrior, Magician, and Lover.

Divine Child

Manifest inherent purity -- re: Christian model - Christ child is the example. Innocent, immaculate, God-incarnate, yet vulnerable, threatened, and needing protection (King Herod). A wondrous mystery; magical events attend his birth -- nature acknowledges his coming: the star, the Wise Men, the shepherds. The longed for promise of hope, joy, light, peace and order on earth.

Divine Child Archetype devaluates to stereotypical polarities of:

(+) High Chair Tyrant: shadow version of Christ -- egoic inversion of center of the universe: others must meet his needs/demands (i.e. tremendous need of support) vs. a Sun/Son as center that radiates blessings free of the need of support. There is never enough; what there is, is never good enough. He will reject true needs (e.g., food, love) and hurt himself in his extreme allegiance to his idea of himself as center: his grandiosity (ring a bell?), arrogance, childishness, and irresponsibility.

(-) Weakling Prince: very little personality, no enthusiasm, needs to be coddled, hypocondriacal: gets the entire family to revolve around his needs. A manipulative, cutting verbal attacker, but a helpless victim if challenged.

Hero

Peak manifestation of masculine energies in the Boy: enables him to assert himself as a distinct being -- a significant aspect being to break free of the mother appropriately: tied to mother, but needs to overcome mother/boy identity bond. <u>Doesn't know or acknowledge his limitations</u>. Doesn't know how to relate to the ordinary -- it's a questing energy that, accessed properly, moves us into manhood.

Devaluation:

(+) Bully: self-centered, urge to dominate and prove superiority over others. A loner. Takes unnecessary risks, and demands them of others (Vietnam). Sense of invulnerability, inflated sense of importance, and abilities. Hot shot salesman.

(-) Coward: can't/won't stand up for self. Allows himself to be run over, invaded, pressured. Lacks motivation to achieve anything.

Precocious Child

Gracious, poised, self-confident, gentle, concentrated, thoughtful, eager to learn and <u>share learnings</u>. Curious about people and the "Why" of the universe.

Devaluation:

(+) Know-It-All-Trickster: creates appearances and sells us on them *(do you see the egoic twist, in these examples, of inherently pure qualities?)* Seduces us, and then pulls out the rug; a braggart, likes to intimidate.

(-) Dummy: lacks personality, vigor, and creativity. Unresponsive and dull: slow learner, physically inept. No sense of humor (secret grandiosity - knows more than he lets on), too vulnerable to come into the world.

Oedipal Child

Tied to mother, <u>as are all immature masculine energies</u>: deficient in the experience of nurturing and mature masculine energy. Passion, sense of wonder, deep appreciation for connectedness (feminine principal) w/inner depths, w/others, w/all things: warm, related, affectionate. Connection to mother is root of spiritual awareness: a sense of mystic oneness *(remember Shakti - mother of all phenomena)*, mutual connectedness of all things; yearning for the infinitely nurturing, good, beautiful Divine (not mortal) Mother -- Maha-Shakti.

Devaluation:

(+) Mama's Boy: tied to apron strings, fantasizes about marrying mother - taking her away from Dad. In an adult body: goes from one woman to another yearning for Mother: <u>never satisfied with mortal woman -- Don Juan</u>. Autocratic, wants to be God in union w/Mother, not mortal man responsible for complex intimate human relationships. Can be compulsive about masturbation and pornography.

(-) Dreamer: takes the spiritual impulses to the extreme: relationships are within w/intangibles and the world of imagination. Feels isolated, cut off from human relationships. Accomplishes little -- appears withdrawn and depressed.

Mature Male Archetypes

King

Two primary functions: 1) to put in order, 2) to provide fertility and blessings. First in importance and underlies all other archetypes: more basic and comprehensive than Father archetype. <u>King energy</u>, *not mortal king* is important. ("The king is dead, long live the King!") Human is vehicle for the greater energy: <u>the mortal king must follow the Tao of King energy in order to set an example and to truly lead</u>. (cf. English royal family) *"He who would command must first obey."* i.e. The highest, the mortal king, is actually totally surrendered to something higher (the trans-ego Tao). Application for therapist & client: *Where is my sense of place, and what in my life needs blessings?*

Devaluation:

(+) Tyrant: no trans-ego commitment, selfish -- he is his own priority. Tries to be King Archetype instead of vehicle for it, i.e. no surrender. Thus cut off from true support, becomes fearful, rageful at not being the center of the universe, fundamentally insecure. Destructive, not creative: fears freshness of life, joy, and spontaneity. Tries to kill the Divine Child (King Herod).
(-) Weakling Prince: repressed grandiosity: explodes to the surface -- becomes Hitler. "Power corrupts; absolute power corrupts absolutely." (cf. Alice Miller's account of Hitler's childhood and oppressive father, in For Your Own Good)

Warrior

Warrior Tao: total Way of Life (cf. Morihei Ueshiba, founder of Aikido, The Art of Peace, by John Stevens (Shambala Publications, Boston, Mass.) Aggressiveness: arouses, energizes, motivates. Always alert, clear-thinking, awake: therefore insures appropriateness of aggressiveness. Pushes us to take the offensive. Because of his clarity: 1) he is a master strategist and tactician, 2) he knows his limitations in any situation (unlike the Hero). Clarity has arisen out of living and training within a continuous awareness of the imminence of death: no time for hesitation; live each moment to the fullest. Mastery of the mind and attitudes (trance states). Transpersonal commitment to something larger than self: God, country, a people, a cause (e.g., Bodhisattva ideal). This eliminates a lot of pettiness (as in personal relationships) -- they become inconsequential in the light of imminence of death. Application for T&C: *What values must I fight for? What actions must I undertake without hesitation?*

Devaluation:

(+) Sadist: embodies cruelty that manifests in two ways: 1) passionate -- wrath of God, 2) w/o passion, cold -- Nazis, capable of horrendous acts, while maintaining a sense of personal goodness. Hatred for the weak and vulnerable, compulsive, self-driven workaholic tendencies. (-) Masochist: pushover, whipped puppy. Cowardly, projecting power onto others and feeling powerless. Takes too much abuse for too long, then explodes in a sadistic rage.

Magician

Archetype of awareness and insight -- "the Observing Ego, the Witness." Knower and Master of technology: guides processes of transformation within and without. Initiated into secret and hidden knowledge of all kinds -- this gives great power. Deflates arrogance, sees through denial: Court Magician - the King's psychotherapist. Present in the Warrior as clarity of thinking. Alone, he doesn't have the capacity to act; he does have the capacity to think. The archetype of thoughtfulness, reflection, introversion. Application for T&C: *What wounds need to be healed; what perspectives and identifications transformed?*

Devaluation:

(+) Manipulator: Magician energies gone awry: power shadow -- detached and cruel, giving information, but not enough; people don't know what they are getting into. Withholding and secretive. Polluters, toxic waste proponents, lobbyists, lawyers and therapists. Knowledge as a weapon to harm, black magic.
(-) Denying "Innocent One": carry over from Dummy; wants power and status, but w/o the responsibility. Doesn't want to share or to teach. Envious, blocking others and seeking their downfall; always hiding his motivation.
Innocent -- "so good." E.g. *"All I want is the best for you."* (in tears). Slippery and illusive.

Lover

The life force, always divine, entering the profane world of matter: the erect penis; blood - the spirit energy of soul. Archetype of play and display of healthy embodiment. Being in one's body w/o shame: deeply sensual, sensitive to the physical world, compassionate and empathetic w/all things. All things bound in mysterious ways: "All beings are my mother," experiencing the whole universe in a grain of sand. Open to the collective unconscious (Jung), not just human consciousness. <u>Feeling</u> connection, passionate, not intellectual. Aesthetic consciousness: all life is art. Source of spirituality and mysticism. Can read others like a book. Capacity to experience deep pain or deep joy. Not bound by conventional boundaries. Application for T&C: *Towards what does my healthy passion move me to passionately engage?*

Devaluation:

(+) Addicted Lover: destructive urge to be unbounded. <u>Lostness:</u> lost in the ocean of the senses; can't get perspective or detach, eternally restless.
(-) Impotent Lover: chronically depressed, lack of connection w/others, very dissociated -- speaks of self in 3rd person. Sense of unreality, life is like a movie. Life status: stressed at work/ angry in relationships/ sexually inactive. Mainlines Warrior or Magician energy.

Reference: <u>King, Warrior, Magician, Lover</u>, by Robert Moore and Douglas Gillette(Harper, San Francisco, Ca.)

Summary

Remember, at the archetypal level, there is an awareness of unity. Each archetypal expression is an aspect of a known wholeness. There is no back-biting because of jealous value judgements about hierarchy. Hierarchy is simply a matter of function, not of inherent value. Therefore it does not instigate any form of shame or competition.

An Eastern metaphor for this is The Lords' Club. A group of Lords gather to put on a play. Some will be assigned roles of royalty, some merchants, some beggars, but no one will complain or be offended or shamed, because a role is just a role, and they never forget that they are all equally and truly Lords. All the roles are fun to take a turn at.

Also, while archetypal polarities fluctuate, "teeter-totter," or swing back and forth, there is no linear order dictating how they must manifest or mix through time. Any archetype can pop up, moment by moment, constantly, noticed or unnoticed, in the spaces of our <u>apparently continuous</u> egoic trance. When noticed, they are experienced as highpoints because of their purity and intensity. Knowledge of archetypal patterns gives us an awareness of their egoic degradations, the stereotypes, identified as the meta-themes, or over-riding characteristics of subpersonality groups - the bullies, the whiners, etc. The whole package manifests as the display of our many-selved self.

Life changes moment by moment, dictating what will be inspired or triggered. Remember, every impulse of energy, moment by moment, is essentially archetypal. If it is not interfered with by egoic contraction, it will reach consciousness as a spontaneous functional response, an inspiration. If egoic contraction is present, the energy will reach consciousness as a triggered, dysfunctional, non-spontaneous, habitual response. Archetypal energies, inspirations, are awake and playful. Stereotypes, triggered habitual responses, are serious, asleep in fearful egoic trance.

The nature of a healthy mind is playful. Therefore, appeal to the playful capacity of the mind to heal the mind. Use techniques that require playfulness. One might say, in more clinical language, non-linear techniques, but <u>playfulness is not bound by either linear or non-linear requirements</u>.

Therefore, the therapist's awareness and delivery are crucial. Think about it, playfully!

◆ ◆ ◆

8. Female Archetypes

There are obvious correlations between the masculine and feminine where a great percentage of the archetypal qualities and functions remain the same or are closely paralleled: King:Queen, Prince:Princess. Material is easily available to fill out these models along the lines already presented.

I have chosen to present here a feminine model that is outside of this easy correlation to a degree in order to expand your conception of the possibilities for distinguishing archetypal patterns. **Think about how your recognition of these qualities, <u>or the disruption or absence of these qualities</u>, in client's stories about themselves indicate strengths and weaknesses. How could such recognitions inform your communications, images, stories, and questions?**

The Circle Of Nine

Primary Energy -- **HECATE** -- Moon Goddess [3 in 1]:

1. New, Crescent, & Full

2. Raw Feminine Energy: the Nine are its display

3. The Circle -- feminine form; receives and contains; bounded space: security and order (vs. chaos)

4. The Nine can occur in any order in the circle (not necessarily as presented here)

5. **Feminine is human property, not exclusive to women**

   a) Take care in identifying with archetypes, particularly in identifying with one. They are aspects of a whole, and <u>non-human</u> in this sense. A human being embodies in potential the entire cluster of qualities. *Identification inappropriately, in a fixated way, is merely an egoic invasion of sacred territory.*

6. The Nine:

3 Queens	3 Ladies	3 Mothers
Act as center of life; How to be; how to maintain; how to draw towards themselves what is needed (cf. magician). **The Heart**	Active energies, doing and giving; create flow out of what is static; **grace & poise,** handle change with ease, Alchemists-turn base material into lightness & charm. The energy field around the body - **The Aura.**	Rulers of structure and order. Know the laws of time and space. From this, make forms and patterns. Take what is necessary for growth and reject the rest. **The Womb.**

The Queen of Night

- Power and energy unrestricted by convention. Knowledge of esoteric forces.

- The tides: night tides, attracting and awakening.

- Strong emotional drives: Draws on currents of energy to fulfill instinctual needs, *unconstrained by honor, justice, compassion, or civilized virtues.* Knowledgeable, magical, primitive. Not attractive as with charm or grace -- can shock & upset.

- Operating at night -- all daily duties left behind. Example: Islamic women -- strict daily life, veiled. Wailing & dancing in the street at night, hair free and unveiled. (Men inside).

- Night - the unknown

- Like the Moon - shape changer, state changer.

The Queen of Beauty

Beauty not fixed -- many faces, infinite range, encompassing the ebb and flow of feminine life.

Dualities

1) Internal & External

Ideally harmonious, both women and men must choose. External more important to women: in pursuit of physical beauty there are initiations, taboos, indignity, ridicule, and suffering (cf. procedures at the hairdressers).

2) Beauty vs. Ugliness

- Age vs. youth (how to express age w/o suppressing it, sexual vs. transcendent, concealed vs. revealed.)

- Physical beauty is a reflection of God's presence in the world. It should aim towards the spirit, but if you try to capture it, i.e. fixate it, own it [egoic trances], you kill it.

- *True beauty has to embrace the polarities (something egoic mind cannot do!)*

- Essential to escape the trap of fixation, i.e., to always be beautiful. Keeping up appearances is deadly. Being put on a pedestal is deadly.

- Beauty has great responsibility -- a woman who embodies beauty must be capable of handling the feelings and energies she arouses - (Gurumayi vs. Marilyn Monroe). The results can be catastrophic -- Helen of Troy.

- Charisma -- the union of physical and spiritual beauty, *requires great discipline.*

The Queen of Earth

- Embodies the Princess, the Enthroned Queen, and the Individual Queen (who makes her mark with her personality, i.e. the <u>named</u> Queen)

- Earth -- bound to cycles of growth: seed, blossom, fruition. Knowledge of seasons, hidden properties of earth.

- Re: sexuality -- 3 Phases:

1) Innocent - the Princess: freedom, wildness of nature, following her own spirit. The earth is her playground - no duties or responsibilities.

2) Awakened - Queen of Earth: ascending to the throne, symbolizes living beauty of earth. Sexuality, earthy passions, rich and flowering. United with her land.

3) Individualized - the Named Queen: can be eccentric, capricious. Can be a powerful force to strengthen her country and unite her people through her relationship to the earth.

The Just Mother

- Courage of the Heart: discrimination, fighting skills
- Dangers to be confronted, within and without
- Has the responsibility of making judgments, then acting, then accepting the consequences, E.g. responding to child-rearing challenges:
- Establishing right and wrong and being tested: to give/ to withhold, to permit/to restrict, to tolerate/to reprimand
- Facing the World - making a public stand (Women's Lib.)
- Weapons (for overcoming superior force, i.e. masculine energy)

  a) persistence - wearing down the obstruction

  b) cleverness - cunning and sharp-witted, finding the way to precision

  c) precision - wise use of timing and energy; knowing the goal. On target.

The Great Mother

- Motherhood - affirmation of Time: i.e. birth implies death, fixed life span discounts individuality - challenge/dilemma of the new mother, "I am not me anymore, I'm mommy!" Can be crazy making.
- Transformation - physical and mental: the womb, the cave(of the heart), the period of darkness, the waiting period(gestation), transcendent knowledge. Confronting the absolute, direct experience -- life & death, reality of birth.
- Motherhood - though it dissolves individuality, it also dissolves barriers: the Bond of Motherhood.

The Weaving Mother

- Requirements: 1)thread that can be bound (raw material), 2)skill to weave them, 3)knowledge of pattern (vision).
- *The organizing principle of the female:*

  a) ties bonds of love, patterns of daily life, and death

  b) turns simplicity into complexity, and complexity into simplicity

  c) knowledge of the beginning and the end of the process - or the middle becomes a hopeless jumble

  d) to form, use, and sever bonds: the first thread -- the umbilical cord, perhaps the strongest bond we ever experience.

The Lady of Light

Feminine version of light -- 3 Manifestations:

- a) Collective level - in-dwelling, suffused, radiates out(vs. Masculine -beam, intense, focused), the power of the group to take in and protect
- b) Polarized level - the other, guiding light: guide, teacher, saint
- c) Individual - the light of creativity: song, dance, artistry

The Lady of the Dance

- ◆ Release from the urge for order: Spirit of the Dance -- joy, spontaneity, freedom of movement of the life force
- ◆ Brings sweetness and charm to life
- ◆ Harmonizing the 3 forces of creation:

    a) initiating (energy of dance) - dancer lifts foot

    b) resisting (governs rhythm of the dance, a structure of repetition) - foot touches the ground(limitation)

    c) unifying/balancing (determines form of the dance, exploration of all achievable combinations of movement) - body adjusts, harmonizing (a) & (b) to continue on with further movement

    The crucial secret, the essence: Finding the **Stillpoint** in movement(no egoic movement- unity of mind & body), staying in touch with it - keeps the dance alive and with spirit.

The Lady of the Hearth

- ◆ The effort to create and maintain a home
- ◆ Sensitive to living environment
- ◆ Links the well-being of the feminine psyche and a healthy living environment
- ◆ Household tasks - carry strong emotional charge, (+) or (-). Strong possibility to (con)fuse devotion/martyrdom.
- ◆ Household routine - powerful ritual, both honored and debased. What will it be - sacred or profane?
- ◆ Lighting and tending the fire:
    - ◆ lighting: beginning new sequence of action; an initiation
    - ◆ tending: sustaining an environment, an atmosphere. Capable of manipulating moods(vs. men who are seized by them)
- ◆ The fire: focus of communication
    - ◆ time to relax, to reflect, to enjoy
    - ◆ time to tell stories: to honor the past, transmitting continuity to a new generation
    - ◆ time to generate a vision of the future

Reference: **The Circle of Nine, by Cherry Gilchrist, (Dryad Press, London).**

◆ ◆ ◆

9. Induction for Accessing Archetypes
Working with Polarities

Begin by discussing the relevant issues/life areas to be addressed, selecting one to enhance in relation to its archetypal "well-spring."

DO INDUCTIONS EMPHASIZING THE CAPACITY TO RELATE TO THE SYMBOLIC PLAY OF IMAGES TO BE INVOKED (versus a discursive, intellectual dialogue, interpretive approach - this approach emphasizes the visual/kinesthetic impact.)

Now experience yourself standing in a meadow *((or another appropriate setting — e.g. go up column of light to superconscious level))*. Experience the meadow; see the plants and trees, feel the wind gently against your face, listen to the sounds of small animals, perhaps birds singing, experience your body erect and at ease upon the earth. Take some time to vividly experience this situation in such a way that you know and feel yourself opening to the communication with _____ *((the archetype governing the life area at issue))* **[therapist repeats and elaborates appropriately to enhance the vividness of the setting and the receptiveness of the client.]**

As you become more in tune with your surroundings, now, in preparation to meet this pure archetypal intelligence which is simply an aspect of your **own** true pure intelligence, you call forth and experience the presence of your Inner Guide, now. *((Pause))* Let me know when your Inner Guide is present and you are ready to proceed.

On the count of 3, with the assistance of your Inner Guide, you will experience before you in the meadow the inner archetype (pure intelligence) whose energy supports this area of your life. *((Option: specifically ask for it to come in human form which is its highest expression in the realm of form.))*

Number one... number two... number three...now there...go with your first impression of what is there. *((Pause))* You can share with me verbally what you are experiencing and, as you do, you will notice that sharing in this way enhances your inner experience in every way. *((Share))* **[To test the**

genuineness of the archetype, send a beam of light from the heart, as done with the Inner Guide.]

Experience the archetype communicating with you <u>by the manner in which it reveals itself</u>. Relax and allow your intuitive sense, and your bodily instinctive sense to absorb this communication completely for your highest benefit, always feeling the support of your Inner Guide... making this process more delightful and effortless moment by moment, now, in every way. Experience the feeling emanating from the archetype. *((Pause))*

Now ask with your whole heart and soul, knowing that you will receive answers for your highest benefit: "What changes do I need to make in order to fully receive the gift of your energies and teachings (guidance) in my life?" *((Receive reply and share))*

Now ask: "What is it within me that has been blocking your pure manifestation in my life?" *((Receive reply and share))*

On the count of three, you will experience this blockage being transformed into a symbol by your unconscious mind... a symbol that embodies its full meaning and significance... one...two...three...experience the symbol and tell me what you experience...*((Share))*...now present this symbol to the archetype and experience the archetypal energies transforming this symbol in such a way that you are freed from its limitations and the problem completely solved. *((Pause -- share))* **[Test: ask archetype if it is done. If yes, ask client if they feel it has happened -- instruct them to sense if any part of them did/didn't participate. Test in this way after each segment.]**

    ((or))

Now, on the count of three, the subpersonality that embodied this problem will appear...one...two...three...experience the subpersonality...*((Share))*...now experience as the archetypal energies envelope the subpersonality blessing and educating it, releasing all limitations, transforming and integrating all that is of value in the subpersonality into your being. *((Pause -- share))*

    ((or))

Now, on the count of three, visualize a characterization of yourself in some situation, some scene personifying this state of limitation...one...two...three... there you are...*((Share))*...now experience the archetype moving into the situation and doing whatever is necessary and appropriate to completely release you from these old limitations, and integrating all learnings and resources. *((Pause -- share))*

    ((Guide the client to give only what verbal information is necessary to allow you to assist them to make the experiences alive and vivid. Avoid analyzing the

symbols. Rather, encourage them to feel the power and significance of the interactions taking place. Tell them to know that many learning are being generated in their being and they will understand consciously whatever is appropriate to understand consciously and to relax and let their greater being absorb ALL the learnings for their highest benefit.))

((As needed or appropriate, do regression here to the origin of the problem, or anything else, of course, that seems right. Since you are going to access the polarity in this script, for time considerations, you will not do the regression section below. However, in a "real" client session, if you're on to something, pursue it and forget the polarity access, e.g.:))

"Now invite the archetype to go back in time with you to the significant emotional experience in the past that gave rise to this problem of _____ IN SUCH A WAY THAT YOU WILL BE FREED FROM ANY REMAINING LIMITATIONS. REMEMBER, YOU KEEP ANY LEARNINGS OR RESOURCES THAT TRULY UPLIFT YOU AS YOU LET THE LIMITATIONS GO. As I count from one to three you will go back in time with the archetype to the experience. One...going back, farther back... back in time...two...floating back farther, effortlessly, comfortably...when I get to three you'll be there, fully aware in such a way that you will be freed of this problem...now...three! Go with your first impression of where you are and what is occurring."

((Continue as necessary with all appropriate procedures to process the experience.))

Experience with your whole being the effect of witnessing the archetype transforming the problem...relax...and...allow your unconscious mind to absorb these blessings and learnings... reevaluating all past experiences with these new resources... and establishing these blessings and learnings in your being in such a way that you will access them fully and appropriately in the future from now on...forever. *((Elicit sharing whenever appropriate))*

Now experience yourself receiving a gift from the archetype on the count of three...a gift that embodies these new resources...1...2...3...accept the gift... experience the energy and significance of the gift... taking it into your being in whatever way appropriate, absorbing completely its blessings, power, and teachings. *((Pause -- share))*

Now...on the count of three...experience yourself giving a gift to the archetype...one, two, three...giving the gift...experience the gift being accepted...experience the archetype absorbing the gift...sensing within yourself the new channels and bonds of communication being created...*((Pause -- share))*

Now invite the archetype to stand aside to witness as you call forth its polar opposite. *((Repeat the process with the polarity beginning with its invocation through the gift exchange, then:))*

Bring both archetypes into your awareness...experience the purity and dynamics of the interplay between the two...*((Share))*...invite them to exchange gifts as you watch...*((Share))*...recognize this relationship is a greater unique energy in itself that encompasses them both and by opening to its presence you allow their wisdom, loving kindness, and beneficial power to flow throughout your being...want that to happen, feel your desire for their True Wisdom, Love and Beneficial Power to heal, guide and teach you. *((Pause -- share))*

In this spirit of openness, close by joining hands with both archetypes and your inner guide, balancing your energies with theirs, accomplishing this desired blessing fully, until your guide signals it is complete. *((When client signals:))*

In a moment you're going to come back to normal waking consciousness, but before you do...[allow this whole experience to dissolve into golden white light] *((repeat))*...[a light that captures all the power, blessings, and guidance of this experience and radiates them throughout your past, causing every experience in your past to be reevaluated in the light of these new learnings and healing powers.] *((repeat))* [Want this Light of True Wisdom, Loving Kindness, and Beneficial Power to fully awaken deep in your being to completely cleanse the younger *((their name))* of your past of all ((his/her)) shame, guilt, fear, and confusion. Experience the younger ((you/name)) growing free of all victimization and need to blame and resent.] *((pause, repeat))* Experience this Wisdom, Love and Power radiating into your future as well... *((pause, repeat))*...experience yourself moving through future anticipated and new situations guided and empowered by these new learnings and resources, guided by your own awakened pure intelligence to perceive your life as a precious sacred gift. Waking into this sacred appreciation of life causes you to experience your thoughts, feelings, and understandings expand beyond the narrow boundaries of small-minded fearful ideas about yourself and others. More and more, day-by-day, you learn how to act truly for the highest good of yourself and all beings.

[Dissolve the light into the body, pervading their whole being, activating and sustaining this process from now on forever in every way for their own highest good - EMBELLISH AND ELABORATE, BE POETIC AND COMPELLING.]

Bring them back.

♦ ♦ ♦

Table of Contents
Phase VI

◆ ◆ ◆

1. The Shadow

The shadow is the composite of all unintegrated energies, "good" as well as "bad." According to our models, it includes all the "stuff" that is negatively hallucinated in order to keep the polarites held in antagonistic suspension, unable to perceive or experience the unity of **being** *and* **intent** that underlies their apparent separateness.

As we look at diagrams on paper and talk about "it," we can easily fall into the trance that we are talking about a thing -- "The Shadow," but it is actually more useful to think of it as a process of consciousness. We have discussed the illusion of the continuum of the conscious, egoic self and our multiplied, moment-by-moment selves that come on line as needed. We have varying ranges of flexibility in our capacities to bring up resources from the unconscious to the conscious, and one could say that, as manifestations of consciousness pop up moment-by-moment, and then recede into the unconscious, that, "where they go," is into the shadow, the darkness. Some information, learnings, skills and problematic material is relatively easy to pull out of the shadows; some of it comes up easily of its own accord, wanted or not, from the conscious point of view.

In a sense, whatever is not in consciousness at any given moment is "shadow" or, in the shadow. What is problematic is the material that is at affect over us that we have forgotten is there - our <u>unexamined</u> likes and dislikes, hopes and fears, etc. The challenge is how to retrieve it to incorporate it into our wakefulness. All the techniques we have been learning and practicing, from this point of view, have been ways of relating to the various aspects of shadow, "bad aspects" (traumas, fears, jealousies, limiting beliefs, etc.), as well as "good aspects" (True Self, inner guidance, positive intent, forgotten or discounted resources, etc.). Therefore, we have been doing shadow work all along.

There can be useful learnings gained from relating to the idea of the shadow as a subpersonality - this amorphous composite "thing." Or the subpersonality approach can be a non-specific way of asking for whatever wants to come out of the shadow in a given session, as opposed to targeting a specific subpersonality.

Since we have already targeted specific parts, the shadow script is structured to access the whole gestalt, if you will, to explore the usefulness of this kind of relationship. *As always, remember, its "thingness" is dynamic, not fixed. Therefore, over several sessions, you may get a variety of manifestations and experiences.*

◆ ◆ ◆

2. Shadow Script

Discuss the concept of shadow with the client so that you both understand that you are going to be inviting this all-encompassing dynamic of unintegrated aspects to come forth to be experienced and communicated with for mutual benefits.

For example, any new feelings of warmth, acceptance, and willingness to work together that are achieved can be communicated by the composite shadow to each and all specific parts as appropriate, outside of consciousness. This would be like having the shadow function as an overseer and intermediary to communicate efficiently with a lot of different parts simultaneously instead of having to process with them one-by-one.

Induction, etc.

Now that you are in this deeply relaxed state...allow your awareness to sense the energy of the shadow, the composite of all the unintegrated energies of your being...let me know when you are in touch with it...feeling its presence and energy...perhaps notice if it's making its presence felt in a particular part of your body...that's right...just allow your awareness of it to gently grow...in a way that you are honoring its existence...appreciate that your awareness of it is a sign of its willingness to communicate...and allow yourself to open to this communication in such a way that it will be mutually beneficial... *((share))*

> *((Option: Invoke the presence and guidance of the Inner Guide to facilitate the whole process, asking his/her opinion and feedback at any point as you proceed.))*

In a moment, I'm going to count to three...when I get to three, the shadow will manifest before you in some form...the most appropriate form that will enable it to communicate with you most effectively now for your mutual benefit...as I am counting I would like the shadow to decide what form it would like to take to communicate...it can be any form in the universe...a rock, a river, a cloud, a bonfire, a person or animal - anything in the universe...on the count of three it will be there. *((repeat this paragraph))*

Now I'm going to begin counting...just relax and go with your first impression on the count of three of how it appears...sometimes people have a sense of what it's going to be before I get to three...and that's fine...just understand that if it is different or the same as what you anticipate...that ...either way, on the count of three, it will be new and fresh and alive in more interesting ways *to communicate for your mutual benefit now...*

Number one...relaxing and preparing to welcome this part into your awareness...

Number two...in such a way that you both feel safe and open to communicate to discover new learnings to benefit you both...

And...three...there it is....experience it there...go with you first impression...share with me what you experience...sharing with me causes you to be more fully involved with your experience, enhancing your capacity to communicate with the shadow. *((If necessary, assist in whatever ways are appropriate to establish the image: 1)small chunks; 2)create devices that will help, e.g. visualize a curtain with the part behind it [open the curtain or, if the part prefers, leave it closed]; 3)generate a house-knock on the door or call the part out; 4)create an idyllic scene with a book, beautiful and ornate on an enchanting pedestal [describe them], have the client go to the book and open it to just the page that has a picture of the part; 5)try anything that comes to you - remember this is theater!))*

That's right...allow it to reveal itself...notice you have a sense now of your connection...also, a sense of how you feel in its presence...and how it feels in your presence...share with me what you are experiencing...understand that it has the freedom to show you various qualities and aspects of itself, and can even change shape to do this, if it wants to...relax and, with a sense of gratitude for its willingness to communicate, make some gesture to it that communicates your respect and desire to establish a more beneficial relationship...*((share))*

Ask: "What are you trying to accomplish in my life by acting and manifesting in the way you do?" ...and tell me its response...*((share))*

Ask: "What areas of my life do you influence or control the most?" *((share))*

Ask: "What do you need from me to make those areas function more freely for our mutual benefit?" *((share)) ((Ask for input from the Inner Guide))*

Appreciate this new level and manner of communication and experience how that feels...feel a bond of kinship and warmth growing as you both recognize you value the same positive intent, the same fundamental goals *((obviously, they first must have achieved this level of recognition in their dialogue, with your assistance))*...freely dialogue about this realization *as it is growing now*...and share with me about your exchange...

((If they haven't already)) ...reevaluate together, the beliefs and the choices of behaviors that the shadow relied on to accomplish its goals in the light of this new recognition of shared positive intent...and make any agreements necessary and appropriate to generate better choices of more effective behaviors that you can do cooperatively to really achieve these goals...

((Have them share, and assist in the negotiation in anyway needed.))

Now that you have established this new bond and sharing of resources in the deeper realization of how you can truly benefit each other...I'd like you to check if there is any residual concern that needs to be addressed...or if you sense that any part of the shadow has any objection that needs to be heard. *((Share, handle whatever comes up - basically repeat the process getting to the fundamental positive intent that everyone can agree on, making new agreements for new behaviors and mutual support.))*

((Option: pick an issue/problem and do regression:))

Now, invite the shadow to help you go back in time to the origin of this problem, *in such a way that your unconscious mind generates the learnings and experiences necessary for you to be free of this problem, now.* *((Repeat))*

As I count from one to three, experience yourself going back in time...guided by the intelligence of your unconscious mind...your unconscious mind can easily and instantaneously access in your memory banks whatever are the appropriate experiences that need to be reevaluated in order for you to be free of this problem, now.

Number one...going easily back...easily back

Number two...farther back...your unconscious mind already scanning and sorting for your benefit...when I say three you'll be there...fully aware...just relax and go with your first impression...

Number three...fully there...go with your first impression and share with me what you are experiencing...*((do any and all appropriate work as necessary: reframing, re-imprinting, replaying, emotional clearing, etc.))*

> *((After processing the experience, as with the subpersonality script, check to see how the work has effected the Shadow and its manifestation. If you wish, go up in the light to the superconscious, archetypal level to experience it in its highest expression. Dialogue and give gifts as done in previously at the archetypal level.))*

Good...in a moment you'll be coming back to normal waking consciousness on the count of 5...but before you do...relax and reflect on all you have accomplished with your shadow in this experience...as you do, allow your shadow and your whole experience to become enveloped in a loving, healing, nurturing golden, white light...[experience yourselves and your whole experience dissolving into this beautiful healing, loving light...enhancing and empowering the bonds you created here today...sense the power this light has to radiate these new learnings, new resources, and new love throughout your past into any and every situation in your past where they may be needed, now... for healing and the releasing of outmoded beliefs, attitudes, judgments or negativities of any kind...] *((pause, repeat this last sentence, [], take a moment to help this sink in, perhaps repeat a third time; with any encouraging non-verbal responses, or simply by imagining yourself talking directly to their unconscious responses, say, "good...that's right"))* ...experience that now in some way...releasing... healing...recapturing your pure innocent life force...*not necessarily in detail or conscious of any specific event*...but relaxing into the presence of this loving light and energy...*it feels good*...imagine that there might be something new, something outside of your awareness, that you could open up to now, that would result in your being truly benefitedcarrying new resources now...into your past wherever they are needed...that's right...want it to happen... ask that it happen ...make an inward gesture giving your permission for it to happen now...that's right...*feeling just how good it feels growing in interesting ways now moment-by-moment*...the more you make this inner gesture with your whole heart...

Now feel that light radiating into your future in the same way...carrying these new resources in your being into your future...imagine yourself in future anticipated and future unanticipated situations perceiving, interpreting, and acting with the awareness and support of a growing cheerfulness and respect for the true integrity of yourself and others...see yourself...feel yourself...hear yourself moving in these future situations with these new ever growing resources...that's right...

Now allow that light to surround your body...feel it permeating your skin as it dissolves into every cell of your body...permeating your entire being...imprinting these new beneficial powers on the awareness of every cell of your body...fell it dissolving into your cells...open to these living, healing resources as they integrate lovingly into your being...that's right...*((repeat appropriate phrases as you sense they are indicated, and feel free to elaborate with your own inspirations.))*

Now...coming back to normal waking consciousness at the count of 5...

One...coming back...feeling this wonderful new energy in your being...

Two...more and more...coming back...

Three... lighter and more awake...wiggle your toes and fingers ((repeat)).. coming back

Four...breathe in a deep breath of fresh air...breathe it in... balancing your energies...clearing your head...that's right...again...fully coming back... and

Five...open your eyes...open your eyes...that's right...fully back...fully coming back now

◆ ◆ ◆

3. Entity Releasing

Entity releasing may sound eery or intimidating, but it is actually quite ordinary. <u>*It should immediately be pointed out that this is not about exorcising demons.*</u> That is a whole different class of work that is outside the realm of this course, and, in human experience, extremely rare compared to the experience of entity attachment in the sense we mean it.

Entities, as related to here, means ordinary people who have died, and, for whatever reason, haven't past on - haven't gone into the light, and are therefore earth-bound. They are in varying states of confusion or absorption (e.g. addictive patterns), and <u>they may not even realize they are dead.</u>

It follows that they don't even notice that the light is available to them, or they actively deny it out of fear (e.g. hell is awaiting), or anger (desiring to get even or just create havoc). Either by discovery of the capacity to attach and influence or, by chance, in ignorance and confusion, they link up with embodied beings (that's us, folks) and create varying degrees of difficulty.

Notice that their relationship to the liberating light is exactly the same as our egoic relationship to our unshamed self, the true light of our being, and the possibility of shared real intimacy. Doesn't the brilliance scare us? Don't we run from it and confuse ourselves so we don't notice we are running or where we are? Don't we deny its existence out of fear, guilt, and resentment? Don't we feel mercilessly compelled to follow our compulsive and addictive urges in spite of "knowing" better, in spite of knowing that release, love, and sanity can only be found by renouncing these urges?

You see, its the same old story as far as the mind goes; it's just that not having a body adds some interesting twists in terms of behavioral possibilities, positively and negatively.

Before exploring entity work in detail, I want to point out the above correlation is a useful perspective to take to relate to lesser phenomena such as confused thoughts and feelings, and to see that this is just a progression of the same basic dilemma of egoic mind. To develop an appropriate dissociation *[appropriate meaning dissociated from the trance/story, while recapturing the energy of self]* from them as "other" puts you at cause over the ways in which thoughts and feelings attempt to influence you. Thus, working with entities isn't really any different. This will become clear in terms of technique and view as we proceed.

From this point of view we can create a hierarchy of unwanted influences:

The least powerful	♦ fleeting thoughts
	♦ strong thoughts/feelings
	♦ entities:
	◆ unwanted influence - not in aura, can push them away
to	◆ attached in aura, slight influence/assumed self
	◆ obsession-strong enough to make you do their thing
the most powerful	◆ possession-they run the show and the body including creating their own illness in host's body.

The model for affliction is analogous to physical affliction. When the immune system is healthy, it is very difficult for disease to enter; when the aura is healthy, it is very difficult for "others" to attach. Many of the same things that weaken the physical immune system weaken the aura:

1) Substance abuse weakens the energy field. The more potent the substance, the greater the possible "opening." As little as two glasses of wine is believed to be enough, based on clients' subjective reported experience, to allow attachment.

2) Powerful prolonged stressful emotions: anger, grief, depression, anxiety, shock (sudden death of loved one, accidents), chronic loss of sleep - all can weaken the energy of the aura. It becomes clear that the aura, the energy field, is intimately linked, in fact, to the physical tone set by the health of the body for those of us who haven't evolved to the point of maintaining our clarity and wakefulness and strength of spirit independent of bodily impact (that's most of us.)

3) Strong attachments of love and the desire to help can cause attachment, as in the case of the child who lost his father, and, in anguish, begged him to stay. The father, prepared to go into the light, stayed, but unwittingly was accompanied by negative spirits who had attached to him in his end of life illness.

4) Accidents that cause unconsciousness, and anesthesia create conditions for possible entry.

5) Outright invitation by inappropriate seance, distraught bargaining (e.g. suicidal pleas), etc. because of their indiscriminate calling can attract negative beings. *Only and always invoke beings of light and love, acting only in accord with your highest good and truth.*

There are special locations of trauma and charged negativity that breed and attract earth-bound spirits: hospitals (they die there in pain and confusion; others are alive there in pain and confusion), battlefields, prisons, cemeteries, bars, crack houses, mental institutions, schools.

To enhance your chances to be attachment-free, you make the same kinds of choice you make to be physically healthy:

1) Abstain from intoxicating and debilitating substances.

2) Cultivate and maintain a positive frame of mind and sense of self-worth.

3) Keep good company.

4) Maintain physical well-being.

In some manner, by meditation and visualization, establish a field of protective light around yourself. It can be done by imagining it, by combining imagination with invocation of the protection from God, protectors, Guides, etc. By preference, it may be a protective bubble, or something that is generated at the core of your being and radiates from deep within you like a sun shining out and around your body to an arms length.

Once you have a method, practice it and maintain it on a daily basis. Remember, repetition and emotional impact make it real. Establish an anchor to pop it on line instantaneously, or to strengthen it instantaneously in an emergency.

Working with Entities

Any symptom can indicate an entity: allergies, obesity, compulsions & addictions, etc. Anything. So, how to tell?

1) Last resort - nothing else works.

2) Symptom accompanied at point of origin by sudden personality shift, e.g. accident/trauma, hospital stay, upon recovery there is suddenly this new problem behavior and/or personality trait.

3) Client feels, *"that's just not me"* - a deep inner intuition; or a strong inner battle not unlike subpersonality splits.

4) On the other hand, client may have the sense of *"always having been this way"* - they have lost the ability to distinguish the desires of the "other."

Case history: Wendy

Age 32, depressed for 20 years. Drugs, psychiatrists, therapies of all kinds, 2 suicide attempts, smokes 3 packs/day, hopeless, life has no meaning. All this began at age 12. Prior to this a happy child in a genuinely happy family.

Standard Therapeutic view: not much hope for change, long term care for maintenance, not for cure.

Entity treatment - 3 sessions

1) Diagnose presence of entity on basis of sudden shift in personality at age 12 following bout of bronchitis. (Suicide attempt shortly after illness; smoking 3 packs/day shortly after illness.)

2) Contacted suicidal entity (a man) - begin releasing process.

3) Next day - contact again and release entity.

After session, all symptoms immediately gone. One month later, no return of symptoms. Radical changes in appearance and lifestyle. Threw away 1/3 of wardrobe - too masculine. Showed therapist "before" (masculine design) and "after" (feminine design) checkbooks.

Regression done to origin of the attachment: at time of illness, treating doctor brought along an entity that was trying to attach to him, but couldn't, so he attached to Wendy.

Reference: video interview, Thinking Allowed tapes, 1-800-999-4415, Edith Fiore, *The Unquiet Dead*, #W415, $49.95('91 prices).

Characteristics of the entity-state

1)They miss their chance to go into the light at death:

a)Fear, confusion, strong attachment or addiction - they intentionally or unwittingly shun the light.

2)They may think they are still alive - until they try to touch someone and go right through them.

3)For fear of hell, or guilt, or strong attachment for a substance, feeling, or experience, they cling to the earth plane.

Based on her experience with thousands of clients, Fiore thinks we all are attached to at one time or another, for greater or lesser periods of time, and because of past-life as well as present life karma.

How to release an entity:

1) **The therapist's first obligation is to the entity.** They are the lost soul. Once they go into the light, the client will be fine.

2) **One must convince, or persuade, the entity to leave** as opposed to forcing it to leave. Gain rapport and trust of the entity. You're going to guide them into the light in the same way you released other fused issues: affirm positive intent, diffuse secondary gain issues, and honor ecological requirements. Fiore discusses her early attempts to force them to leave by calling in the "Big Guns" like Jesus and angels and such. She quickly discovered that, if that didn't work, she had "shot her wad" and lost all prestige and credibility. *My hit on this is that it doesn't mean that the "Big Guns" were somehow defeated by the entity, but that from their higher perspective, they were aware of a greater karmic context for the beings involved, including the therapist. Basically, until all parties involved learned the lessons they needed to learn, they were going to be stuck with each other, and a fundamental theme of the lessons seems to be constructive communication for mutual benefit of client and entity.*

a) convince them that their own body is dead. They may not have noticed.

1] have entity look in a mirror

2] have entity feel the body in case of cross sex attachment to notice discrepancies

3] do regression to origin of attachment or to death of entity (client has access to entity's memory banks) to gain information that will cause the entity to notice and remember death event.

b) Explain that there is no hell. Tell them to notice that whatever spiritual teachers have authority for them are here now in the light to explain this to them.

c) Tell them to notice that any appropriate loved one is here now in the light to welcome them.

d) Appeal to any desire for substance, or sex, or whatever: it is waiting for them in the light: a new ever-young healthy body, etc.

Fiore has found that whatever they need, whatever she has thought to say is there, is there instantaneously. Her attitude is that "Assistance" is guiding the process from other planes; she isn't coming up with this stuff on her own or making it work on her own. *I think you should take this attitude with all your work, not just entity releasing, and actively invoke "Assistance" prior to each session and give thanks after each session.*

e)examine the bond, the motive for possession. It could be love or hate; it could be karmic between them, or random circumstance (still karma, but not identity specific). Go to the origin in this or a past life, as with any problem. There may be a bond of several lifetimes, and some attachments have a karmic link that just has to be lived out. The general implication seems to be that when a person encounters entity release work, it coincides with the end of the karma.

3) **Examine the patient's need to be possessed.** Check worthiness issues of the client - are they inviting attachment out of guilt? If so, just seeing the origin in regression is enough to release it. There is no need to do forgiveness or emotional work. Just having the remembrance is enough to release it. (But if you find an exception, do whatever is necessary).

4) **The entity may need time to re-evaluate,** so it may take more than one session for them to leave. *To cover any concerns they may have, I simply tell them, "if anything I have said about going into the light is wrong, you can come back." This is a simple and comprehensive way to cover all ecological concerns.*

5) **Hypnosis** is not necessary to do the process, but it **may enhance the client's clairvoyance to give you information**. The Unquiet Dead has a verbatim depossession script. Most of the procedures listed here are options if Fiore's "simple depossession" method doesn't work. *The simple method is to clearly explain that the entity has made a mistake; that it is dead and not really happy living this way; that it can now notice the light and go into it to receive whatever it needs for its own benefit to move on in its development; send it away with your blessings. She always tries the simple and easy way first, and adds from these other options as necessary.*

6) **Check for other entities.** Enlist the help of the first one you get free. Possessing entities can be possessed themselves. [Father and son example above.] Possessing entities can "follow" a being and pick them up again on their next incarnation.[Don't ask how.]

7) **If the entity is hiding, regress the client to the point of attachment to see the entity and the occurrence.** This gives them both a sense of boundary, and food for thought and re-evaluation.

8) **Identifying addictions as the entity helps the client say no to the urges,** "If you want that, leave and go get it in the light." Note: it is important to release them into the light, not just release them. If you don't send them into the light, they may just go attach to someone else.

9) **Releasing curses** - earthbound spirits mobilized to attach by darker forces, often as a result of past-life misuse of psychic power by client - karmic debts to pay. Ritual to release curses:

- visualize the person who cursed you; visualize the bonds of the curse (usually yucky).

- visualize having a sword of light. Sever the bonds as you proclaim "I release you to your highest good."

- that should do it; if not, regress to past life origin of the need of client to accept curse (guilt).

The test of whether the process has worked will be instantaneous changes in behavior and absence of the symptoms.

Reference: Edith Fiore, <u>The Unquiet Dead</u>,

4. Entity Release:
Simple Depossession Script

With hypnosis: Inductions.

Without hypnosis: have client sit comfortably with eyes closed.

Have client scan their body for the "residence" of the entity if necessary. If the entity is readily available for communication, begin:

You are free to listen to what I have to say and evaluate it for your own true benefit. Nothing we do here today is in any way proposed as a conflict, or to take anything from you, or to deny you anything you truly need. Do you understand? *((response))*

I'd like you to reflect on your situation with (client). Since you don't have your own body on the physical plane, this arrangement can't really be as satisfactory as you might like, can it? *((response, follow up on it appropriately — pacing their reality, and leading with your outcome clearly in mind, i.e. to make it inviting for them to turn to and to go into the light.))*

For some reason, when you died, you missed an opportunity to experience a wonderful release from all the pain and disappointments you may have suffered in your life. I don't know what they were, or how you died, but ...maybe you remember those things, now...I want you to know that wonderful opportunity still awaits you and never really left you...you have just kept overlooking it for some reason...but now you can notice it...I'd like you to sense the presence of a pleasantly bright white light, and to look up into it...as you do you will sense and see in that light proof of what a wonderful experience awaits you when *you decide to go into that light*...you may see an important loved one there now, or something you really want and need, and never thought you could have...look and see...tell me what you are experiencing *((since this script is assuming a simple depossession, they will report something wonderfully compelling which will motivate them to easily go into the light. If not you would proceed with other options previously discussed.))*

Good...just let go and move into the light feeling the welcoming presence of (what/who) awaits you there...as you move into the light all old afflictions and problems and regrets will fall away...you will receive all kinds of revelations about your true path and the knowledge of an infinitely loving support system that will always guide you and assist you...just let yourself open to all of that as you move into the light and experience it happening now...*((sharing from entity and/or client about its progress--respond as appropriate))*

Assuming release, to client: Now that the entity has left...fill that space in your aura with healing golden white light to heal and seal your aura...call upon your own true guides and assistance to make this happen completely and thoroughly. *((Pause))* Let me know if you sense any reservation about this process being successfully completed. *((pause/share))*

Do you sense there is any part of your own being where you may be harboring the notion that you are somehow unworthy and therefore deserve to be possessed in some way again? *((Share - process as necessary to clear such notions if they are present, i.e., regression to the origin of the notion, etc.))*

Now before we close...[imagine a brilliant sun shining out from the core of your being...radiating healing, loving, purifying energy out throughout your body and out surrounding your body in every direction to an arms length...this loving light dissolves all forms of negativity that may have been present as darkness in your being and aura...waking up every cell of your being to its sacred purity...making it easy to release all dark thoughts now...as you imagine and feel this radiant sun and its blessings...you (press together the thumb and forefinger of your right hand) *((or some other anchor, perhaps asking that they or their inner guide choose it))* to establish an anchor to remind you of the presence of this sun of the purity and goodness of your true being and of your growing allegiance to it and conviction in it...that's right...from this moment forward you will cultivate *the image and felt presence* of this radiant sun by taking time several times a day to quietly focus on it and contemplate it and *feel* it...also becoming aware in some way of the encouragement of higher loving forces guiding and supporting you in every facet of your life...relax into that realization now...offering any doubts you may be sensing into this loving light...] *((Repeat [ ]))* *((share))*

After you have spent some time invoking this sun in this way on a daily basis, each time activating your anchor...you will find that by simply activating your anchor, you will feel and sense the vivid presence of this support and protection anytime you feel you need it...imagine what that's going to be like as you move into your future now...that's right.

Bring them back.

◆ ◆ ◆

5. Checklist of Indicators of Attachment

1. Chronic sense of being drained, depressed, little or no energy.

2. Abrupt and rapid shifts in emotions and mood.

3. Habitual relationship to self in the second person; talking to yourself as "other."

4. Having used alcohol or drugs at any time, particularly to excess.

5. Impulsiveness, bingeing, engaging in thoughtless and reckless activity.

6. Minor or major blackouts relative to time, activities or objects. "Where are my keys?" "In your hand."

7. Diminished capacity to concentrate, fogginess, preoccupation and restlessness. Trying to read but having the sense that your eyes aren't quite reaching the page.

8. Susceptibility to sudden fits of anxiety or depression seemingly without cause.

9. Difficulties recovering from a hospitalization or surgery.

10. Emotional discomfort or distraction when trying to think about the possibility of entity attachment.

If your response to items 2,3,4, or 10 are affirmative, it could be indicative of the presence of an entity. If your response to several of these is affirmative part of the time, it could indicate the presence of an entity. Use your own judgment, what do you sense? Clean house anyway!

6. Accessing & Evaluating Probable Futures

Edgar Cayce was one of the foremost seers and psychics of our age - of any age. He was unique in that he left a large body of recorded, verifiable data about diagnosis and treatment of physical ailments that he did in trance, at a distance, with only the patient's name and location.

He also gave profound metaphysical discourses and foretold future events, many of which are coming true like clockwork.

He would go into trance to access his knowledge and powers and named the Akhashic Record, an imprint of all knowledge of the universe, as the source of his ability.

Well, if it's there to be accessed, people may choose to explore the possibility of becoming properly aligned with it.

The process presented here relies on the format we have used to go into the past with appropriate modifications:

1) Pick an outcome: a] a specific time period or date, b] probable future outcomes of current possible choices (e.g. what job to take in what town), c] an exploration - just for fun and curiosity.

2) Do inductions

3) Go to an appropriate staging area (for other outcomes we have used meadows, libraries, desert mesas, etc.)

4) Choose an appropriate vehicle and give it some character - may I suggest a time machine. May I also suggest that to maintain objectivity, you have the Inner Guide be the pilot so the client can be passively receptive to where he is taken. The goal here is to support the client in being free from the tendency to color or effect the outcome based on any hope, fear, or prejudice, giving him the best chance to be an impartial observer.

5) As in regression, on the count of three, or whatever, go to and arrive at the destination - first impression.

6) Elicit a detailed vivid association with the situation. Assist and question to ascertain all significant information about this future probability.

7) Consult with the Inner Guide and the Higher Self about the appropriateness of aligning with and committing to actualizing this future.

8) Accept it, change it according to their feedback, or proceed to an alternate probability and evaluate the new choice in the same way.

9) Once a future choice has been decided upon, associate into it, and with the support of your Higher Self and Inner Guide, look back toward the present and see the choices and steps you took/will take to arrive at this future outcome.

10) Suggest: *that the unconscious mind will organize these steps completely, now... whether your conscious mind is aware of each step. Allow yourself to sense in some way, to trust, this unconscious process occurring, now...as you also attend to whatever specific steps you are aware of.*

11) Bring them back with full access to the information and resources they have contacted.

At this point, I think you're up to the challenge to fill out this outline into a script for yourselves. The language in #10 is provided to be part of that script, if you wish.

◆ ◆ ◆

7. Hypnosis with Couples

The Presenting Problem:

1) **With Regression:**

a) go to their respective originating experiences relative to the limitation the issue embodies, e.g. lack of intimacy, trust. Process each accordingly.

b) go to a past life **shared** experience, if any, for which the current situation may be the karmic consequence. Note that you may get this when asking for [a] above.

c) do both of the above. Typically, if there is a [b], it will come first, but the learnings and/or limitations that led them to create that situation will have prior significant causes, or will have created other significant and distinct dramas, as in [a], whose clearing will enhance the release of the presenting problem.

2) **With Subpersonality Work:** as in mediation for one client, do the process for both. Have them dialogue in such a way that the parts that get triggered in each other get to understand how those irritating parts in their partner correspond to and are merely reflections of their polarity aspect in themselves (i.e., the shadow: What we hate in another is what we hate in ourself, but may not be aware of, i.e., successfully negatively hallucinating). Such recognition should drain the hostility and blocks to resolution. You have parallel mirrored intrapersonal mediation and integration going on simultaneously with interpersonal appreciation: mutual clearing and bonding allowing the partners to see each other more clearly as they come out of the trance of projecting disowned parts on to each other. The analogy would be group therapy.

3) After using [1] or [2] above, you can lead into archetypal approaches, and, of course, accessing higher self or Inner Guide assistance is always an option.

The Induction:

1) Play them off each other - directly: *"as you hear me guiding her deeper, you will find yourself gliding easily into trance..."* or indirectly: with a sense of confidentiality, to the second about the first, *"he's taking the suggestions really well and I'm certain he is going into a wonderful state..."* (it sounds like you're confiding in her, but he can overhear, so it becomes an indirect suggestion for him.)

2) When focusing individually, always suggest to the other that what they overhear will just enhance their ability to continue appropriately in their own experience.

3) Switch back and forth at points where you have established them in an experience they can process for a time, leaving them with the resources to do so (and/or suggesting that, as they relate to their experience, their awareness of your interaction

with their mate in the background will trigger them to access resources and inspirations as needed.)

4) Be prepared to switch quickly to the subject who may need you, e.g. if emotional abreaction comes up. Think about how you could do this and make quick, effective, and non-disruptive asides occasionally to the other subject.

5) Weed out unnecessary drifting off the subject at hand.

6) As they clear limitations, have them share with each other, in whatever ways may be appropriate. If it's not appropriate, don't interrupt a client's process, even with "good news" from the other.

7) As in individual sessions, you will bring them to a positive outcome, generalizing the new resources into the past and future. Once you have them both out of the particulars of their inner experience, have them share in the awareness of the formless light surrounding each of them which contains all the new energy.

8) In their inner world, have them give gifts to each other honoring the changes each has made.

9) Bring them back together.

10) Have them make or buy and give a physical gift representative of the inner gift.

◆ ◆ ◆

8. Group Hypnosis

For the most part the basic rules of hypnosis apply, with what should be some obvious considerations for the fact that it is not an individual session:

1) Pre-induction talk - cover the same points as with an individual; review Phase I material.

a) ask for specific concerns from the group; anticipate problems or concerns - especially in groups diffuse performance anxiety. Emphasize that they honor their own experience, without comparing to others.

b) give them permission to follow their own inner directions, even if it means they aren't following you at some point in the induction.

c) clarify styles of accessing - some may be visual, some auditory, etc. Explain what those distinctions mean. Explain that visualizing is with the mind's eye, not on the back of the eyelids. Make sure everyone understands that they know how to visualize, and that they do it, even if it isn't their preferred mode. (e.g., imagine your bathroom - everyone should realize with such an example, that they can "see.")

d) before you begin with the induction, ask for feedback, making sure everyone knows they are in control of their own safety and comfort, and that they can relax and enjoy the experience without expectation. There is no right way to do it; there is no right experience they are supposed to have.

2) Induction - except for instructions that require individual responses, you are free to use any techniques you like. Include some form of eye-strain, eye closure, progressive relaxation, and deepening.

3) Calibrate trance induction; do limb challenge to test. With a group it can be useful to establish a common inner gauge of depth such as the yardstick so you can get indications from them as to their depth of trance. (remember the yardstick? 36 down to 25= light trance, 24 down to 13= medium trance, 12 down to 1= deep trance).

4) Inner work - with a group, generally guide for positive experiences. Use dissociated states such as floating above the life stream, using movies to represent past situations, etc. If individual attention is needed, make it O.K. for everyone by suggestion. Make sure you are pacing everyone as best you can, allowing enough time for experience according to your suggestions. Bring in Inner Guides to give personalized attention in lieu of the therapist's attention.

5) Bring them back with full recall, after standard generalizations, and dissolution into the light.

6) Share in the group about experiences. People need not share content. Sharing about the general quality of trance experience should be safe territory for everyone.

Encourage them to nurture their experience by writing about it, drawing the inner scenes, or creating some ritual to maintain a connection with any valuable energies they may have contacted.

9. Creating and Nurturing a Dynamic Practice

In my opinion it is very important to start with the right view, the right appreciation of context, and the right perspective when approaching the "business" of therapy.

As has been emphasized in this course relative to therapy, there is a **unifying ground** to the work that must be recognized and kept in awareness. An important sameness, the egoic process, underlies and pervades all problematic states. This same egoic process stands ready to infiltrate your mental equilibrium when your focus turns to livelihood. It is fine to have subpersonality departments that run different areas of your life, as long as they are fluid and transparent, integrated, light and joyful.

When it comes to livelihood, **survival issues**, it is very easy for rigid, fear-based, egoic thinking to take over. If there are hard-line divisions between "parts," the therapy part and the business part, it can happen that a Jekyl and Hyde personality shift arises, whose hardness and contradictions can go largely unnoticed by the therapist in question, due to our capacity to negatively hallucinate shadow parts.

It is important to always remember that the underlying principles we rely on in therapy, *the most basic and root reliance being an ever-expanding connection to the inherently pure guidance of Self/Source,* apply in everyday life, **to us as well as our clients**, *even when it comes to money.*

As Dave Elman would say to a "resistant" client, "Some people are willing to do it the easy way, and some people want to do it the hard way."

The hard way is the way of fear-based, survival driven/self reliant, (self = fragmented trance state self, the doer, "I have to do it right, work *hard* (i.e.,contracted, no joy or lightness, no trust or faith), competitive effort. It's all very well to open to inner guidance in hypnosis to work on emotional issues, but this is **money** we're talking about - every man for himself! **The hard way includes pride in doing/"helping" (which is fear-based as well). Don't <u>ever</u> give something to a client - <u>*have them give it to themselves*</u>. Can you let go of your "accomplishment"? Can you be invisible? Moreover, can you accept dishonor?**

If we are honest with ourselves , we will notice this egoic urge coming up on a daily basis, on a moment-by-moment basis. Don't get moralistic about it, as in, "I shouldn't be thinking/feeling this." That just buys into the egoic trip, and you go into denial, coming under the complete control of that which you are denying - that you could have fear-based, money grubbing thoughts. Let egoic minding be; be nice to it; tickle it; display it humorously; let it arise and fall; don't act/react in relationship to it; focus on the higher/deeper intent and open to That guidance. *Consider this an essential expression of generosity to oneself.*

This will help you stay tuned to:

The Easy Way. The easy way is the way of faith, the way of unwavering greater vision, even when brushing your teeth or wiping your...face. It is the way of always taking the first step first, the right step first, the "beginner's mind" step first. It is the way of remembering the source of formlessness, purity, and timelessness, before entering into endeavors in the world of form and time. To accomplish this, it is necessary to understand the way in which each moment is its own first step. the way in which the formless pervades each moment of form, thereby making guidance and support abundantly ever-present. *This is a description of humility -- vs. the pride/fear of the "Doer" -- recognize it?* **Are you willing to cultivate it?**

Going the easy way, **there is no competition, therefore, no grievance.** There is no "other" because your relationship is with the flow of your interdependence with the universe, your synchronicity factor, not with the world of "others," the world of hope and fear, as constructed by the egoic mind of time and poverty. Therapy, business, housework, shopping -- everything is inside the circle of sacredness. Everything counts, and is touched by the power and law of this sacredness. When we deny it, we create/give-in-to the power and law of the world, the egoic mind trance.

The mark of this easy way is not thinking about it, but a *felt sense* of light-heartedness, **humility**, cheerfulness, with the capacity to feel deeply without shame or avoidance.

> *"Comparing is the root of fear."* --Upanishads

To compare you need an "other." **Keep the transparency of the apparent "other" of the world apparent.** Reflect on the Warrior's qualities of clear-thinking and discrimination, and the foundation of these qualities, and cultivate them on a moment-by-moment basis so that you achieve an habitual mode of self-correction, of wake-up calls, of deep releasing breaths, as you think about the nuts and bolts details of action.

For there are nuts and bolts details of action to be done. **It just makes all the difference in the world what your inner state and view is while you're doing them.** Opening to inner guidance, and letting a Higher Power take over, doesn't mean you don't do anything. *It means you do the common sense things without getting caught by hope and fear, praise and blame, good and bad, gain and loss, because none of those standards are your standards.* They are egoic standards; your standard is to impeccably honor the sacredness of life through right action, and *to find out what that means in an ever new and expanding way, moment-by-moment, for ever.*

Your work is not a survival issue anymore - survival is a matter of faith. Your work, like everything else, is a way of celebrating and honoring life, fearlessly.

With this view, let us examine some of the common sense nuts and bolts tips of starting and sustaining a business.

1) **You need to know who you are.**

   a) recognise your areas of interest and strengths

b) create a succinct conversational presentation in 25 words or less describing your work. That way when you meet people and they ask, you won't find yourself saying, "Uhhhh..." unless you want to.

2) People need to know you exist.

a) Who are you?

b) What service do you offer?

c) Why do they need it?

d) Where are you?

3) Advertise

a) Target your clientele

b) Utilize advertising that will reach your targeted clientele. E.g. The New Times, PCC Newsletter, or, if business people are your clientele, for example, local business news periodicals.

c) Find as many forms of free advertising as you can

    1) Give free talks at service organizations

    2) Radio or TV talk shows

    3) Calendar listings are often free

    4) Press releases

    5) Networks and support groups

d) Yellow pages

e) Flyers, brochures, and business cards

f) Put yourself in circulation. Go to meetings where your work may be of interest and benefit.

g) Write articles for local periodicals

h) Bulk mail

i) Teach seminars and classes

j) Host a booth at appropriate fairs. Share information, do demonstrations, offer free sessions through a drawing. (A note about free drawings: set a time limit on the prize. The point is to get people to act. Of course all the losers are interested people who now are part of your mailing list.)

4) What to charge?

a) You need to do your own soul-searching about this. You need to be able to ask for compensation without hesitation or shame. The egoic mind can master such a presentation as a convincing act, but there will be a contraction within it, no matter how well disguised. I suggest you take an approach with more genuineness. It will necessitate not merely deciding on a figure, but getting clear on what your relationship to money and time is in a comprehensive way.

b) Re: advertising - don't treat it like rent, treat it like an investment. That is, rent is something you pay because you need a place to live; you don't examine your return on the money spent. But with an investment, if it's not giving you more than you put into it, you try something else. With advertising you have to be patient in an appropriate way to give it a chance, just like an investment. Give anything you try at least 6 months, perhaps a year.

c) Here are some money books to enrich your thinking:

1) <u>Guerilla Marketing</u>, Levinson

2) <u>The Unabashed Self Promoter</u>, Phil Laut

3) <u>Money Is My Friend</u>, Phil Laut

4) <u>Marketing Without Advertising</u>, Michael Phillips and Sally Raspberry

5) <u>7 Laws of Money</u>, Michael Phillips and Sally Raspberry

5) **Establish a daily habit of meditation** -- for the sake of all beings if you must have a goal. As an expression of faith, opening, humility, and gratitude, if possible - even if you don't think or feel so. *That doesn't matter - just do it with that conviction no matter what you think or feel.*

6) **Therapy and Mentorship** -- a form of self-nurturing and guidance. It will help you with your skills. It will help you avoid the trap of becoming the dried up kind of therapist who does it for others as a way of avoiding their own yucky stuff (a technical term). We all have blind spots, and we can forget the perspective and struggle of the client re: trusting , becoming vulnerable, and opening - **it will help our cultivation of humility.** (*I am available for graduates in either capacity, on an individual and group basis, and refer clients to those so engaged.*)

7) **Go For It!**

> "Until one is committed
> There is always hesitancy, the chance to draw back,
> Always ineffectiveness.
> Concerning all acts of initiative and creation
> There is one elementary Truth, the ignorance of which, kills countless ideas and splendid plans;
> That the moment one definitely commits oneself,
> Then Providence moves, too.
> All sorts of things occur to help one that would otherwise not have occurred.
> A whole stream of events issues from the decision
> Raising in one's favor all manner of unforseen incidents and meetings and material assistance which
> No man could have dreamed would have come his way.

> -- Excerpted from the Scottish Himilayan Expedition by W.H. Murray

> 'Whatever you do, or dream you can do, do it.
> Boldness has genius, power and magic in it.
> Begin it now.'

> -- Goethe

You may know of Goethe as one of the great writers of all time, but you may not realize he was an initiated adept of esoteric spiritual teachings. Take what he says, and Murray's eloquent understanding of the same principles, as the words of a Magician who realized in his own life the faith and synchronicity of which he speaks.

This quote explains a technical dynamic of the phenomenal world, but it arises out of a deep thoughtfulness. **The point of this course is to cultivate, for clients and self,**

thoughtfulness - heartfulness, soul-fulness, not merely technical competency.
(Then cars going by, birds cooing, or the commotion of others won't be distracting.
From??...our experience of being sacredly, gratefully, alive...moment-by-
moment...*now!*)

◆ ◆ ◆

10. Spare Parts (and Review)

1) Don't just listen for the problem; **listen for their resources**, and teach them to apply them in the problem contexts.

2) Listen to the problem in a way that allows you to extract the resources from the problem. This is always fundamentally the same thing:

If you start with a) basic purity, and b) identity with an infinite source of creative energy, and c) the recognition that everything is theater, i.e., constructed, then the problem from this perspective, in spite of the suffering it causes, is proof of the existence of their power and creativity. *"Look at what you have created...you've taken this brilliant powerful light and manufactured a convincing representation of a black hole where no energy exists...what a powerful creative feat! You obviously have all the resources you need to create a beautiful set of representations **as your life from now on**...it just hadn't occurred to you **until now** to go in the direction of that beauty with your power and creativity, instead of **that old way** of creating those **old horror movies."***

3) Duality means agendas. As soon as the split occurs, balance is gone. The parts arise as competing agendas. Their underlying positive intent is to restore balance, but that goal is lost sight of because of the root Fear inherent in the split. Everything gets turned upside down and backwards; **egoic trance logic repeatedly takes you just where you don't want to go.**

Watch yourself engaging in agendas on a large and small scale, and become sensitive to how **attachment to an agenda** (in a contracted way, which means some part is running the show) **limits your intelligence, perception, clarity, awareness of choice, and capacity to think/inner dialogue about the situation.** (Fearful parts insist: *"It has to be this way!"*) It feels stuck. Become sensitive to the feeling of stuckness in yourself and breathe into it, relax into it with patience and love, without keeping score (*"How'm I doin'?" "How long is this gonna take?" "What if it doesn't work?"*)

Become sensitive to client's statements and non-verbals as they point out where and how they create stuckness and how they regard it - usually negatively.

4) Behavior, change, and meaning are context dependent. Behaviors, words, feelings, and intentions have no meaning, indeed they cannot arise, independent of a context - so stop comparing yourself to others, the context is never the same! Understand?

5) Distinguish between the being and the behavior. Accept the being--a manifestation of your very own life force, & vice-versa--change the behavior. But, remember, **everyone is doing the best they can with what they have** (re: awareness of choice, understanding, and perspective). Therefore, to change behavior, you don't stop it with force, or take it away by force. You give them better choices, greater understandings, expanded perspectives of context, that eliminate shame. With these new resources, they will make the changes naturally.

6) We are in command of our minds (granted, for most of us it doesn't seem that way "consciously"), and our thinking/feeling processes, therefore we are in command of our outcomes. Our experience is not what happens in the so-called external world, but our internal choice of response to our perceptions of it. We create our internal representations by choice, therefore we create our reality. If it doesn't feel this way; when it doesn't feel this way - don't fight it. If you don't know what to do; don't do anything! - except persist in non-doing until something shifts:

> *"Do you have the patience to wait*
> *till your mud settles and the water is clear?*
> *Can you remain unmoving*
> *till the right action arises by itself?"*
> --Tao Te Ching

7) *"Once you realize your innocence you can accomplish anything."* --Jack Elias

8) Confusion: con = with; fusion = to pour, to join together. The inappropriate joining of::

a) being and behavior -- "I'm bad; I spilled the milk."

b) cause and effect -- "I could have stopped her from dying." (8 year old boy re: mother's death.)

c) perspective and evaluation -- "He won't like me once he gets to know me." vs. "I'm going to give him the chance to get to know me."

d) meaning and context -- "horses are animals, therefore all animals are horses."

9) The glue that holds con-fusions together is anchoring and mental speed. The thought/feeling/trancing speed blurs the process, like a magician's slight of hand, so that bogus connections, con-fusions, go unchallenged, unnoticed, undiscriminated. And as you know, if you don't say "No," you automatically say "Yes."

10) Stop thinking in terms of success and failure. There is only learning going on in the realm of Divine Ignorance.

> *"In great attempts, it is glorious even to fail."* --Fortune cookie

11) The Way of No Resistance: Therapist listens and observes to understand the value in the problem, and helps the client see the value, the true need, that needs to be met. Once value is understood to be **independent of any particular means of achieving it,** it is very easy to let go of a **particular** means to achieve it, especially one with negative side-effects. The therapist helps the client understand that the negative behaviors can be surrendered, without surrendering the power or right to meet the need. Until then, they have con-fused the negative behavior with the genuine need. It's a corollary to the old verse: "Love and marriage, love and marriage, go together like a horse and carriage...you can't have one without the other."

12) The ironic and paradoxical path out of the dark states: Be willing to be small and disgusting; be willing to be all the things you're afraid you might be, and that's the beginning of the end of shame and the end of those dark feelings. This is an internal effort and it's an opening in the realm of being; *do not misinterpret it as an instruction to act out harmful actions.*

13) Keep a perspective on the objects of your internal states. Treating internal elements like objects, like possessions can provide a useful dissociation from them and therefore power over them (e.g., your internal dialogue vs. my internal dialogue: your pictures vs. my pictures.) If I can do something you can't: if you have a problem I don't, and you can locate these key object/factors, you can get control and change things. Maybe you need some of my kind of pictures. Maybe I need some of your internal dialogue.

14) Playing with the image of the first band of archetypes being like white light through a prism displayed as the spectrum of colored light: at the superconscious level, create a ritual of having a choice of resource circles to step into - each circle of a different color, a column of pure energy of that color. One steps into the column to be immersed and penetrated by the healing power of that color, that archetypal energy. Step into it with appropriate parts: cradling your inner child, guiding your parent clones, your enemy, a shadow aspect, etc. Get the idea!? Create wonderful healing experiences.

15) Seeing life as ritual. Not just our movements, but all of nature, and the universe, including our movements, as the mysterious display of an awesome symbolic expression, symbolic of...who can say? How does thinking about all our actions, especially the repetitive and mundane, as essential steps in this ritual change the way we regard our lives moment-by-moment, on the spot in each moment? Well, we first have to step out of our trance about what is going on, don't we? Think about it...now think about it more deeply...now...and so on.

Being deeply immersed in non-trance thought (what is that?) is to be awake in the real ritual, the Great Symbol. (Translation of Buddhist term: Mahamudra)

16) *A snake doesn't know its true nature until it is put in a bamboo tube.* --Old Buddhist saying.

Your client's mind is the snake; let your techniques be the tubes. As you digest the techniques, you integrate their core learning. This releases you from the hook of any technique's tendency to be an agenda (*"complete me, complete me"*). You can afford to do something with inquisitiveness instead of having to count on a particular outcome - even if it is predictable, you still have beginner's mind.

So you try things mainly to notice what happens - what comes up is what you want.

You are not doing a technique to be successful, but merely to put the snake in the bamboo pole. First step is to watch and notice the way the snake bumps around in the pole - that dictates your next move, moment-by-moment.

17) The archetypes are important tools of self-inquiry. Their exposure of basic patterns releases us from identification with our precious secret stuff. *"You mean everyone has been going through this for ages?!"* By exposing the patterns, they expose how we pervert our basic goodness, our innate sane intelligence.

18) Subpersonalities - energy bundles, closed circuit and in-process. To do emotional clearing, get to their primordial statements and get the client to express them:

  -I am this.

  -I do this.

  -I am afraid of this.

  -I need this.

-I want this.

-I'm sad, angry, scared, etc. (not lost, abandoned, etc. Watch for situational adjectives masquerading as emotions.) Because of the dualistic split, a person can go around in circles for a long time: in a trance, the world not changing, but repeating - a constant replay of unchangeable elements. There is:

- -limited perception
- -limited (flexibility in) dialogue
- -limited choices
- -limited recognition of responsibility

The commitment of one's emotional energy is to the past, which is nothing more than a holographic mental representation, a ghost - seductive and powerful, but unreal.

19) Present time situations are dreams of the samskaras (Sanskrit term for the unresolved karmic residue of experience. They are the closed circuit trance states representative of the past: parts). One's life energy, the meaning of present time, is transfigured and determined by the samskaras/past. They manipulate the present to give it meaning. One is <u>dreaming</u> present time from the vantage point of the past where one is alive. The past infuses present time with energy to the degree present time approximates the past "real" situation, providing the possibility to relive and resolve it.

There is a constant flux of samskaric activity, moment-by-moment, working in tandem, cooperating-operating in managing the present as the means to their ends. But the ends are futile - the ends, resolutions, have to be in the past. The past is over: samskaric intelligence can't admit that. It would have to feel the pain, the loss, the grief. It would have to let go, giving up resentment, giving up the hope of resolution. It can't see beyond that suffering to the freedom, the open space, of the release. It only sees <u>into</u> the releasing process, and it doesn't like what it sees. The intuition of the open space is fearful because egoic mind fills the open space with the projection of a repeat of the past harm, usually as a formless foreboding. (The forms have to be kept hidden, otherwise one might notice it's a projection of something that's over. A full realization of this fact would break the trance.)

The openness, as itself, is not fearful. It's a 4 year-old staring into a goldfish pond for the first time.

20) When you are whole, when you have gathered all the parts into the pool of your being, **even momentarily**, you can turn your mind off - and there It is, where It has always been, all around you - open space, ordinary and free. It's like turning off a spigot. Try it! Good luck!

APPENDIX

Recommended Reading List

for

◆

The Institute for Therapeutic Learning

TRANSPERSONAL HYPNOTHERAPY/NLP CERTIFICATION TRAINING

Phases I-VI

◆

Hypnotherapy Books

Hypnotherapy, Dave Elman, Westwood Publ. Co., Glendale, Ca. *(required)*

Master Course in Hypnotism, Harry Aarons, Power Publ. Inc., S.Orange, N.J.

Hypnosis for Change, Hadley & Staudacher, Publ. Group West; *(required)*

The Unlimited Human, James Maynard, Transpersonal Press, L.A., Ca.

Miracles on Demand, Charles Tebbetts, Westwood Publ., Glendale, Ca.

Ericksonian Hypnotherapy

Ericksonian Approaches to Hypnosis and Psychotherapy, Jeffrey K. Zeig, Ed., Brunner/Mazel Publ., N.Y., N.Y.

My Voice Will Go With You, The Teaching Tales of Milton H. Erickson, Sidney Rosen,Ed., W.W. Norton & Co., N.Y., N.Y.

Uncommon Therapy, The Psychiatric Techniques of Milton Erickson,M.D., Jay Haley, W.W. Norton & Co., N.Y., N.Y.

An Uncommon Casebook, The Complete Clinical Work of Milton H. Erickson, M.D., O'Hanlon & Hexum, Eds., W.W. Norton & Co., N.Y., N.Y.

Therapeutic Trances, Stephen Gilligan

NLP (Neuro-Linguistic Programming)

Frogs Into Princes, Bandler and Grinder, Real People Press, Moab, Utah

Patterns of the Hypnotic Techniques of Milton Erickson, Bandler and Grinder

Using Your Brain - for a Change, Richard Bandler

Change Your Mind, and Keep the Change, Steve Andreas

Trance Formations, Bandler and Grinder

Heart of the Mind, Steve and Connirae Andreas

Core Transformations - *Reaching the Wellspring Within,* Connierae Andreas with Tamara Andreas

Psychology, Psychology of Shame, Medical Psychology

The Drama of the Gifted Child, Alice Miller

For Your Own Good, Alice Miller

Thou Shalt Not Be Aware, Alice Miller

The Family, John Bradshaw (PBS Video series available for sale or in Public Library)

Healing the Shame That Binds You, John Bradshaw

Homecoming, John Bradshaw

High Risk Children Without a Conscience, Ken Magid and Carol A. McKelvey

Becoming Naturally Therapeutic, Jacquelyn Small *(required)*

Transformers, Jacquelyn Small

Psychotherapy: Purpose, Process and Practice, Foundation for Inner Peace *(required)*

Mind Games, Jean Houston & Robert Masters

Beyond the Brain, Stanislav Grof

Minding the Body, Mending the Mind, Joan Borysenko, Ph.D.

Love, Medicine & Miracles, Bernie S. Siegal, M.D.

Metaphysical/Archetypal

Reliving Past Lives, Helen Wambach, PhD.

What We May Be, Piero Ferrucci

The Unquiet Dead, Edith Fiore, Phd.

Many Lives, Many Masters, Brian Weiss, M.D.

The Hero Within, Carol S. Pearson

The Circle of Nine, Understanding the Feminine Psyche, Cherry Gilchrist

Archetypes of the Zodiac, Kathleen Burt

Mythology, Edith Hamilton

King, Warrior, Magician, Lover, Robert Moore, & Douglas Gillette

The Cry for Myth, Rollo May

The Power of Myth, Joseph Campbell

A Course in Miracles, Foundation for Inner Peace

Return of the Bird Tribes, Ken Carey

You'll See It When You Believe It, Dr. Wayne W. Dyer

Empirical Religion

Zen Mind, Beginner's Mind, Shunryo Suzuki, Roshi

Returning To Silence, Dainin Katagiri

Cutting Through Spiritual Materialism, Chogyam Trungpa

Myth Of Freedom, Chogyam Trungpa, Rinpoche

Shambala: The Way Of The Peaceful Warrior, Chogyam Trungpa

Journey Without A Goal, Chogyam Trungpa, Rinpoche

Rainbow of Liberated Energy, Ngakpa Chogyam

The Tibetan Book of Living and Dying, Sogyal Rinpoche

The Supreme Adventure, Peter Hayes

Kindle My Heart, Gurumayi Chidvilasananda

Where Are You Going?, Swami Muktananda

I Have Become Alive, Swami Muktananda

Rolling Thunder, Doug Boyd

The Gospel According to Jesus, Stephen Mitchell

Tao Te Ching, Stephen Mitchell

The Book of Job, Stephen Mitchell

Quantum Psychology & Physics

Quantum Healing, Deepak Chopra

Ageless Body, Timeless Mind, Deepak Chopra

Trances People Live, Stephen Wolinsky

Quantum Consciousness, Stephen Wolinsky

Parallel Universes, Fred Alan Wolf

The Dancing Wu Li Masters, Gary Zukav

Chaos, James Gleick

The Tao of Physics, Fritjof Capra

Ⓢ *Institute for Therapeutic Learning*
Transpersonal Hypnotherapy/NLP
Trainings & Other Offerings

To master and integrate the principles discussed in <u>Finding True Magic</u>, the Institute presents certification trainings in Transpersonal Hypnotherapy/NLP and various educational seminars. Many of these programs, recorded live, are offered as audio and video tapes, as well as individual healing tapes.(See below)

◆◆ Live Training Certification Options

For information about <u>certification</u> training, live or by independent study, complete details are available in hardcopy by snailmail, or in *"essential facts"* format by e-mail. Call, write, or e-mail (**jelias@sprynet.com**) your request for free catalogs. <u>Non-certification</u> independent study (no teacher/student interaction & no homework protocols) is also possible with the Independent Study Tapes Investment Option below.

◆◆ Independent Study Investment Options:

⊠ Complete Six Phase Course Set includes:

1) **Finding True Magic,** 300 page book by Jack Elias, founder and director of the Institute for Therapeutic Learning, serves as text for the course

2) **71** audio tapes(90 minute tapes) recorded at live certification trainings, rich with stimulating discussions, instruction, and demonstrations. (Stored in 6 compact 12 tape binders)

3) **6** demonstration videos, one per phase, 90 minutes each.

> **Complete Set Investment: $760.00** (includes S&H - U.S. & Can.)

"It seems like I can't find any boundaries to the application of this material in my work with other people to assist their healing, as well as my own personal & spiritual growth. I'm near bursting with enthusiasm and ideas around the medical practice as well as the bodywork I do and variations on group meditations for working with medical problems. All in all, a pretty good deal, Jack!

Julie H., Physician [M.D.], Washington

"I received knowledge from [Finding True Magic]..., and understanding from listening to you on the tapes. Thank you."

Tim B., Naturopathic Physician [N.D.], Georgia

⊡**Per Phase Investment Option:** For those who don't want to jump in all at once, it is possible to purchase one phase at a time. Purchase **Phase I**. If you like it and then want to complete the set, you can still take advantage of the **Complete Set** price of $760.00! Take a look below at some of the topics covered, then consider **Test the Waters!** below.

"My objectives were to learn more about the subconscious and the counseling process to improve my effectiveness as a Shamanic Counselor. I have gained so much from this course, I'm now feeling Shamanic counseling will be something I do as part of Hypnotherapy, rather than the other way around."   R.H., Shamanic Counselor

)(**Phase I** (10 tapes+*Finding True Magic*)- $185.00*
   Induction techniques
   Deepening techniques
   Structure of Effective Suggestions
   Transpersonal fundamentals of Hypnotherapy

)(**Phase II**(19 tapes)- $195.00*
   Regression
   Pastlife Therapy
   Higher Self Invocation
   Transpersonal Models of the Psyche

)(**Phase III**(10 tapes) - $130.00*
   Subpersonality Therapy
   Inner Guide Access
   Managing Trance
   Subpersonality Regression Work

)(**Phase IV**(15 tapes)- $180.00*
   Shame & Addictive Personality
   Treatment of Addiction & Compulsions
   Anesthesia & Pain Relief
   Clinical Scripts

)(**Phase V**(8 tapes)- $120.00*
   Archetypes, Myths, Poetics of the Psyche
   Accessing Superconscious Archetypes
   Comprehensive Treatment Planning
   Masculine & Feminine Archetypes

)(**Phase VI**(9 tapes)- $125.00*
   Shadow Work
   Entity Releasing
   Couples Hypnosis
   Creating A Dynamic Practice

*price includes a 90 minute demonstration video with each phase +S&H for US & Canada

---

Cumulative Investment, Phase by Phase: $935.00 incl. S&H, US & CAN

This outline is a partial list of topics covered in each Phase of the course. The per Phase option should be exercised in sequence since material is not strictly compartmentalized from phase to phase. For example, NLP and Ericksonian principles and their correlation with transpersonal perspectives pervades the entire course. What may look basic or elementary in the outline may not be at all because such perspectives are brought to bear. It is important to experience the flow and development that moves through the class from day to day.

"Six years of university training in psychology...twenty as a counselor...countless years of spiritual quest...culminating in the discovery of this course...a psychology firmly rooted in profound spiritual wisdom."   J.M., M.A. Psychologist

Finding True Magic is authored by Jack Elias, founder and director of the Institute for Therapeutic Learning, Seattle, WA. An internationally known Transpersonal Hypnotherapy/NLP trainer, Mr. Elias has been a Buddhist student and practitioner with recognized Masters for over 30 years.

Test the Waters!

(of your unconscious mind)

With **Phase I** of the Independent Study Program (ten 90 minute audio tapes + one 90 minute video, + **Finding True Magic)**, the book containing the curriculum for the entire six phase course, **in a matter of days**, you will learn:

- ◆ **How to safely induce a hypnotic trance**

- ◆ **How to safely induce different levels of trance**

- ◆ **How to structure a hypnotic session**

- ◆ **How to make hypnosis tapes for yourself and others**

- ◆**How to safely do quick inductions**

- ◆ **How to safely do self-hypnosis**

- ◆ **How to give yourself and others the ability to go into a deeply relaxed state whenever needed in a matter of seconds**

- ◆ **How to guide someone into a relaxed state that many say is the most profound experience they've ever had!**

- ◆ **How to construct powerful and effective suggestions to transform any area of your life: relationships & sexuality, business, sports or academic performance, compulsions, fears, & addictions, depression and anxiety, weight loss, smoking and more.**

Unbelieveable!?! All this and more is possible because you receive **word for word** scripts in **Finding True Magic**, and full explanations about the nature and history of hypnosis and how to do it responsibly. Plus the tapes, **recorded at live trainings**, give you the opportunity to share in discussions, explanations and demonstrations of the scripted procedures that you can then practice. You will witness these procedures demonstrated on the video. You'll be amazed at how simple it can be!

You can have this wealth of inspiring knowledge - **10 audio tapes, 1 video, + Finding True Magic**, for only **$185.00** (includes shipping & handling in the U.S.A. & Can.) Begin to change your life for the better. Send check or money order to:

Jack Elias
Institute for Therapeutic Learning
P.O. Box 17229
Seattle, WA 98107

Email: jelias@sprynet.com   **Website: http://home.sprynet.com/~jelias**

Allow 2-3 weeks delivery.   Phone: (206)783-1838

"I have made important and necessary changes in my life as a result of your course - in my relationships, diet, daily schedule, therapeutic skill, and self esteem. I feel like I'm coming alive to my life in a way not experienced before."

A.B., Drug Addiction Counselor

Audio & Video Tapes - Individual Selections

(See Independent Study Course for information on Audio tape Training Series.)

1.Stress Release, Rejuvenation, & Creative Empowerment - This tapes teaches you to drain the stress from your body and mind. You learn how to "get out of your own way" so the inner genius of your unconscious mind can rejuvenate you and give you greater creative intelligence to meet life's challenges. **$12.00**

2.Releasing and Removing Allergies- The allergic response is generally an unnecessary phobic response on the part of the immune system to essentially harmless irritants. Experience how quickly the immune system can change its response to these irritants, protecting you and leaving you allergy free!! Safe and effective. **$12.00**

3.Ending Insomnia - Restoring Restful and Healing Sleep- Recapture the "sleep of innocence." Inspire your inner wisdom mind to utilize your sleep, and your dreams, to generate creative solutions, physical and emotional healing and rejuvenation. **$12.00**

4.Strengthening the Will; Successfully Defining & Accomplishing Beneficial Goals- Cut through uncertainty and self-sabotaging attitudes to recognize and accomplish goals to enhance your life. **$12.00**

5.Cultivating Fearlessness and Compassion- A simple yet powerful spiritual practice inspired by the Buddhist practice of Tonglen that will open your heart and fill it with light and strength. **$12.00**

6.Entity Releasing and Energy Field Restoration- Instructions to free yourself from entity attachments and negative influences. Guidance through the releasing process and through the restoration and maintenance of a healthy energetic field. **$12.00**

7.Dissolving Shyness- A dramatic and insightful resolution of a life-long limitation. Requested by students to be offered for sale, this tape demonstrates a rapid and comprehensive generative shift in attitude and sense of identity, with lasting beneficial and transforming results as reported by the subject. Instructive for professional therapeutic use and personal use. **$12.00**

8.Clarifying Confusion- Working with hypnotherapists in a mentorship class, important questions and confusions about the client/therapist relationship are addressed. Instructive and moving as it takes the therapists to the heart of their own personal issues hidden at the core of their concern for their clients. **$12.00**

☒**9. Shame & the Addictive Personality -** One day workshop. Insights into the origin and structure of shame and trauma. Techniques to release the shame and trauma at the core of addictive and self-defeating behaviors, freeing people to focus on healthy new behaviors and choices. **4 tape set - $40.00**

☒**10. Subpersonality Workshop -** One day training. Explore the hypnotic qualities of our familiar personalities. Without realizing it we all become skilled self-hypnotists to cope with growing up. Recognise your problems and limitations as self- hypnotically imposed trances. Learn techniques to wake up from these dream prisons in order to live a joyful abundant life. **4 tape set - $40.00**

☒**11. The Art & Skill of Therapeutic Inquiry -** One day training. Through effective inquiry we connect with our authentic Self, with what we truly value, and with the ability to act with clarity and courage creating genuinely beneficial outcomes. Mastering inquiry skills increases intelligence and awareness - a must for professional competency and personal growth. **4 tape set - $40.00**

☒☒☒**Invest in all three workshops (9-11 above) and receive a 15+% discount!! Together they will give you a comprehensive new set of insights and tools to achieve genuine benefit and success in any area of life.** <u>**Total for all three: $100.00**</u>

❖**12.The Nature of Archetypal Energies; Discovering the Archetypal Self.** A two hour public talk. Also known as the Rainbow body, the Archetypal Self is our spontaneous, free, fully empowered and joyfully actualized True Being. **$12.00**

❖**Video Tape Selection - The Rainbow Body-** A 2 hour public talk exploring and clarifying the obstacles created by the mind that block our full experience of our Rainbow Body - our body of joy, peace, power, creativity and spontaneity. **$23.00**

❖❖ **This audio and video selection are a great complementary combination. Invest in both and save 15%. Total for both: $30.00**

<u>Price includes shipping & handling for U.S.A. & Canada.</u> **International orders require additional shipping charges. Send check or money order to: Jack Elias, Institute for Therapeutic Learning, P.O. Box 17229, Seattle, WA 98107, (206)783-1838. Allow 2-3 weeks delivery.**
E-mail: jelias@sprynet.com   Website: http://home.sprynet.com/~jelias